High-Imp

Terrorism

Proceedings of a Russian-American Workshop

Committee on Confronting Terrorism in Russia

Office for Central Europe and Eurasia
Development, Security, and Cooperation
Policy and Global Affairs
National Research Council

In cooperation with the Russian Academy of Sciences

NATIONAL ACADEMY PRESS
Washington, D.C.

NATIONAL ACADEMY PRESS • 2101 Constitution Avenue, N.W. • Washington, DC 20418

NOTICE: The project that is the subject of this report was approved by the Governing Board of the National Research Council, whose members are drawn from the councils of the National Academy of Sciences, the National Academy of Engineering, and the Institute of Medicine. The members of the committee responsible for the report were chosen for their special competences and with regard for appropriate balance.

This study was supported by Grant No. B7075 between the National Academy of Sciences and the Carnegie Corporation of New York. Any opinions, findings, conclusions, or recommendations expressed in this publication are those of the author(s) and do not necessarily reflect the views of the organizations or agencies that provided support for the project.

International Standard Book Number 0-309-08270-6
Library of Congress Catalog Card Number 2002102001

A limited number of copies of this report are available from:

Development, Security, and Cooperation
National Research Council, FO 2060
2101 Constitution Avenue, NW
Washington, DC 20418
Tel: (202) 334-2644

Additional copies of this report are available for sale from:

National Academy Press
2101 Constitution Avenue, NW, Lockbox 285
Washington, DC 20055
Tel: (800) 624-6242 or (202) 334-3313 (in the Washington metropolitan area)
Internet, http://www.nap.edu

Printed in the United States of America

THE NATIONAL ACADEMIES

National Academy of Sciences
National Academy of Engineering
Institute of Medicine
National Research Council

The **National Academy of Sciences** is a private, nonprofit, self-perpetuating society of distinguished scholars engaged in scientific and engineering research, dedicated to the furtherance of science and technology and to their use for the general welfare. Upon the authority of the charter granted to it by the Congress in 1863, the Academy has a mandate that requires it to advise the federal government on scientific and technical matters. Dr. Bruce M. Alberts is president of the National Academy of Sciences.

The **National Academy of Engineering** was established in 1964, under the charter of the National Academy of Sciences, as a parallel organization of outstanding engineers. It is autonomous in its administration and in the selection of its members, sharing with the National Academy of Sciences the responsibility for advising the federal government. The National Academy of Engineering also sponsors engineering programs aimed at meeting national needs, encourages education and research, and recognizes the superior achievements of engineers. Dr. Wm. A. Wulf is president of the National Academy of Engineering.

The **Institute of Medicine** was established in 1970 by the National Academy of Sciences to secure the services of eminent members of appropriate professions in the examination of policy matters pertaining to the health of the public. The Institute acts under the responsibility given to the National Academy of Sciences by its congressional charter to be an adviser to the federal government and, upon its own initiative, to identify issues of medical care, research, and education. Dr. Kenneth I. Shine is president of the Institute of Medicine.

The **National Research Council** was organized by the National Academy of Sciences in 1916 to associate the broad community of science and technology with the Academy's purposes of furthering knowledge and advising the federal government. Functioning in accordance with general policies determined by the Academy, the Council has become the principal operating agency of both the National Academy of Sciences and the National Academy of Engineering in providing services to the government, the public, and the scientific and engineering communities. The Council is administered jointly by both Academies and the Institute of Medicine. Dr. Bruce M. Alberts and Dr. Wm. A. Wulf are chairman and vice chairman, respectively, of the National Research Council.

NRC COMMITTEE ON CONFRONTING TERRORISM IN RUSSIA

Siegfried S. Hecker, Chair
Senior Fellow and Former Director
Los Alamos National Laboratory

Michael L. Moodie
President
Chemical and Biological Arms Control Institute

Raphael F. Perl
Specialist in International Terrorism Policy
Congressional Research Service

Staff

Glenn E. Schweitzer
Project Director
National Research Council

Kelly Robbins
Senior Program Officer
National Research Council

A. Chelsea Sharber
Program Specialist
National Research Council

Rita S. Guenther
Program Assistant
National Research Council

RUSSIAN ACADEMY OF SCIENCES ORGANIZING COMMITTEE

Nikolai P. Laverov
Vice President
Russian Academy of Sciences

Yevgeny P. Velikhov
Director
Khurchatov State Research Center of Atomic Energy

Viktor Luneev
Institute of State and Law
Russian Academy of Sciences

Yury Shiyan
Foreign Relations Department
Russian Academy of Sciences

Preface

In June 1999, the presidents of the National Academy of Sciences (NAS) and the Russian Academy of Sciences (RAS) agreed that a joint project on combating especially dangerous crimes, particularly terrorism, would be of considerable interest to both Russian and American specialists in a variety of fields. The president of the NAS requested the president of the National Academy of Engineering (NAE) to assume responsibility for developing and implementing the project. Representatives of the RAS and NAE decided that a bilateral interacademy workshop on the topic of high-impact terrorism would be a good first step in carrying out such a project. The Carnegie Corporation of New York has been very interested in enhancing Russian capabilities to address terrorist threats and provided the funds required for the workshop.

The workshop was held in Moscow on June 4-6, 2001. A number of Russian governmental and academic organizations with responsibilities and interests in the field accepted the invitation from the RAS to participate in the workshop, and Russian specialists with a variety of backgrounds made presentations at the workshop. Several dozen other Russian specialists attended the sessions, and their comments greatly enriched the discussions. The NAE selected eight American specialists to make presentations on governmental and nongovernmental experiences in the United States in the fight against terrorism. Some of the presentations by Russian and American specialists reflected a remarkable degree of similarity in views on the terrorist threat (e.g., radiological terrorism, agricultural terrorism), while others indicated different levels of appreciation of vulnerabilities and response requirements (e.g., the long-term Russian attention to protection of industrial facilities, the extensive American concern over cyberterrorism). The agenda for the workshop and the written presentations comprise the body of this report.

We will not attempt to summarize the papers or the discussions here, but simply note that the workshop provided an excellent forum for informative discussion and exchange of ideas on the broad topic of high-impact terrorism. The statements made in the enclosed papers are those of the individual authors and do not necessarily represent positions of The National Academies.

ACKNOWLEDGMENTS

This proceedings has been reviewed in draft form by individuals chosen for their technical expertise, in accordance with procedures approved by the NRC's Report Review Committee. The purpose of this independent review is to provide candid and critical comments that will assist the institution in making its published proceedings as sound as possible and to ensure that the proceedings meets institutional standards for quality. The review comments and draft manuscript remain confidential. We wish to thank the following individuals for their review of papers in this proceedings: Vinton G. Cerf, WorldCom; David R. Franz, Southern Research Institute; Charles T. Owens, Civilian Research and Development Foundation; Suzanne E. Spaulding, formerly Executive Director of the National Commission on Terrorism; Roger L. Schneider, Rho Sigma Associates, Inc.; and Alvin W. Trivelpiece, formerly Director of Oak Ridge National Laboratory.

Although the reviewers listed above have provided many constructive comments and suggestions, they were not asked to endorse the content of the individual papers, nor did they see the final draft of the proceedings before its release. The review of this proceedings was overseen by Marilyn Baker of the National Research Council. She was responsible for making certain that an independent examination of this report was carried out in accordance with institutional procedures and that all review comments were carefully considered.

We wish to thank Rita S. Guenther, Rita Kit, Kelly Robbins, and A. Chelsea Sharber for their translation of the Russian language papers into English. Special thanks also to Florence Poillon, Kelly Robbins, and A. Chelsea Sharber for editing of the proceedings.

SIEGFRIED S. HECKER
Chair, NRC Committee on Confronting Terrorism in Russia

GLENN E. SCHWEITZER
Director, Office for Central Europe and Eurasia, NRC

Contents

BIOLOGICAL TERRORISM

CHEMICAL TERRORISM

NUCLEAR TERRORISM

EXPLOSIVES TERRORISM

CYBERTERRORISM

AGRICULTURAL TERRORISM

FUTURE TRENDS AND INTERNATIONAL COOPERATION IN THE STRUGGLE AGAINST MODERN TERRORISM

APPENDIXES

High-Impact Terrorism

Opening Remarks

Siegfried S. Hecker
Los Alamos National Laboratory

I would like to thank the Russian Academy of Sciences, especially Academician Nikolai Laverov and my cochair, Academician Yevgeny Velikhov, for hosting this workshop. Very special thanks go to Glenn Schweitzer and Yury Shiyan, who were the principal organizers of the workshop.

During the next three days we will discuss one of the most important issues facing the world today—that of terrorism in high-technology society and modern methods to prevent it and respond to it. Terrorism knows no boundaries. The problem is international, but the effects are felt locally. Every day, someone in the world dies at the hands of terrorists, be it in Volgograd, Oklahoma City, Israel, or Indonesia.

Terrorism is a very big problem with many dimensions. We will focus on terrorism in a high-technology society or what we can call high-impact terrorism. Hence, we will cover terrorism with the potential for mass destruction (such as nuclear, chemical, and biological) and terrorism with the potential for mass disruption (such as cyberterrorism and the use of conventional explosives against high-value targets).

Terrorism is a problem of great importance to government. It threatens the lives of its citizens. Moreover, it threatens government itself. I view terrorism as the number one threat to all democracies of the world, especially those nations in which the roots of democracy are still very shallow.

So, why are the National Academies of Russia and the United States hosting this workshop? I believe that since this problem has so many dimensions, it should be viewed from as many different points of view as possible, including those of scientists and engineers. Also, high-impact terrorism has a significant science and technology dimension. There are many areas in which specialists can help. The U.S. National Academies have a long record of involvement in this area. Finally, sometimes our governments fail to cooperate on the very problems that need cooperation most. In such cases, an informal dialogue can often help to catalyze necessary government actions. My cochair, Academician Velikhov, can give us such examples in the area of nuclear arms control.

Therefore, I believe it is quite appropriate that the National Academies of Russia and the United States provide the forum for this workshop. We thank the Carnegie Corporation of New York for its financial sponsorship. I want to remind participants that this is a workshop. Hence, we encourage discussion and the building of personal networks.

The objectives of the workshop, as I see them, are to (1) share our experiences in combating terrorism and (2) explore together how we can collaborate in the future to more effectively combat terrorism. Terrorism is one area where over the years we in the United States have more experience, simply because terrorism is a greater threat in a more open society. In that spirit, our specialists have brought not only their own work, but other key references in the field. It is our hope that you will be able to build a library here in Russia, with these references complementing your own.

The desired outcomes for the workshop are that we learn much from each other and that we define specific follow-up actions and build future collaborations, both on a personal level and as a group through the Russian and U.S. National Academies.

TERRORISM AND THE LAW

The Legal Basis for Counterterrorism Activities in the United States

Raphael F. Perl
Congressional Research Service

I thank you for the opportunity to be here in this great country and to speak before this distinguished group. It seems somewhat of an irony, on reflection, that the end of what we in the West referred to as the Cold War may have made the world somewhat safer for terrorists and criminals. The very peace we sought has brought with it new challenges for combating terrorism within the legal context of an open society.

My presentation today will address the threat posed by the convergence of terrorism and technology and the current status of the U.S. legal response. I will begin by discussing trends in terrorism and technology and the present U.S. legal framework. I will then discuss the role of the U.S. Congress in antiterrorism legislation and the role of the executive branch in implementing such legislation. My remarks will conclude with observations on specific U.S. laws that seem effective and new legislation that could be proposed.

In their desire to combat terrorism in a modern political context, nations often face conflicting goals and courses of action: (1) providing security from terrorist acts (i.e., limiting the freedom of individual terrorists, terrorist groups, and support networks to operate effectively in a relatively unregulated environment) versus (2) maximizing individual freedoms, democracy, and human rights. The constitutional limits within which democratic societies must operate are sometimes seen as conflicting directly with a desire to protect citizens against terrorist activity.

Technology has the potential to help terrorists establish networks, communicate, and avoid detection. Technology also provides terrorists with the means to commit acts that can increasingly damage societies. The greater the damage caused by a terrorist act, the greater is the potential for government responses that may help ensure security, but can conflict with the civil liberties of all individuals.

Efforts to combat terrorism are complicated by a global trend toward deregulation, open borders, and expanded commerce—enhanced movements of people, money, goods, information, and services. Such developments pose complex challenges to law makers and policy makers on how best to use law, treaties, and other mechanisms to promote international cooperation in this new environment. In a world that knows no borders, law must become increasingly transnational if it is to be effective.

The world is changing and terrorism is changing as well. Terrorism is becoming more violent, more the product of loosely affiliated private groups, and more reliant on information technology. Terrorism today is often focused on inflicting damage on the enemy, with little need for restraint or public credit for the acts committed. In an age of asymmetric power, there can be an increased blurring between peace and war, between terrorism and war, between law enforcement and national security, and between terrorism and crime. In November 2000, Polish authorities arrested two Russian organized crime members, who they suspect are connected to the August 8, 2000, bombing under Moscow's Pushkin Square, which killed eight persons. I understand that recently prosecutors have come to believe that the bombings were meant to settle economic scores. If such suspicions prove correct, what could more clearly demonstrate a blurring between terrorism and organized crime? In the area of cybercrime or cyberterrorism in particular, the distinctions between terrorism and crime are becoming difficult to discern.

Moreover, it is widely believed that moral constraints concerning the use of weapons of mass destruction in terrorism have declined. In such an environment, the potential use of biotechnology and genetic engineering to attack humans, livestock, and the food chain in general warrants increased attention. Information technology is seen as aiding terrorists to network, operate undetected, and attack national infrastructures. The ability to damage computer systems and other electronic devices by electromagnetic pulses, high-power microwaves, and high-energy radio-frequency devices is a capability that is becoming increasingly available to terrorists.

Increasingly, terrorism is becoming anonymous. Often, terrorists do not claim credit for their acts, and technology provides a means to "mask" these acts. In the twenty-first century, an increasing challenge to societies will be not only to detect and find terrorists, but also to recognize that damage to particular systems may in fact have been caused by terrorist acts.

When speaking of the United States and its legal system, it is important to keep two points in mind. Under the U.S. Constitution, all authority not specifically granted to the federal government is reserved for the states and the individual. So we begin with the premise that authority rests with the individual or the 50 states. The right of the federal government to act does not exist unless it is authorized by law. Secondly, but also very important, the United States does not have a parliamentary form of government. A significant difference from the parliamentary system is that in the United States, our legislature—the Congress—exercises the major role in shaping the federal budget—the so-called power of the purse. Because the United States is a federal system, laws are passed at the federal (national) level and also at the state level. Ordinances (locally passed laws) may also be passed and enforced at the county and city levels.

My remarks today will focus on the federal or national legal response to combat terrorism. U.S. laws that respond to terrorism can be divided into four categories: (1) laws that empower the government to combat crime in general, such as murder or kidnapping; (2) laws that specifically apply to terrorism, such as fundraising for terrorist organizations; (3) laws and constitutional guarantees that, by protecting civil liberties such as the U.S. constitutional right to privacy or the constitutional right against self-incrimination, may limit the power of government to investigate or prosecute terrorists in the interests of protecting civil liberties; and (4) laws that apply to government control in emergency situations during or after a major catastrophic terrorist event. Public health regulations governing quarantine procedures over persons or livestock exposed to or infected by disease are examples of the latter category. Regulations governing government use of communications airwaves during and after a mass casualty terrorist attack provide another example (see also the National Emergencies Act, 50 USC 1601ff, and the Robert T. Stafford Disaster Relief and Emergency Act, 42 USC 5121ff and 5193ff).

U.S. policy against terrorism was shaped, in large part, by the reaction to the murders of Israeli athletes at the 1972 Munich Olympics. Much of the policy remains unchanged, but the thrust became increasingly assertive as terrorist attacks against U.S. citizens abroad became increasingly frequent and deadlier in the 1980s. Congress passed a series of laws to clearly identify terrorism as a crime, to set up procedures for gaining jurisdiction over persons who commit terrorist acts against U.S. persons or property outside the territory of the United States, and to require or permit sanctions on countries supporting terrorism.

In the United States, no all-encompassing federal law explicitly addresses domestic terrorism. For example, a terrorist act may be an actual or attempted bombing, armed robbery, arson, assassination, assault, hijacking, kidnapping, or foreign embassy takeover. All of these activities are violations of federal or state laws and, depending on the motive, may be acts of terrorism. The Federal Bureau of Investigation (FBI) defines terrorism as "the unlawful use of force or violence against persons or property to intimidate or coerce a government, the civilian population, or any segment thereof, in furtherance of political or social objectives."

In the current federal statutory structure, terrorism is addressed in a variety of ways. Extraterritorial acts of hostage taking or terrorism aimed at U.S. nationals or actions intended to coerce the United States are federal offenses. Under the

1996 Omnibus Antiterrorism Act, P.L. 104-132, certain acts of terrorism transcending national boundaries are federal offenses, as are conspiracies within U.S. jurisdiction to kill, kidnap, maim, or injure persons or damage property in a foreign country. Foreign murders of U.S. nationals by U.S. nationals are also subject to federal criminal penalties, as are crimes committed by or against U.S. nationals on certain foreign vessels. Other federal offenses include acts of violence against maritime navigation, on maritime platforms, or at international airports. Within the United States, federal law prohibits material support to terrorists, as well as certain financial transactions involving terrorist states (see 18 USC 2331ff). In addition, many federal laws target offenses that may be terrorism related, such as use of weapons of mass destruction; torture; genocide; destruction of aircraft, trains, or motor vehicles or related facilities; threats or crimes of violence against diplomats, members of Congress, Cabinet officers, members of the Supreme Court, the President, or the Vice President; firearms offenses in federal facilities; malicious mischief against federal property or property within the special maritime or territorial jurisdiction of the United States; alien smuggling; air piracy; mailing injurious articles; chemical weapons offenses; and explosives offenses, among others. In addition to violations of federal law, terrorist acts may also be subject to prosecution under state law, depending upon the specific circumstances involved.

Current immigration law permits exclusion of aliens who have engaged in terrorist activity or aliens who a consular officer or the Attorney General knows, or has reasonable grounds to believe, are likely to engage in terrorist activity after entry.

Under U.S. law, sensitivity to constitutional protections is necessary when responding to the risk of terrorist activity at home and abroad. For example, during investigations of allegations of possible terrorist activity, the prohibition against unreasonable searches and seizures in the Fourth Amendment, the protection of the freedoms of speech and association in the First Amendment, the protection of the right to bear arms in the Second Amendment, and the due process rights under the Fifth and Fourteenth Amendments may be implicated. The constitutional framework sets the outside limits within which any official investigations must operate.

In addition to these constitutional parameters, the tools to be used in such investigations are dictated in part by statutory provisions addressing wire, oral, and electronic surveillance in the context of criminal investigations, and foreign intelligence surveillance and physical searches relating to foreign intelligence activity. Access to stored electronic data is also statutorily limited. The division of labor among federal departments and agencies for criminal and foreign intelligence investigations is governed by statute and executive order. The Attorney General's guidelines on domestic security and terrorism provide guidance as to the initiation, methodology, and scope of Justice Department investigations in this area.

Congress exercises its authority by enacting laws (its legislative function) and by holding investigations and hearings to ensure that the laws are being properly implemented (its oversight function). Increasingly, funding drives government policy, and Congress authorizes and appropriates funding for antiterrorism programs. Strong areas of congressional interest include (1) reforming the structure of government to enhance responses to terrorism; (2) mandating homeland defense initiatives to respond to catastrophic terrorism, (3) possible consolidation and coordination of the federal antiterrorism budget; (4) sanctioning state sponsors of terrorism; and (5) protecting the homeland against bioterrorism.

Among the topics of special congressional interest are those discussed below:

Reforming the Structure of Government to Enhance Responses to Terrorism. A topic of intense congressional focus is how best to structure the federal government to create and implement a national strategy to respond to terrorism. Congress has created a series of commissions dealing with proliferation, homeland defense, and terrorism. All agree on the need for a national strategy and policy reform. On June 5, 2000, the National Commission on Terrorism, a congressionally mandated bipartisan body, issued its report, which included a blueprint for U.S. counterterrorism policy with both policy and legislative recommendations. The chairman of this commission, Mr. L. Paul (Jerry) Bremer, is with us today and will address the findings of his group.

Mandating Homeland Defense Initiatives to Respond to Catastrophic Terrorism. A number of bills have been introduced in Congress to enhance the nation's ability to respond to catastrophic terrorism. In addressing these initiatives, President Bush announced on May 8, 2001, that he would order the federal agency charged with domestic disaster relief, the Federal Emergency Management Agency, to establish an Office of National Preparedness to coordinate a response to attacks involving biological, chemical, or nuclear weapons. The executive order establishing the office is being prepared by the White House. President Bush also announced that U.S. Vice President Richard Cheney would lead a new task force on terrorist threats to determine how best to respond to catastrophic disasters.

Consolidating the Federal Antiterrorism Budget. Forty-six federal agencies have varying aspects of counterterrorism responsibilities. An issue of concern is that the budgets of these agencies should reflect—and be integrated into—a coordinated interagency threat assessment and consolidated federal antiterrorism budget.

Sanctioning State Sponsors of Terrorism. An important area of congressional legislative focus is sanctioning state sponsors of terrorism. The Export Administration Act (Section 6 [j]) allows the President to regulate export of dual-use technology and to prohibit or curtail the export of critical technology or other technological data. U.S. sales of technology, particularly high-technology processes, have been considerable, and sales restrictions or prohibitions are known to have put pressure on states reluctant to control terrorism. Under this act, exports of various sensitive articles to the seven terrorist countries on the U.S. terrorist list (Cuba, Iran, Iraq, Libya, North Korea, Sudan, Syria) and Afghanistan are strictly controlled or prohibited. The Omnibus Antiterrorism Act of 1996 (P.L. 104-132) prohibits the sale of arms to any country that the President certifies is not cooperating fully with U.S. antiterrorism efforts. Sections 325 and 326 of this law also require that aid be withheld from any country providing lethal military aid to countries on the terrorist list. The Arms Export Control Act authorizes the President to restrict the sale of defense articles and restrict or suspend defense services to states fostering terrorism. Specific authority for the Libyan trade embargo is in Section 503 of the International Trade and Security Act of 1985, while Section 505 of the act authorizes the banning of imports of goods and services from any country supporting terrorism.

Protecting Against Bioterrorism. By Executive Order 12375 of November 16, 1990, former President George Bush made a finding that chemical and biological weapons proliferation is a threat to U.S. national security and declared a national emergency to deal with the threat. This finding was refined, amended, and updated to include proliferation of nuclear weapons by Executive Order 123998 of November 14, 1994, and it continues to be updated yearly.

In the Biological Weapons Antiterrorism Act (P.L. 101-298, Section 3[a]), as amended by the 1996 Omnibus Antiterrorism Act (Section 511), Congress made it a federal crime to threaten, attempt, or conspire to use a biological weapon (including biotechnologically engineered products) and directed the Secretary of Health and Human Services to issue regulations identifying potential biological agents and governing their transfer.

The National Defense Authorization Act of 1997 (Section 1414) directs the Secretary of Defense to develop and maintain at least one rapid response team capable of assisting officials to detect and deal with chemical, biological, and related weapons of mass destruction.

Recurring policy issues arising before Congress in the terrorism arena include the following:

1. What level of resources should be committed when responding to low probability but potentially high casualty threats?

2. To what degree should terrorism be treated as a national security threat and to what degree as a law enforcement threat?

3. How can civil liberties be best protected while still allowing for the controlled use of wiretaps and the possible recruitment of "shady" informants?

4. How can the intelligence community protect sources and methods and, at the same time, share information?

5. How can economic interests be protected while restricting the export of commercial products and technology that terrorists might use?

The executive branch often drafts and recommends new legislation or changes in existing legislation to Congress. Presidential decision directives often provide broad policy direction on issues of national security. Executive orders may implement legislation or presidential authority by setting federal guidelines. In addition, individual agencies may issue their own internal guidelines.

For example, on May 22, 1998, President Bill Clinton issued Presidential Decision Directive 63 ("Critical Infrastructure Protection"), which established within the National Security Council a National Coordinator for Security, Infrastructure Protection, and Counterterrorism, who also provides advice regarding the counterterrorism budget.

On August 20, 1998, President Clinton signed Executive Order 13099, freezing assets owned by Saudi-born Islamic terrorist leader Osama bin Laden, specific associates, and their self-proclaimed Islamic Army Organization, and prohibiting U.S. individuals and firms from doing business with them. Previously, the Clinton administration had frozen the assets of 12 alleged Middle East terrorist organizations and 18 individuals associated with those organizations. Executive Orders 12957 and 12959 prohibit U.S. development of Iran's oil industry and U.S. exports to and imports from Iran, as well as third-country reexport of U.S. products to Iran.

Federal agencies may also issue documents with legal consequences pursuant to the need for detailed information required by specific laws. For example, on October 8, 1997, the State Department (pursuant to Section 219 of the Immigration and Nationality Act) released a list of 30 foreign terrorist organizations. As of January 2001, the number of organizations on this list stood at 29. The 1996 Antiterrorism and Effective Death Penalty Act makes it a crime to provide support to these organizations, and their members shall be denied entry visas into the United States.

An example of federal agency internal guidelines is found in the U.S. Justice Department's domestic terrorism investigations guidelines. Investigations pertaining to acts of terrorism occurring in the United States are conducted in accordance with the Attorney General's Guidelines for General Crimes, Racketeering Enterprises, and Domestic Security/Terrorism Investigations. The guidelines were required by the Privacy Act of 1974 (5 USC 5222a [e][7]). First issued in 1976 by then-Attorney General Edward Levi, the original guidelines were superseded by those issued by Attorney General William French Smith in 1983, Attorney General Richard Thornburgh in 1989, and Attorney General Janet Reno in 1995. Under the guidelines, the FBI may open a domestic terrorism investigation if, after carefully checking out initial leads, it is determined that the credibility of the initiating source and the compelling and serious nature of the potential charges warrant that the matter be further investigated.

A number of U.S. laws and practices merit specific mention when discussing the U.S. legal response to counterterrorism. These laws and the concepts underlying them may have broader applicability in a global environment. They include (1) racketeering-influenced corrupt organizations (RICO) legislation, (2) conspiracy legislation, (3) wiretap authority legislation, (4) foreign intelligence surveillance legislation, (5) rewards and witness protection provisions, (6) passport and visa forgery legislation, (7) cyberterrorism and cybercrime legislation, and (8) the U.S. plea bargaining system.

Racketeering-Influenced Corrupt Organization (RICO) Legislation. Title 18 USC 1961ff (part of the Organized Crime Control Act of 1970) is designed for combating organized crime but can have a broader reach. RICO was designed to address types of activities that Congress perceived to be characteristic of organized crime regardless of who committed those acts. Consequently, application of RICO is triggered by the commission of underlying offenses, including specified violent crimes, extortion, and drug trafficking. RICO applies to any person or entity who invests in, acquires, maintains, conducts, or participates in the affairs of an entity that engages in the patterned commission of various state and federal crimes or who conspires to do so. Patterned activity constitutes two or more offenses that suggest a pattern of continued activity or threat.

Unlike the general federal conspiracy statute, a RICO conspiracy does not require an overt act by the parties to complete the offense. It is enough that two parties agree to invest in, acquire, or conduct the affairs of an enterprise engaged in interstate or foreign commerce in a manner that violates 18 USC 1962(a), (b), or (c). Penalties include fines, forfeiture, and imprisonment. Conspiring to carry out such activity is an offense as well. A person wrongfully injured by RICO can collect treble damages through a civil suit against the person or entity who engaged in the RICO offense. RICO does not prohibit any conduct not otherwise illegal under state or federal law. Rather, it expands the civil and criminal penalties for certain state and federal crimes.

RICO is aimed primarily at the commission of crimes that provide profit; it targets groups that profit from crime. However, RICO has been used to prosecute bombers of abortion clinics in the United States and to address mail bombings by Croats against political rivals. From the perspective of a prosecutor, RICO has seven advantages:

1. It provides for stronger penalties (e.g., felonies that may result in only 5- to 10-year jail terms under state or federal law may have 25-year sentences under RICO).

2. RICO brings state crimes into the purview of federal prosecution.

3. RICO provides for forfeiture of property used in the illegal activity and of proceeds generated by the misconduct, remedies not always available under underlying state and federal laws.

4. Because RICO activity is a *continuing* crime, statutes of limitations that bar prosecution for the underlying offenses may be avoided.

5. RICO encourages plea bargaining by defendants because of its higher

penalties and because common criminals often do not want to be convicted "racketeers."

6. Victims of RICO can initiate civil suits for treble damages.

7. Under RICO, the government can obtain injunctive relief, such as the reorganization of a corporate entity.

Conspiracy Legislation. Under 18 USC 371, it is a crime for two or more people to conspire to commit a federal offense when one of those people commits an overt act in furtherance of that criminal purpose. Conspiracy to commit a series of specified terrorist acts is explicitly covered by 18 USC 2331-2332.

Wiretap Authority Legislation. Generally, interception of wire, oral, or electronic communications is prohibited by federal law (18 USC 2510 ff) unless the interception fits into a specific exception to the general rule. Usually, before authority is granted to wiretap, a judge must find that there is probable cause to believe that a specified offense has been committed, is currently under way, or is about to be committed and that information from the wiretap will provide evidence of the crime. Normal investigative techniques must have been tried and failed, or the court must find that normal investigative techniques reasonably appear unlikely to succeed or are too dangerous to use. Criminal penalties exist for misuse of the information by law enforcement. Wiretaps are not permitted to be used in investigating all federal offenses. Rather, wiretaps can only be used to investigate certain specified crimes such as bribery, unlawful use of explosives, obstruction of a criminal investigation, kidnapping, violent crimes connected to racketeering, assassination of government officials, destruction of certain aircraft or aircraft facilities, money laundering, sabotage of nuclear facilities, and chemical and biological weapons offenses. Similar judicial standards apply to pen registers (which record phone numbers of outgoing calls) and trap and trace devices (which record phone numbers of incoming calls) (18 USC 3121ff).

Foreign Intelligence Surveillance Legislation. Among other things, the Foreign Intelligence Surveillance Act (50 USC 1801ff) provides a statutory framework for electronic surveillance and physical searches of foreign "powers," which is defined to include, among others, groups or agents of groups engaged in international terrorism or engaged in preparation of international terrorism. Under such circumstances, the President, through the Attorney General, may order surveillance for up to one year to collect foreign intelligence data without a court order.

Rewards and Witness Protection Provisions. Money can be a powerful motivator. Rewards for information have played a role in Italy's efforts to weaken the Red Brigades and in Colombia in apprehending drug cartel leaders. A State Department program is in place, supplemented by the aviation industry, offering rewards of up to $5 million to anyone providing information that would prevent or resolve an act of international terrorism against U.S. citizens or U.S. property or that leads to the arrest or conviction of terrorist criminals involved in such acts. This program was at least partly responsible for the arrest of Ramzi Ahmed Yousef, the man accused of masterminding the 1993 World Trade Center bombing, and of Mir Amal Kansi, the murderer of Central Intelligence Agency personnel. The program was established by the 1984 Act to Combat International Terrorism (P.L. 98-533) and is administered by the State Department's Diplomatic Security Service. Rewards greater than $250,000 must be approved by the Secretary of State. The program can pay to relocate informants and immediate family members who fear for their safety. The 1994 crime bill (P.L. 103-322) helps relocate aliens and immediate family members in the United States who are reward recipients. Some observers have suggested expanded participation by the private sector in funding and publicizing such reward programs. In addition, 18 USC 1513 also provides criminal penalties for retaliation against a witness, victim, or informant; and Section 1512 provides penalties for tampering with a witness or informant (see also P.L. 84-885, Section 36 [h], and 18 USC 3071, 3072, and 3077).

Passport and Visa Forgery and Violations. Under 18 USC 1541-1544, it is a criminal offense to forge or knowingly misuse passports or visas or to make false statements when applying for passports or visas.

Cyberterrorism and Cybercrime. The provisions of 18 USC 2701 make it unlawful to intentionally access stored wire and electronic communications and transactions without proper authorization. Authority for government access is provided in some circumstances, with civil penalties stipulated for those who violate statutory procedures. Under 18 USC 2709, the director of the FBI, without court order, can request telephone, toll, and transactional records from a service provider upon certification that such records are needed for counterintelligence purposes and that there are specific facts giving reason to believe that these channels have been used to communicate with persons engaged in international terrorism or clandestine intelligence activities that may violate federal criminal laws. Service providers are prohibited from disclosing that the FBI has sought or obtained access to such records.

Plea Bargaining. This practice is useful to prosecutors in obtaining cooperation from criminal defendants. Under the practice, prosecutors have the discretion of reducing charges against a defendant in return for cooperation. The charges dropped, however, must have been supported by the evidence (see Rule 11 of the Federal Rules of Criminal Procedure).

I will conclude my remarks today with some observations on areas for legislative focus. A growing area of debate in the counterterrorism policy, national security, and law enforcement communities is whether new or revised laws are required to combat the changing nature of terrorist threats and organized criminal activity or whether existing laws are adequate. One option intended to strengthen laws would be to create a continuing criminal enterprise (RICO-type) statute that targets the types of activities terrorists and their organizations engage in, may engage in, or may conspire to engage in. These would include committing crimes of violence, smuggling or acquiring weapons of mass destruction and components thereof, forging documents, or crossing borders illegally.

To the degree that new legislation is needed to combat terrorism, it will likely be in areas where new and innovative technologies provide terrorists with both shields and swords not anticipated by lawmakers. One option is to build flexibility into legislation by allowing regulations to specify, amend, or fine-tune prohibited acts that fall into broadly established guidelines. However, granting such administrative authority to the executive branch could to some degree be seen as diminishing the authority or role of parliaments in formulating counterterrorism legislation and policy. Establishing national, bilateral, or multinational commissions or study groups composed of experts on emerging technologies, law, terrorism, and perhaps also organized crime may be another option for legislators to consider. Such groups could evaluate the adequacy of law in light of changing technology and current and potential patterns of terrorist and criminal behavior.

Areas of focus of such terrorism-oriented groups would undoubtedly include cyberterrorism or cybercrime and the growing potential in the field of bioterrorism. Moreover, the ability to damage computer systems and other electronic devices by electromagnetic pulses, high-power microwaves, and high-energy radio-frequency devices is a capability potentially available to terrorists. Such technology is increasingly available in the marketplace—available to both criminal and terrorist groups—with no international controls currently regulating sale and export.

Technology spreads quickly, and technology can be a double-edged sword. The challenge to policymakers is to minimize the advantage technology offers to the terrorist and criminals who seek to employ it, while maximizing the advantage it offers the state—all without unduly compromising the freedoms that democratic institutions are pledged to protect. It is no easy challenge. But it is clear that law is an important and essential component of a successful counterterrorism response. Given the rapid pace of technological development, the law may no longer want to sit still, wait for events to happen, and then be revised to cover new circumstances. There may be merit in suggestions that legislators and the laws they enact need to be increasingly proactive and forward-looking, especially in areas where technology has a major impact on society.

Russian Legislation and the Struggle Against Terrorism

Mikhail P. Kireev [*]
Academy of the Ministry of Internal Affairs

Terrorism, terrorists, and terrorist activity—these concepts appear in the media practically every day, bringing horror and fear to the population and giving rise to unease and well-founded alarm for our present and our future.

Let us try to get an understanding of the position of Russian legislation in the manner in which Russian laws protect the citizen from crimes of a terrorist nature, crimes with terrorist aspects, and terrorism itself, from the criminal-legal standpoint.

Objectively speaking, terrorism represents a complex and multifaceted phenomenon, the subjects of which infringe in various ways on many legally protected common goods in the pursuit of the most varied goals. This naturally gives rise to difficulties in developing a universal understanding of just what terrorism means.

One of the most serious problems is that of defining the criminal-legal concept and correctly applying existing laws in the struggle against terrorism. A survey conducted among law enforcement agency personnel (more than 1000 individuals were polled) showed that 31 percent anticipate a stabilization in the level of terrorism, while another 31 percent expect a small rise and 13 percent forecast a significant rise. The data collected evoke concern, since the fundamental object of the struggle lies in relations of the security of civil society, characterized by stability and protection of those social conditions necessary for the normal activities of the population and the stable functioning of social institutions. At the same time, terrorism creates a threat not only to the security of society, but also to the security of the individual and to the lives and health of

---

[*] Translated from the Russian by Kelly Robbins.

people, as well as to the security of the state and the capacity of state institutions to fulfill their duties to society.

Of course, the question immediately arises as to the extent to which the actions of law enforcement agencies affect the stabilization of the situation. Among those polled, the overwhelming majority of 70 percent responded that these actions had a partial impact, 21 percent replied on the contrary that there was no such effect, and only 9 percent indicated that stabilization was entirely dependent on the actions of law enforcement.

The Criminal Code and the 1998 Federal Law on Combating Terrorism represent the key elements of Russian antiterrorism legislation. The Criminal Code of the Russian Federation defines actions that are considered to be terrorism or terrorist acts, including the differences between such actions and sabotage or other crimes. It also sets forth the punishments if such actions are committed. The code largely formulates the tasks of law enforcement agencies and intelligence services in uncovering, preventing, and suppressing terrorist activity and defining their goals, organizational structures, and means of using the results of preventive, antiterrorist, administrative, procedural, and other activities aimed at fighting terrorism.

The correct criminal-legal evaluation of information obtained by law enforcement agencies is highly significant in increasing the effectiveness and productivity of the struggle against terrorism. Evidence of this may be found in the results of our research. We shall point out the reasons, in our view, for the unsatisfactory state of the struggle against terrorism. Among the reasons most commonly cited, 24 percent of those surveyed blamed insufficient coordination and 18 percent pointed to a lack of decisiveness on the part of law enforcement officials during decision making.

On the whole, the 1996 Criminal Code of the Russian Federation regulates matters of responsibility for terrorism and terrorist acts in a new way. This is connected with certain changes and additions made in the texts of the corresponding articles of the Special Section of the code, other changes in many criminal-legal standards and institutions, and reforms in the state legal system of our country.

The criminal-legal concept of terrorism is set forth in Article 205 of the Russian Criminal Code. The objective aspect of this crime lies in the perpetration of bombings, arson, or other actions creating a danger of loss of life, significant property damage, or other socially dangerous consequences (an analysis of statistical data shows that 35 percent of terrorist acts involve bombings). The characterization in the new Criminal Code of certain possible consequences of terrorism as "socially dangerous" requires some limiting commentary.

Indeed, if the above-mentioned expression were interpreted literally, then any intentional crime committed in the aim of violating societal security would have to be viewed as an act of terrorism. After all, any crime is a socially dangerous action, that is, it entails or threatens to entail socially dangerous consequences. Furthermore, in such a literal interpretation, the boundary would disappear between a deliberately false report of an act of terrorism (Article 207 of the Criminal Code) and a deliberately false report of a crime (deliberately false accusation) (Article 306). In the normative language on terrorism, the law has in mind not any dangerous consequences, but only those for which the danger is comparable to the danger of loss of life and significant property damage. In addition, the actions carried out must be capable of facilitating the achievement of terrorist goals as described in Article 205, that is, frightening the population, violating societal security, and influencing the decisions of organs of power. Therefore, the category of "other consequences" might include causing harm to the health of many people, making it impossible for the population to exercise its civil rights and freedoms, causing serious disruptions in the operation of vital services and organs of power, or leading to other such socially dangerous outcomes.

At the same time, the new Criminal Code is similar to previous legislation in that it does not require that the above-listed consequences actually occur in order for terrorism to be recognized as a committed crime. Moreover, even if in a case of bombing or arson, the real danger of loss of life, serious property damage, or other such consequences never actually arose due to measures taken, terrorism must be deemed as having been committed formally under Russian legislation.

The Criminal Code does not provide an exhaustive list of actions recognized as terrorism. It is supposed that these could include not only single one-time actions (arson, bombing, landslide, destruction of a building, gunfire, contamination of a local area, and similar acts, including technological and nuclear terrorism), but also continuing actions made up of a number of connected attempts against life, health, or property united by a common plan and goal of frightening the population, violating societal security, or putting pressure on organs of power. This element, in our opinion, also differentiates terrorism from other serious crimes.

An example of this would be campaigns of murder and violence carried out among a population on ethnic, religious, or other lines or group armed attacks and mass murders carried out in such forms and using such weapons, means, and methods as are clearly intended to frighten residents and create panic. Such pogroms and attacks can be viewed as single socially dangerous actions aimed at achieving terroristic goals.

It should be emphasized that the goal of affecting decision making by organs of power presupposes a striving to influence both organs of state power (including executive, legislative, and judicial branches, as well as both federal and federation-subject organs) and organs of local self-government, through which the people realize the power pertaining to them in accordance with the Constitution of the Russian Federation. In a criminal-legal assessment of information on facts that might involve the commission of an act of terrorism, it is essential to keep in mind the following circumstances.

In its external aspects and in the socially dangerous consequences it presents, terrorism resembles certain other crimes against life and health, societal security, and the security of movement and transportation. This concerns such crimes as negligently causing death or harm to health (Articles 109 and 119 of the Criminal Code of the Russian Federation); violating rules of fire safety (Article 219) as well as safety rules at atomic power facilities (Article 215), potentially explosive sites (Article 217), or mining, construction, or other work sites (Article 216); violating rules for the storage and use of explosives (Article 218) or use of transportation (Articles 263 and 268); or handling radioactive materials illegally (Article 220). However, in the cases listed above, the danger to property or human life arises as a result of the negligence of the guilty party. Terrorism here does not represent an intentional crime. An individual committing an act of terrorism recognizes the societal danger of his actions, foresees the unavoidability or possibility that socially dangerous consequences will ensue, and hopes for such consequences in order to achieve his goals.

Terrorism must also be differentiated from certain intentional crimes that are similar from an objective standpoint, such as the intentional destruction or damage of property by universally dangerous means (Part 2, Article 167), the intentional destruction or damage of military property committed by a perpetrator in the course of another military crime (Article 346), or murder committed by universally dangerous means (Article 105, Part 2, Section E). The descriptions of these crimes lack any indication of special terrorist goals. But it is these very goals—the violation of societal security, the frightening of the population, and the influencing of decision making by organs of power—that are pursued by an individual committing an act of terrorism.

The criminal directs his will toward achievement of these goals, and to realize them, he selects the time and appropriate weapons and tools of the crime as well as the situation. As a rule, the terrorist accompanies commission of universally dangerous actions with notification of the authorities and the population that new bombings, arsons, or similar acts are possible. In this way, he is counting on attaining the terrorist goals that have been set. Even mere reports of possible actions that would create the danger of loss of life, significant property damage, or similar consequences are capable of creating panic among the population, producing disorder, disrupting the operations of transportation and other enterprises and institutions, and compelling state agencies to take complex and expensive preventive measures.

It is for this reason that the new Criminal Code classifies as a completed terrorist act even a threat of universally dangerous actions made for terroristic purposes. Furthermore, the making of an intentional false report of an act of terrorism is also deemed to be a crime (Article 207 of the Criminal Code), regardless of the motives and goals of such a report.

A footnote to Article 205 of the Criminal Code concerns the absolution from criminal responsibility of individuals who have participated in preparations for a terrorist act. Its text is practically unchanged from that of a footnote to Article

213/3 of the 1961 Criminal Code of the Russian Soviet Federated Socialist Republic. At the same time, the juridical content of this footnote requires new interpretation. This is due to the appearance in the General Section of the Criminal Code of standards concerning the voluntary refusal of participants in a crime to carry that crime through to completion. In accordance with Part 2 of Article 31 of the Criminal Code, there are no grounds for assigning criminal responsibility to an individual who has voluntarily and finally declined to carry a crime through to completion. Furthermore, an accomplice to a crime bears no responsibility if in addition to voluntarily and finally declining he has also taken all possible measures to prevent the crime. The same would be true for the organizer and instigator of the crime if he in fact managed to prevent the criminal attempt (Part 4, Article 31). It must be emphasized that in this case we are referring not to an absolution of criminal responsibility, but rather to the *complete absence of grounds for such responsibility.*

By comparing Article 31 of the Criminal Code and the footnote to Article 205, one may conclude that the referenced footnote refers only to those cases in which the criminal becomes involved in preventing a terrorist act voluntarily and not through pressure or force (for example, by being discovered and held to account) or because an individual stops a planned terrorist act in order to carry it through later at a more convenient time. In other words, the footnote to Article 205 could be applicable only if there is no evidence of a voluntary and final withdrawal from participation in a terrorist act. If not, then Article 31 would apply, stipulating not an absolution of responsibility, but rather an absence of grounds for responsibility.

In making a criminal-legal assessment of information on planned or completed bombings, arsons, or similar actions, one must make a distinction between a terrorist act and an act of sabotage. Indeed, along with language on responsibility for terrorism, the new Russian Criminal Code also includes a standard on sabotage. Sabotage is defined as a bombing, arson, or other action aimed at destroying or damaging vital service facilities, enterprises, structures, means of communications, or the transportation infrastructure if committed for the purpose of undermining the economic security and defense capability of the Russian Federation (Article 281 of the Criminal Code). Differentiating between the elements involved in these two crimes, terrorism and sabotage, is done by means of objective characteristics (sabotage does not necessarily presuppose the creation of danger of loss of life or serious harm to health, and it does not necessarily require the use of universally dangerous means of harming the above-mentioned facilities) and subjective characteristics (the saboteur pursues certain goals that do not coincide with the goals involved in an act of terrorism).

Sabotage is categorized among crimes against the foundations of the constitutional structure and state security (Chapter 29 of the Criminal Code). According to the law, the fundamental difference between sabotage and a terrorist act lies in the goals of the criminal. A terrorist bombing is directed against societal security and against the population. It is carried out with the aim of disrupting the foundations for the existence and functioning of civil society, the foundations for the organization and self-organization of the social sphere. If the goal of the criminal is to attack national (state) security and harm its basic values, including first of all its economic security and defense capability, criminal law labels the actions as sabotage. It is no accident that the law does not require the act of sabotage to create the threat of loss of life. Indeed, the saboteur achieves his goals not by frightening the population, but primarily by affecting material objects created and functioning in the interests of protecting the country and defending its economic interests.

The choice of the target that the criminal aims to destroy or damage is the primary evidence indicative of sabotage-related goals. The Criminal Code lists the following possible targets in this category: facilities providing vital services to the population (heating plants, bakeries, medical and pharmacy establishments, water intake sites, etc.); other enterprises and structures; radio, telephone, telegraph, and other communications-related facilities; bridges; roads; means of transportation; and other transport infrastructure-related sites.

Further evidence of sabotage-related goals may be found in the choice of the time, place, and specific circumstances of the crime (for example, the commission of a crime during war or danger of war or during a period of economic crisis, and an attempt to undermine Russian sovereignty using these circumstances). Other evidence may be found in the specific target selected for destruction or damage (for example, a facility that plays a key role in a strategically important economic or vital services sphere). Let us emphasize once more that this sort of case does not require the damage to be caused by universally dangerous means. The means chosen by the criminal are primarily aimed at harming the economy and military power of Russia.

In the course of applying the new Criminal Code of the Russian Federation, a question might arise regarding the possibility of an ideal combination of terrorism and sabotage, that is, a situation in which the perpetrator fulfilled the requirements for committing both crimes in a single action (for example, an action carried out in a zone of internal armed conflict). It seems that the law does not rule out such a possibility. In carrying out his task of weakening Russia's military potential, the criminal takes a defense-related facility out of commission, choosing to use the most terrifying and universally dangerous means and intending to elicit a certain reaction from the authorities.

It should be considered that the law does not rule out the possibility that the criminal may have goals related to both sabotage and terrorism simultaneously. This is possible if, for example, a perpetrator on assignment from a foreign organization and in the aim of undermining the country's economic security takes a strategically important industrial facility out of commission, using means that frighten the population (a powerful explosion) and intending to force the authorities to meet the criminal's individual demands. In such cases, commission of such a bombing includes characteristics of both sabotage and terrorism, which means that it would be qualified under two different articles of the Criminal Code of the Russian Federation.

When the criminal destroying targets aims to frighten the population so as to diminish Russia's defense capability and its social-moral potential in some manner (for example, in conditions of war or armed conflict), then it is a matter only of sabotage-related goals. No additional qualification of the action as terrorism is required.

Another circumstance also merits attention. In the majority of instances, both acts of sabotage and acts of terrorism are planned and carried out on the basis of a preliminary agreement among a group of individuals or an organized group. It is no coincidence that the Criminal Code includes the appropriate qualifying standards in Parts 2 and 3 of Article 205 and Part 2 of Article 281.

Therefore, it is highly likely that a situation could arise in which the goals of individual participants might not coincide. This is possible, for example, if for the purpose of undermining the economic security and defense capability of Russia, the head of a saboteur group plans a bombing to be carried out by another individual unaware of the group leader's true motives. This individual in fact might be pursuing goals linked with frightening the population or other terrorist purposes. In such situations, the actions of each participant should receive an independent criminal-legal evaluation regarding the orientation of their intentions. The actions of participants in a bombing must be categorized according to the article on terrorism or on sabotage, depending on the goals established and held by each criminal involved.

Examples of terrorism in the political sphere are not found only in universally dangerous actions aimed at influencing the activities of organs of power. Such terrorism can also appear in the form of specific terrorist acts committed for the purpose of halting the political activity of individual persons (Article 277 of the Criminal Code).

Serious changes were made in the 1996 Russian Criminal Code standard on responsibility for terrorist acts. These changes primarily involved characteristics of the objective aspect of the crime. According to the new Criminal Code, a terrorist act is considered to have been committed not only in the event that it causes the death of a state or public figure, but also in the case of attempts on the lives of such individuals. Shifting the moment at which a terrorist act is deemed juridically complete to the assassination attempt stage makes it possible to apply the maximum measure of punishment to the culprit, including the death penalty, even if the intended victim is not killed (although it is true that a death penalty moratorium is currently in effect in Russia).

The list of those potential target individuals who are covered under the crime analyzed above is narrow: the law excludes representatives of organs of power, since responsibility for their murder must fall under Article 295 ("Attempt on the Life of an Individual Involved in Facilitating Justice or Preliminary

Investigations"), Article 317 ("Attempt on the Life of Law Enforcement or Military Service Personnel"), or Part 2 of Article 105 ("Murder in Connection with Employment in an Official Capacity").

The subjective aspect of the terrorist act has now taken on new characteristics as well. A requisite component of this crime is the motive of revenge for the state or public activity of the victim or the goal of halting the victim's state or public activity. The above-mentioned motive and goal may be present simultaneously.

The question of types of intent in committing a terrorist act also merits independent evaluation. For Russian criminal law, only direct intent has traditionally been included as a criterion for this crime. This is because the subjective aspect of an act of terrorism for a long time presupposed the mandatory presence of special "counterrevolutionary" or later "anti-Soviet" goals. The presence of this special goal as part of the crime of terrorism understandably narrowed down the possible types of intent, leaving only direct intent. However, the present law also recognizes as an act of terrorism an assassination attempt without any special goal, or only with the motive of revenge for political activity. Thus, "with regard to causing death to the victim, there can be both direct and indirect intent, as the presence of a motive necessarily presupposes direct intent with regard to the action but not necessarily to the result of that action."

The motive can determine the action itself but can be aimed at another result; in that case, indirect intent is possible with regard to the anticipated result of the terrorist act (death). This occurs specifically if out of revenge for political activity, the criminal wishes to harm the health of a state figure, creating the possibility of his death in the process. In the event that death is actually caused, intent must be considered indirect.

An expansive approach is lacking in recent doctrinal commentaries regarding the concept "state figure." More accurately, emphasis is placed on the circumstance that the figure is primarily an individual who makes decisions, that is, a leader or member of a collegial governing agency influencing the functioning of the state mechanism or a public association, not merely executing but rather forming their policies.

At the same time, efforts to place only federation-level figures in this category are clearly unfounded. Leaders of cities and districts and similar individuals involved in local self-government must be regarded as public figures, and in this capacity they cannot be excluded from the category of potential victims of terrorist acts.

It should be kept in mind that the new criminal law does not preclude the designation of foreign government officials or figures from international and foreign public organizations as victims under the article on terrorist acts (Article 277), provided that these persons are conducting their activities in our country in accordance with the Constitution of the Russian Federation and Russian legislation.

In conclusion, another new legislative enactment also merits attention. It is commonly known that Part 3, Article 12 of the 1996 Criminal Code of the

Russian Federation sets forth the "real" principle of criminal law activity with regard to actions infringing upon the interests of the Russian Federation.

It signifies that Russian criminal law can be applied to a foreign citizen or stateless person who has committed a crime on Russian soil aimed against the interests of our state. This standard is applied in the event that such an individual is not convicted in a foreign country and is subsequently tried in our country. This means that in accordance with the above-outlined principle in our law, foreigners who have committed the following acts could be held criminally responsible: a terrorist act aimed at influencing the decisions of Russian authorities (Article 205 of the Criminal Code); sabotage of a Russian military or economic target located outside the borders of the Russian Federation (Article 281); a terrorist act against a Russian state or public figure who is temporarily abroad committed in connection with the victim's official activities but in the interests of our country (Article 277).

From this analysis, it is obvious that the struggle against terrorist activity is effective when it is legal, uncompromising, and correctly qualified, that is, differentiated from other types of crimes that may include elements of terrorization.

Russian Legislation and the Fight Against Terrorism

Viktor E. Petrishchev [*]

Russian State Duma

In the early 1990s, terrorism in the Russian Federation underwent a transformation from a number of unrelated, rare, and somewhat unique manifestations of violent crime to a systemic and large-scale threat to the state and society in general. Prior to that period, the Soviet Union had legislation in place that provided for rather harsh repression of socially and politically motivated criminal acts. Therefore, potential perpetrators of terrorist acts (such as ultranationalists, religious fanatics, and extremists) who were plotting violent changes of the existing sociopolitical order, and so forth, were usually identified by law enforcement agencies in the early planning stages. Potential perpetrators were subjected to open and clandestine operations aimed at correcting their behavior and redirecting their activities into legitimate channels. In addition, the nationwide system for preventing extremist and terrorist acts seemed to be quite effective. For instance, the distribution of anticonstitutional propaganda and the creation of organizations for this purpose were punishable under the Criminal Code. State censorship eliminated possibilities of mass production and legitimate dissemination of materials proclaiming ideas of national, religious, or racial superiority; licensing and permit requirements created serious obstacles to procuring firearms and explosives.

Given all of the above circumstances, the few isolated terrorist acts that occurred, such as the bombing of the Moscow Metro perpetrated in 1977 by a group of Armenian nationalists and the hijacking attempt by a group of youths in Tbilisi Airport in 1984, were justifiably considered to be unique occurrences, atypical for our country. As a result, only two types of crimes were classified as terrorism under the Soviet legislation of that period: a terrorist act and a terrorist

---

[*] Translated from the Russian by Rita Kit.

act against a representative of a foreign state (Articles 66 and 67, respectively, of the Criminal Code of the Russian Soviet Federated Socialist Republic [RSFSR]).

However, by the early 1990s the situation had changed considerably. Riding on the wave of the so-called democratic reforms, the country experienced an outbreak of destructive processes creating a favorable environment for increased crime, extremism, and terrorism. Among these factors were economic decline, deterioration of interethnic relations, growth of separatism, and loss of the values that formerly bound the society together, such as civic duty, patriotism, and internationalism. While the head of state, Mikhail Gorbachev, traveled overseas promoting his new policies and universal human values, his very own state was collapsing. Overall, the self-centeredness and nearsightedness of those at the highest levels of political office, the lack of executive control over developments in the outer regions of the USSR, and the political manipulation of various nationalists and extremists by a new breed of ambitious politicians seeking to seize political control resulted in the breakdown of law enforcement. Unauthorized meetings, demonstrations, and marches became more prevalent. They increasingly took on an antisocial nature and more frequently turned into riots and civil unrest. The Kremlin failed to respond swiftly and decisively, and as a result, law enforcement and the military were held hostage by an indecisive head of state. Eventually, these processes resulted in the de facto collapse of the state.

However, a new political "elite," actively employing nationalistic and separatist ideas as well as political and religious extremism in their political fight with the central authorities, failed to recognize the fact that the destructive processes they had supported so actively were gaining a substantial momentum of their own. Having achieved widespread support among various groups of the population, extremism turned into a considerable threat to the newly emerging post-Soviet administrative and political entities. Underestimation of this threat by the leaders of the newly created states, illustrated by Boris Yeltsin's appeal to the subjects of the Russian Federation "to take as much sovereignty as they can possibly swallow," resulted in a number of large-scale conflicts, some of them armed.

Widespread legal and moral nihilism and the loss of general social values and spirituality greatly contributed to increased incidents of terrorism in Russia and other members of the Commonwealth of Independent States. In addition, on numerous occasions, the highest authorities themselves demonstrated a total disregard for the rule of law and the national constitution. Illegal violence was regularly employed by those in power to protect some unclear "vital interests" (as defined by the head of state and his closest staff). In the Russian Federation, this trend reached its peak in October 1993, when the Russian "White House" was assaulted in Moscow.

One can argue that the above comments go far beyond the scope of discussing Russian antiterrorism legislation and venture into the field of political science, but I felt obligated to bring them up here, given the truly decisive role these negative developments played in the late 1980s and early 1990s.

Other factors contributing to the spread of terrorism in the Russian Federation in the early 1990s include the following:

- Overall decline in economic activity;
- Increased tensions in interethnic relations, frequently resulting in armed conflicts of varying intensity;
- Increasing numbers of social problems—unemployment, declining material well-being of the active work force, lack of a targeted youth policy, loss of ideological and moral values;
- Weakening of the licensing and registration system for weapons and an increase in illegal trafficking in firearms and other aids to violent crime;
- High level of corruption among government bureaucrats, resulting in a rise in both organized crime and street crime; and
- The relationship between religious and political extremism on the one hand and increased overall levels of criminal activity in society on the other.

In this context, starting in the early 1990s, statistics in the Russian Federation showed a steady increase in crime. For example, during 1994-1995, only 64 bombings were reported, but during 1996-2000, the annual number of such explosions was 600-700 (155 such cases were reported in the first quarter of 2001). Special attention should be paid to changes noted in the nature of crimes committed using explosive devices. Most frequently, these crimes do not fall into the trivial "gang warfare" category, but rather seem to meet all of the criteria of terrorist acts. According to the Federal Security Service of the Russian Federation (FSB), only 16 out of the total number of 600 reported bombings in 1997 could be treated as terrorist acts, while out of approximately the same number in 2000, 150 could be considered terrorist acts. Using the same criteria, 61 of the 155 bombings in the first quarter of 2001 were deemed to be terrorist acts.

In addition, one needs to emphasize a trend toward increasing human and social impacts of the bombings committed in the Russian Federation in recent years. For instance, in 1997, 153 lives were lost as a result of bombings; in 1998, 163; in 1999, 506; and in 2000, 207, with hundreds more wounded. So far this year, dozens have been killed or injured.

In the mid-1990s legislators had to respond to the growing threat of terrorism and to broaden the definition of criminal acts classified as terrorism. Adopted on January 7, 1994, Federal Law 10-FZ introduced into the RSFSR Criminal Code Article 213(3), entitled "Terrorism." This marked the first legal definition of the term terrorism in our country. The article defines terrorism as "bombings, arson, and other acts causing a threat to human life, major property loss, and other negative consequences committed against public safety or with the aim of influencing decision-making of the government authorities."

The new Criminal Code of the Russian Federation, which came into force on January 1, 1997, defines terrorism in Section IX, Chapter 24 (crimes against public safety and public order), Article 205. In my opinion, the primary aim of terrorist attacks is much broader than public safety—terrorists commit their acts against the constitutional foundations of society and its governing structure. Therefore, it would have been more appropriate to include the article on terrorism in Section X of the Criminal Code, which deals with crimes against government authority. Indeed, are the consequences of a terrorist act less significant to the state and society than an attempt on the life of a law enforcement officer? The law punishes an attempt on the life of a law enforcement officer with the death penalty, while committing a terrorist act (without aggravating factors) carries a sentence of only five to ten years of imprisonment.

The definition of terrorism in Article 205 seems to be incorrect as well. In this article, terrorism is defined as "bombings, arson, and other acts representing threats of loss of life, major property loss, and other negative consequences, provided that these acts were committed against public safety, with the aim of spreading fear among the population or influencing decision-making of government authorities, and/or a threat of committing these acts with the same purpose."

An analysis of this definition shows that it fails to adequately describe the nature and substance of terrorism. In fact, terrorists may pursue goals that go beyond influencing the decision making of government authorities. According to M.P. Odessky and D.M. Feldman, terrorism, in its broadest possible definition, is "a way of governing society through fear."[1] Therefore, terrorists may also target people outside the government. The targets can be based on nationality, race, politics, economics, religion, or some other criteria; in some cases an entire population can be targeted.

I would also like to question defining "spreading fear among the population" as the primary objective of terrorism. Indeed, spreading fear among the population is a very important component of terrorism. (The authors of the Article 205 of the Criminal Code of the Russian Federation should be credited with mentioning this component—it was not included in the body of Article 213[3] of the RSFSR Criminal Code.) However, this component serves merely as a tool for achieving terrorist objectives and is not an ultimate goal by itself.

Finally, the text of Article 205 of the Criminal Code fails to adequately reflect the substance of terrorism, even when taken not as a sociopolitical phenomenon, but as purely a criminal one. One can easily see that in this article, the legislators provided a list of various manifestations of terrorism—arson, bombings, and other acts. Therefore, the title "Terrorist Acts" would have been more appropriate for this article, rather than the present title, "Terrorism." This substitution of definitions resulted in a number of difficulties in drafting the Federal Law "On Combating Terrorism," which is described below.

The institution of criminal penalties for terrorist acts nevertheless failed to address the problem of terrorism as an extremely dangerous sociopolitical phenomenon. (In addition to Article 205, "Terrorism," the Criminal Code of the Russian Federation contains Article 206, "Hostage Taking"; Article 207, "Making Knowingly False Statements About Terrorist Acts"; Article 277, "Attempt on the Life of a Government or Public Figure"; and Article 360, "Attack on Persons and/or Entities Enjoying International Protection.") The need for a comprehensive nationwide system of counterterrorist measures was first realized in the early 1990s by the agencies most familiar with terrorist acts, namely, the security services and law enforcement. In late 1996, a working group charged with drafting the Federal Law "On Combating Terrorism" was created under the auspices of the Committee of the State Duma. The Chairman of the Duma, Mr. V.I. Ilyukhin, headed the working group. Although the working group was rather small in number, dozens of scientists, experts, and practitioners from various ministries and agencies contributed to the final draft. In addition to several documents already prepared by the Federal Security Service, Ministry of Interior, and Office of the General Prosecutor of the Russian Federation, the working group studied materials from a number of conferences held on this topic and the legislation of some foreign countries, including Great Britain, Israel, Spain, Italy, Peru, the United States, Turkey, and Germany. I would like to emphasize that the vast majority of Duma deputies, regardless of their party or political affiliation, supported the activities of the working group. I believe that this overwhelming support can be explained by the fact that terrorism is an "equal opportunity" threat—it makes no exceptions for race, class, nationality, or ethnicity. As recent history has shown, victims of terrorist attacks can be found among heads of state, public figures, entrepreneurs, and innocent passersby.

By the time of the first reading of the draft on September 10, 1997, terrorism was defined by the authors as a sociopolitical phenomenon manifested through "illegitimate violence (or threat thereof) against persons and entities or destruction/damage (or threat thereof) of property committed with the aim of undermining public safety, international entities, and the established system of national government through forcing government bodies to make decisions desired by the terrorists." In this wording, the authors clearly stepped aside from the narrow legal definition of the term—and they were perfectly right to do so, since this is not a criminal law, but a federal one, designed to establish a nationwide approach to combating terrorism as a dangerous sociopolitical phenomenon. This is the wording that was adopted almost unanimously by the deputies of the State Duma during the first reading of the draft law.

However, during the comment stage, the authors received substantial number of similar comments[2] urging them to bring the definition into accordance with the wording of Article 205 of the Criminal Code of the Russian Federation. Among others, the President and the Government of the Russian Federation submitted similar requests. Unfortunately, the influence and authority of those commenting prevailed, and the definition was subsequently narrowed down to a mere list of terrorist acts as described in Articles 205, 207, 277, and 360 of the Criminal Code. This change inevitably resulted in the narrowing of the statewide prevention role. On the one hand, changes in the definitions shifted the emphasis toward combating terrorist crimes, which fall under the jurisdiction of the security services and law enforcement agencies. On the other hand, the narrower definition removed a number of factors from their focus, which played an important role in defining terrorism itself. However, these factors have to be addressed not only from the legal standpoint, but also through a nationwide system of economic, social, ideological, and other measures.

I must bring to your attention yet another shortcoming of the draft, which appeared after it was adopted at the first reading on September 10, 1997. This issue relates to the status of the Federal Interagency Anti-terrorist Commission, which was created by the Russian Federation Government Decree 45, dated January 16, 1997. The director of the Federal Security Service of the Russian Federation was appointed to head the commission, whereas in most other countries antiterrorist activities are conducted under the auspices of the highest executive office in the nation. This status would have been very beneficial in present-day Russia. That is why the authors of the Federal Law in the article titled "Interagency Antiterrorist Commission of the Russian Federation" provided that the Government of the Russian Federation would create the commission and the deputy chairman of the government would head it. The same article provided a relatively detailed outline of the mission statement, authority, and responsibility of this federal coordinating body. In addition, the law provided for establishing similar bodies at the federation subject level (or regional level, including several federation subjects). All of these measures were reflecting the proposed nationwide vertically integrated system of antiterrorism measures. Unfortunately, given persistent requests from the Office of the President, this provision was changed as follows: "To provide for proper coordination of anti-terrorist activities, the President and the Government of the Russian Federation may set up regional and federal antiterrorist commissions."[3] Only later was this corrected (Russian Federation Government Decree 1302, dated November 6, 1998). The decree also appointed the chairman of the Government of the Russian Federation to head the commission.

In the final analysis, the Federal Law "On Combating Terrorism" that went into effect on August 4, 1998, remained an imperfect document. However, it contributed to solving a number of earlier problems. It provides for certain legal and social guarantees for individuals directly involved in counterterrorist operations. This provision was especially important for law enforcement officers. The law also establishes clear definitions and introduces major terms, which is helpful not only for the theoretical analysis of the situation, but also for the practical work of several executive agencies, the security apparatus, and the general public.

The law provides a clear list of entities directly responsible for counterterrorist operations. Article 6 establishes that there are six such agencies in the Russian Federation: the Federal Security Service, the Ministry of Internal Affairs, the Foreign Intelligence Service, the Federal Protective Service, the Ministry of Defense, and the Federal Border Service. Unfortunately, their respective jurisdictions were not clearly defined. For example, Subarticles 2 and 3 of Article 7 provide that prevention, identification, and investigation of politically motivated terrorist crimes fall under the jurisdiction of the Federal Security Service, while prevention, identification, and investigation of financially motivated terrorist crimes fall under the jurisdiction of the Ministry of Internal Affairs of the Russian Federation. However, the law fails to provide clear definitions and a distinction between political and financial motivations.

The law also stipulates that in addition to the above-listed agencies, the Government of the Russian Federation provides a list of other federal executive agencies that may be called upon to contribute to counterterrorist activities within their respective competencies.

Establishing the list of specific ministries and agencies directly responsible for counterterrorist activities is important, and it is far from being a mere formal declaration. One should take into account the fact that at the earlier stages of drafting this law, heads of some of these bodies attempted to rid themselves and their agencies of this responsibility, arguing that this function was not delegated to them under earlier legislation. Had this position prevailed, the legislators would have been forced to delegate this responsibility to two agencies only—the Federal Security Service and the Ministry of Internal Affairs of the Russian Federation. Indeed, prior to drafting the Federal Law "On Combating Terrorism," these two agencies were the only ones responsible for such activities (see Federal Law 40-FZ "On the Federal Security Service of the Russian Federation," dated April 3, 1995; Federal Law 27-FZ "On the Internal Troops of the Ministry of Internal Affairs of the Russian Federation," dated February 6, 1997; and Decree 1039 of the President of the Russian Federation "On Approving of the Regulations Regarding the Ministry of Internal Affairs of the Russian Federation"). The authors of the Federal Law "On Combating Terrorism" based their work on the assumption that the new law can modify agencies' responsibility in accordance with the earlier enacted legislation.

Chapter III ("Management of Counterterrorist Operations") of the Federal Law "On Combating Terrorism" deserves positive mention as well. This chapter provides a general outline for establishing and managing task forces for conducting counterterrorist operations, which brings much needed clarity into mounting and running such operations. The commander of the task force is given broad authority—he decides on the scale and scope of the operation, determines the timeframe of the operation, determines what forces and assets will be utilized, determines what kind of information is given to the media, et cetera. The article "Management of Counterterrorist Operations" specifically provides that "interference by any person regardless of his/her position in the day-to-day management of the counter-terrorist operation is strictly prohibited." The provisions of Chapter 3 passed real-life tests during the special counterterrorist operations in Chechnya, when the Federal Law "On Combating Terrorism" de facto replaced the failed Federal Law "On Emergency Situations."

The Federal Law "On Combating Terrorism" also imposed severe restrictions on deals that can be offered to terrorists in order to save human lives. Should negotiating with terrorists be deemed necessary, negotiators must be specifically authorized by the task force commander. No individuals can be turned over to terrorists, no weapons or hazardous materials can be given to them, and no political demands could be considered in exchange for calling off the terrorist act.

Finally, the law attempts to break away from the recent trend of narrowing the definition of counterterrorism to a mere response to terrorist acts. (Once again, deficiencies must be pointed out in the definition of terrorism used in the language of Article 3 of the Federal Law.) Nevertheless, immediately after declaring the principle of the rule of law, Article 2 ("Fundamental Principles of Combating Terrorism") of the Federal Law states that "priority shall be given to terrorism prevention." The goal of terrorism prevention is emphasized numerous times in other provisions of the law, along with the need for obtaining timely information about the planning and preparation of such attacks.

There is no need to argue that when facing terrorist acts, law enforcement officers are facing the consequences of chronic processes that lead to crime, processes that are outside their direct control. These include social, political, and economic developments, interethnic relationships, relationships between the federal government and federation subjects, and so forth. Therefore, the law makes an attempt to shift the emphasis to terrorism prevention, including holding government officials liable for poor administrative and political decisions.

Let me elaborate on the previous statement. The primary causes of terrorism in modern Russia lie in the current economic and social crisis, worsening interethnic relationships, and increased political tensions. Therefore, any terrorist act is a result of the dynamic interaction of adverse societal conditions and personality disorders, usually attributed to the perpetrators of terrorist acts. I dare say that there is a trend perfectly illustrated by both international and Russian experience. When the national economy is stable, the government's social policies are well balanced and supported by the majority of the population and people's incomes are far above the poverty line. When an individual can freely and fully satisfy his or her spiritual and material needs and exercise his or her rights and freedoms, there are no adverse societal conditions feeding terrorist acts, and personality disorders become the primary motivation. On the contrary, when the national economy, social policy, and spiritual well-being are suffering from a major crisis, terrorist acts are driven primarily by these adverse conditions.

Psychologically motivated terrorist acts could be best illustrated by the actions of Theodore Kaczynski (labeled by the Federal Bureau of Investigation [FBI] as the Unabomber), who terrorized the entire United States from 1978 until 1985, or Charles Whitman, whose 1966 shooting spree in Texas left 12 dead and 30 wounded.

On the other hand, the increase in terrorist activity in Russia over the past decade can be explained primarily by adverse societal conditions. Their combined effect is largely responsible for the outburst of terrorism in Chechnya as well.

Given the fact that terrorism is becoming an increasing threat to countries all over the world, many nations are actively seeking ways to enhance their national antiterrorist legislation. Obviously, in spite of the increasing trend toward globalization, each country is searching for its own unique ways of protecting itself against terrorism. In light of this, studying international experience in the area of counterterrorism policies, approaches, and regulatory framework is becoming increasingly important. Such studies provide researchers with a set of tools and techniques, enabling them to better analyze the threats facing their own countries and to devise the most effective nationwide systems for preventing and eliminating terrorism.

In fact, despite the diversity of national legal systems and approaches to terrorism prevention, most were developed in response to the same fundamental set of internal and external factors. These include the nature of the external threat, the domestic political situation, crime levels in the country, the nature of long-term domestic conflicts, the history of various ethnic groups and their cultural and religious traditions and norms, the level of cultural and legal awareness of the population, the development of the societal institutional framework, and so forth. Analysis of the impact of the above-mentioned factors on the development of antiterrorist legislation in various countries and application of this international experience to the specific circumstances in your country may result in development of the most effective model for a national approach to combating terrorism. Implementation of this approach while fully utilizing international experience may save time on empirical testing of various models and may raise the level of academic research and practical work in your own country to a higher level.

Comparative studies of antiterrorist legislation and law enforcement practices throughout the world enrich all specialists, enabling them to view the problem in its entirety, thus putting them in a position to propose promising approaches for enhancing national legislation in this area.

Let me briefly touch upon Russian and American approaches to combating terrorism, which I hope will be interesting given the topic of our seminar. To save time, I will not go into a detailed analysis of the causes of terrorism in our two countries, because this issue could become a subject for a separate discussion.

Mr. David Tucker, who has specialized in research on special operations and low-intensity conflicts over the past 25 years for the U.S. Department of Defense, has outlined the following principles of antiterrorist operations:

- Following a policy prohibiting deal-making with terrorists;
- Expanding the jurisdiction of national legislation to allow for the pursuit of terrorists outside of the United States;
- Actively promoting international antiterrorism conventions and treaties;

- Designing and implementing various defensive antiterrorism measures;
- Attacking the causes of terrorism and preventing it from spreading;
- Implementing forward-looking measures designed to prevent terrorist acts; and
- Carrying out special operations to destroy terrorist organizations from within.[4]

There are similarities in the antiterrorism policy of both Russia and the United States, including restrictions on mass media coverage of terrorism-related events; possible deployment of military assets to respond to large-scale terrorist acts; utilization of undercover methods to penetrate terrorist organizations; social guarantees and protection of personnel involved in antiterrorist operations; et cetera. Analysis of the principles of antiterrorism policy outlined in Article 2 of the above-mentioned Russian Federal Law reveals the following similarities:

- Rule of law;
- Higher priority for terrorism prevention;
- Inevitability of punishment for terrorist acts;
- Combination of transparent and undercover methods;
- A comprehensive approach, including preventive measures, political, legal, socioeconomic, and public relations actions;
- Priority protection of the right of victims of terrorism;
- Minimal yielding to terrorist demands;
- Single line of command for counter-terrorist operations; and
- Minimal reporting of tactics and methods of counterterrorist operations, as well as minimal disclosure of information about the personnel involved.

A comparative analysis of the Russian Federal Law "On Combating Terrorism" and the U.S. Antiterrorism and Effective Death Penalty Act of 1996 shows some common features, despite major differences in the two documents. For example, U.S. and Russian legislators give different definitions of terrorism; they differ in their identification of the primary causes of terrorism; and they give the government different authority to deal with external threats. In addition, the legal framework is different in the two countries. Besides, the Antiterrorism and Effective Death Penalty Act is a very detailed document, while the Russian law is relatively short (containing only 29 articles) and provides only general regulation of counterterrorism activities.

Obviously, the financial resources of these two nations are vastly different. In fact, the adoption of the U.S. Antiterrorism and Effective Death Penalty Act resulted in additional multimillion-dollar appropriations to the agencies involved in counterterrorism work, including the FBI, U.S. Customs Service, Immigration and Naturalization Service, Drug Enforcement Administration, Departments of Justice and Treasury, U.S. Secret Service, and others. To illustrate the Russian situation in this area, let me provide the following examples. In the beginning of 1999, the Security Council of the Russian Federation acting in accordance with the decree of the President, drafted the Federal Program on Strengthening Counter-Terrorism Activities. Having "cleared" all stakeholders (i.e., agencies directly involved in this work), the draft was then "killed" by the Ministry of Economy and the Ministry of Finance because there were no funds to pay for the proposed measures. It should be noted that preventive measures were prevalent in that program, with special emphasis on active countermeasures against the dissemination of extremist and terrorist ideologies. I believe that the absence of these measures contributed to the failure of attempts to combat the Wahhabi and Chechen separatist agendas, which drew Russia into a long-term armed conflict in the North Caucasus region.

To continue discussing the importance of preventive measures, one cannot help but appreciate the strong preventive components build into the U.S. Antiterrorism and Effective Death Penalty Act. For example, in this act, American legislators demonstrated their deep understanding of and concern over newly emerging terrorist threats involving modern technologies. Building upon detailed models of potential terrorist threats involving weapons of mass destruction, the act provides for a number of measures aimed at preventing such terrorist acts, which could possibly lead to massive loss of human life.

Potential terrorist acts involving the use of explosives and modern weaponry and technology may be prevented by imposing strict regulations requiring the proper safeguarding and storage of materials that could be used to carry out terrorist acts. In addition, the law imposes criminal charges for activities conducted in preparation for committing a terrorist act or creating a favorable environment for it. For example, Article 503 obligates the Attorney General and the Secretary of Defense to exercise personal oversight over thefts of firearms, explosives, and other hazardous materials and to report their findings to Congress.

Article 511 imposes harsher punishments for illicit trafficking in weapons-grade biological materials and imposes stricter regulations on their storage and use for scientific research. In particular, the Secretary of Health and Human Services is required to compile, approve, and update as necessary a list of potentially dangerous biological preparations. The Secretary is also responsible for designing and enforcing safety rules for dangerous biological materials, for ensuring that personnel working with these materials have the proper training and retraining, for providing adequate equipment and establishing proper procedures for secure storage, and for designing countermeasures to neutralize potential threats in the event of theft.

Section VI of the act regulates enforcement of the Convention on Plastic Explosives. This is very important, since these explosives are extremely powerful and difficult to detect with scanning equipment. Several measures were built into the law in order to prevent the commission of crimes with this type of explosive. Article 603 (mandatory identifier) imposes criminal penalties for manufacturing plastic explosives without special identifying ingredients. Criminal penalties are also imposed on the export, import, possession, transportation, and receipt of unidentifiable explosives. Violators can be punished with up to 10 years in prison.

There are several other examples of preventive measures built into the act, which should be of great interest to Russian legislators.

At the same time, strengthening preventive measures is by no means the only method of enhancing Russian antiterrorist legislation. There are several other problems that have to be addressed. For example, there is a great need to extend the period that individuals reasonably suspected of belonging to terrorist organizations can be detained by the authorities. There are several provisions of the criminal law effectively nullifying the principles of inevitability of just punishment that are no longer acceptable in the present situation. In general, the Russian public fails to understand why a terrorist whose atrocities were documented, witnessed, and proven in a court of law should remain reasonably certain that the maximum penalty is life in prison. Members of the public wonder why the government is sending the message that it is safe to commit even more murders. They ask what happened to the principle of adequate punishment. Why spend taxpayers' money to feed "scumbags" covered in the blood of countless victims? Is it not time to suspend the moratorium on capital punishment for individuals who were found guilty of intentionally killing large numbers of people? I believe that in this regard we have a lot to learn from our American colleagues. Let me remind you of the name of the corresponding American law—the Antiterrorism and Effective Death Penalty Act! The Russian law has serious loopholes in the area of preventing and responding to high-tech terrorism as well.

I believe that the American side can also benefit from an analysis of the appropriate Russian legislation and its application to operations in Chechnya, especially taking into account the fact that the United States has had a long and difficult history of dealing with Islamic extremists of the type currently operating in Chechnya.

In conclusion, I would say that enhancing national antiterrorist legislation, bringing it into compliance with the norms of international law, and harmonizing national approaches toward combating terrorism and reducing terrorist threats appear to be the most promising methods available to the international community to fight terrorism.

NOTES

1. Odessky M.P., D.M. Feldman. 1997. The Poetry of Terror and the New Administrative Mentality. Moscow: Russian State Humanitarian University, p.19.

2. More than 300 comments and amendments were offered after the first reading of the draft.

3. President's Comments on the Draft Federal Law "On Combating Terrorism" (No. Pr-1705, October 18, 1997).

4. *The Washington Quarterly.* 1998, No. 1.

Organized Crime and Terrorism

Viktor Luneev *
Russian Academy of Sciences Institute of State and Law

Criminal terrorism (a journalistic term, inasmuch as any type of terrorism is punishable by law) holds a special place in the range of various types of terrorism. It can include all or a majority of types of terrorist activity classified according to various characteristics. A significant number of contract murders of businessmen, officials, politicians, and law enforcement officers, as well as bombings inflicting massive casualties on innocent people, are committed for reasons of greed or other criminal motives. Such actions represent about 25-30 percent of all terrorist activity.

By its nature, criminal terrorism can be international and domestic. In terms of location, it can occur on land, air, and sea and involve the use of traditional and technological means—that is, nuclear, chemical, biological, cybernetic, and other means using highly toxic ingredients and especially destructive powerful explosives, as detailed in the reports of other seminar participants. As a rule, criminal terrorism is internationalist, apolitical, and atheistic. But it does not hesitate to cooperate with terrorist organizations occupying various ideopolitical platforms (ideological, nationalist, or religious). Such cooperation could occur in the form of criminal terrorists supplying such organizations with resources and weapons and using them to put pressure on the authorities with the aim of protecting themselves or ennobling or covering up their own purely criminal goals. If conditions are favorable, they are not above jointly taking power hand in hand with opposition forces using terrorist methods of struggle.

---

* Translated from the Russian by Kelly Robbins.

The omnivorous nature of criminal terrorism represents a particular social, national, and international danger. In this regard, it is a special type of terrorist activity with a specific causative base, and it is necessary that special measures be taken to control and combat it.

• • •

Like any other type of terrorism, criminal terrorism can be committed by lone individuals or groups. Acts of terrorism carried out by lone individuals are today a relatively rare phenomenon and do not present particular social, national, or transnational danger.

The leading figures in criminal terrorism are organized criminal groups, societies, and organizations of a national or transnational nature. The merging of organized crime and terrorism leads to the significant expansion of the financial, material, and purely operational capabilities of terrorist organizations, along with strengthening them structurally.[1]

Organized crime groups use fear and direct violence in various forms as their main means of influencing the government, its representatives, lobbyists, and their competitors in illegal and legal business in the aim of redistributing spheres of influence, property, financial income streams, and types of criminal and legal activities.

Premeditated contract killings of government officials, law enforcement personnel, judges, entrepreneurs, and bankers who hinder criminal activities, fail to meet the demands of criminals, or compete with them in criminal or legal business have become a daily phenomenon in our country and several others, as have bloody conflicts to settle scores between the criminal groups themselves.

Examples of cooperation between terrorism and organized crime are especially widely observed in the states formed from the territory of the former USSR.

• • •

Given the fact that Russia has not overcome criminal ties with regard to the "money-property-power" and "power-property-money" chains, the terrorist activity of organized crime has a tendency toward a certain political orientation in order to pursue several goals. These include weakening the activities of law enforcement agencies, slowing legislative initiatives unfavorable to the criminal world, demoralizing the population, getting criminal kingpins or their helpers or sponsors elected to organs of legislative power, obtaining important posts in the federal and regional executive branches, and gaining immunity from legal prosecution for crimes committed.

The striving of organized crime toward these desired political results is used by some far from politically clean parties, which receive serious financial support from organized criminals in the form of "black" or "gray" contributions to their political interests. They repay this support by lobbying for the interests of criminal groups, placing organized crime figures in their electoral lists, and providing other political help to the criminal world. Such actions are facilitated under current Russian conditions by the imperfect nature of legislation on parties and elections. Efforts have begun to substantially rework this legislation, but they are proceeding in a contradictory fashion as a result of the struggle of opinions of various political formations both within the Duma itself and outside its walls. During discussion of the draft law on parties in May 2001, sharp exchanges focused on the question of unregistered financing of parties by private individuals. A similar practice also exists in some other countries. Let us recall the case involving secret financing given to the party of Helmut Kohl as just one example.

• • •

Organized crime in the United States appeared during the period of Volstead's Prohibition (the Eighteenth Amendment to the Constitution), which was adopted in 1919 and rescinded in 1933 during the world economic crisis. It still takes the form of illegal activity carried out by criminal associations. It has long infiltrated legal businesses, unions, and political organizations. U.S. President Richard Nixon once defined the three goals of organized crime in the United States as exploitation, corruption, and destruction. The last form of criminal activity also represents criminal terrorism, to a certain extent.

U.S. organized crime in the 1920s through the 1960s developed relatively slowly and was accompanied by the gradual formation of social and legal controls aimed at it: laws on racketeering (1946), narcotics (1956), street crime control and security (1968), ongoing criminal enterprises (1970), racketeer influenced and corrupt enterprises (Racketeer-Influenced and Corrupt Organizations Act [RICO], 1978), et cetera.

The political, socioeconomic, and organizational-legal conditions in our country were different when organized crime seriously made its appearance (the 1970s and 1980s). The appearance and development of our native mafia is based in the foundations of the shadow economy, socialist distribution relations, and the awkward system in which state property seemingly belonged to no one. During the period of perestroika and market reforms, social and legal controls over crime in general utterly collapsed, and organized crime was completely beyond control.

For more than 15 years, there was heated disagreement over the need for passing a law on combating organized crime. Only in 1997 did we see the creation, more or less, of a basis in criminal law for the fight against organized crime (the 1996 Criminal Code of the Russian Federation). During this time, organized crime has grown, strengthened, and stratified, in practice penetrating a significant portion of the economic and political life of our country. During a visit to Moscow in 1994, Federal Bureau of Investigation (FBI) Director Louis Freeh said that Russia had very quickly realized the danger of organized crime, something that had taken America 50 years to accomplish. I think that he flattered Russia too much. The Russian judicial community indeed began to recognize the enormous danger of organized crime in the mid-1980s, but the government proved to be immune to such a realization.

•   •   •

The law enforcement agencies set up some sort of accounting of organized crime based on their operations data. In 1989, 486 organized groups were counted, while in 1995 the figure was 8222—almost 17 times higher. Organized crime groups were working more intensively to establish international and regional ties. The degree of corruption of organized crime grew even more intensively (by an order of magnitude). These data are very subjective. Given the lack of legal criteria and in the interests of demonstrating successful actions, the internal affairs agencies often listed common crimes committed by groups under the heading of organized crime.

Unfortunately, many law enforcement agencies merely engage in window dressing. Former U.S. Attorney General Ramsey Clark writes: "How much effort have law enforcement personnel devoted to chasing petty thugs so that some district attorney or police chief or federal agency head could create a reputation for himself." By the way, there have been hundreds of books about organized crime written in the United States, but there are still no federal statistics on this sort of criminal activity. U.S. federal databases register only eight types of "serious" crimes (murder, rape, assault, robbery, theft, etc.) and include no data on organized crime or terrorism.[2] Meanwhile, these data may be found indirectly in prison statistics. In 1999, for example, U.S. prisons held individuals serving sentences for drug dealing (39.7 percent), pornography and prostitution (17.5 percent), fraud (11.2 percent), and other activities in which organized crime groups are significantly involved.[3]

It was inflated operational data and loud pronouncements by opposition Russian politicians that served as the basis for the 1997 study on Russian organized crime conducted by the Center for Strategic and International Studies under the leadership of William Webster. This study included many topical observations and useful conclusions, but on the whole it was of a political nature designed to scare its audience. This is despite the fact that by our calculations, Russian organized crime figures comprise no more than 5-10 percent of U.S. mafia structures even if you include all the organized crime elements who came from the former USSR but have no relation whatsoever with Russian organized crime (with Russian being defined as pertaining either to the Russian Federation or Russian ethnicity, as the term is commonly understood in the United States).

I say this not to engage in any sort of self-justification or to minimize the real danger of Russian organized crime. The mafia in all countries is becoming increasingly transnational. As shown by the case involving the Bank of New York and other U.S. banks, Russian-organized groups could conduct "dirty" deals there only with the participation of American organized crime clans. In this regard, exchanges of scary stories leads to nothing—it is mutual actions that are needed. We might recall the words of the great Russian writer Lev Tolstoy. He said that if bad people join together, then good people must also join together. We Russians, for example, are very pleased by the positive agreements made by Russian and American representatives regarding the struggle against Afghan terrorism.

• • •

A relatively reliable database of actions committed by organized crime groups is being established in Russia on the basis of existing legislation. These actions are entered into the database only when they have been clearly established and the subsequent criminal case has been fully investigated and submitted to a court.

In 2000, for example, 27,362 crimes committed by organized crime groups were registered, including 195 murders and 1734 crimes against public security (3 terrorist acts, 8 cases of hostage taking, 404 gangster robberies, 77 instances involving the organization of a crime society or criminal organization, and other actions). That same year, 135 cases of terrorism were registered on the whole (an increase of 576 percent in comparison with 1999), along with 49 cases of hostage-taking and 513 of gangsterism. As a rule, these actions, which fall into the category of criminal and other types of terrorism, are committed by organized crime groups or illegal armed formations, which are also fundamentally related to organized crime. A significant portion of the crimes cited remain unsolved; therefore, they are not included in the organized crime database. For example, of the 135 registered cases of terrorism in 2000, only 3 terrorist acts committed by organized crime elements were officially established after investigation. Another 11 cases of terrorism were discovered, but the participation of organized crime elements was not proven, and the remaining 121 cases of apparent terrorism were never solved. As of May 2001, internal affairs agencies have recorded 133 cases of terrorism this year, of which only 6 cases have been solved and officially registered. The fact that terrorists operate with impunity in the world and especially in Russia is a problem of exceptional significance.

• • •

Terrorism researchers, or "terrologists," as they might be called, are predicting the growth of various types of terrorism, especially those connected with radical political, separatist, nationalist, religious, and fundamentalist tendencies. This prediction is coming true in reality. Negative trends are also predicted with regard to criminal terrorism. Terrorism has substantially changed over the past century. It has become more severe and has taken on a relatively massive scale and worldwide significance. A review of the chronology of global terrorism in recent years presents the following statistical picture: in 1993, there were 45 terrorist acts registered; in 1994, 55; in 1995, 78; in 1996, 90; in 1997, 94; and in 1998, 117.[4] This represents an increase of 160 percent in five years. The average annual rate of increase was more than 10 percent. In 1999-2001, this trend is intensifying. Corrupting organized crime, with its enormous material and organizational resources and its power (through its sponsors), could very well gain access to high-tech means of terrorism. In the world today, there are 23 countries that openly or secretly possess nuclear weapons, but there are grounds for believing the number actually to be 44 countries, including totalitarian regimes.[5] American films showing organized crime using nuclear weapons to blackmail governments could turn out to be reality.

•   •   •

The overall intensification of terrorism in the current century will be closely linked with worldwide processes of globalization. This is already creating fierce and even violent resistance on the part of many thousands of various segments and groups of the population, as confirmed by the events in Davos and Seattle, where globalization problems were being discussed. It should be emphasized that this resistance was coming from well-off Americans and Europeans. Imagine what can be expected from those peoples left on the sidelines of globalization.

Globalization is the key problem illustrating the main trend of world development and the main contradiction of the twenty-first century. The key problem of the second half of the twentieth century was the conflict of two world systems. Now it is the interaction of fourth-generation civilizations against the backdrop of accelerating processes of globalization and localization. These processes are seriously affecting the lives of each one of us and the lives of each country and the world as a whole. They have long concerned the thinking segments of the population in various countries, inasmuch as they bring with them not so many positive changes as negative ones.

•   •   •

In our country alone, more than 10 domestic and foreign books have been published in the past year devoted to various aspects of globalization and the world and national threats it presents. For the sake of objectivity, I shall cite only the foreign books: *Entering the Twenty-First Century* (report of the World Bank on world development for 1999-2000, including an introduction by J. Wolfensohn);

The Crisis of Global Capitalism (G. Soros); *The Grand Chessboard* (Z. Brzezinski); and *The Global Trap: The Assault on Democracy and Prosperity* (H.P. Martin and H. Schumann, well-known editors of the German magazine *Der Spiegel*).

The books were written by people of very different sorts, but their essence is identical: globalization, which is on the one hand objective and on the other actively pushed by transnational, monopolistic financial and industrial entities, the political and economic elite of the golden billion, and especially the United States, carries with it disastrous consequences for world civilization.

Obviously, the same words sound different coming from the lips of different people. Therefore, I will touch on a few issues and predictions advanced by Western researchers, since it is more difficult to suspect them of tendentiousness.

In their well-argued internationally-published work *The Global Trap: The Assault on Democracy and Prosperity*, the German authors consider such urgent questions as the following:

- The 20:80 society;
- World rulers en route to a different civilization;
- Globalization and global disintegration;
- Dictatorship with limited liability, and playing with billions;
- The "Law of the Wolves" and the job crisis;
- The myth of the fairness of globalization;
- *Sauve, qui Peut* and the disappearing middle class;
- The poor global players and the welcoming back of compulsion;
- Who does the state belong to—the loss of national sovereignty;
- The dangerous world policeman, et cetera.

The authors present the contemporary world as if from an unseen side, revealing harsh economic realities and leaving no rosy illusions regarding free competition, freedom of speech, and equality for all. They show the world of the industrial-financial elite that today rules the world economic order, which the authors demonstratively call the global trap for all of modern postindustrial civilization. Globalization will substantially expand the socioeconomic base (social inequality, ethnoreligious contradictions, uncontrolled intergovernmental relations and conflicts, problems of refugees and poverty, et cetera) for various types of terrorism, and primarily for criminal terrorism.

• • •

I am not a specialist in globalistics. As a criminologist, I am interested in such matters only within the scope of certain criminologically significant circumstances at the international level.

The first criminologically significant problem is that of employment. Globalists describe it with the help of the figures 20:80 and the concept of "tittytainment." In the twenty-first century, 20 percent of the population will be needed. The other 80 percent will be left on the world periphery, extras without work or the means for survival and having colossal problems of a criminal nature. They must be satisfied only with tittytainment, a term coined by Brzezinski. As expressed by a participant in discussions at the Fairmont Hotel in 1995 (San Francisco), the dilemma will be "to have lunch or be lunch."[6]

There are no Russian citizens on the golden list of the world's billionaires. For almost a hundred years, with all their enormous territorial, natural, economic, demographic, physical, and intellectual capacities, Russians have been unable to break away from need and poverty for reasons of both an internal and an external nature. The American scholar Thomas Graham, Jr., writes that the United States has enormous interest in Russia's recovery, but he is "even more concerned that the lessons of the 1990s have shown that we [Americans] have greater potential to do harm than good (by means of direct intervention in Russia's internal transformation)." These words are not news to his fellow countrymen who are well aware of the price of our market reforms as recommended by advisers from Harvard and elsewhere. It is this century of humiliation that forms the basis for many reasons explaining current Russian crime problems of a national and global nature. The influence of globalization as planned by the world economic elite could provide a strong impetus to the growth of crime in Russia and could intensify organized crime and criminal terrorism. Many years of mass frustrations provide a foundation for the strengthening of aggression, violence, and terrorism.

The second criminologically significant problem is that of financial speculation markets. More than 80 percent of financial capital is in free circulation and does not have any real material form. This is a market in which money makes money, that is, a market for roulette players. Thanks to computer technologies, the financial market—the lion's share of which is the financial speculations market—has been like an iron ring drawing in all countries around the major financial magnates of the countries of the golden billion. This makes it possible for them, depending on their own interests, to place this or that country on the verge of financial collapse. Indeed, the system of such collapses began long ago, including for Russia.

This same conclusion is reached not only by Russian authors, but also by the outstanding entrepreneur, philanthropist, and author of the theory of reflexivity, George Soros. In his next to last book, *The Crisis of Global Capitalism* (1999), he cites words he spoke at the U.S. Congress: "The global capitalist system, which has been responsible for the remarkable prosperity of this country in the last decade, is coming apart at the seams. The current decline in the U.S. stock market is only a symptom, and a belated symptom at that, of the more profound problems that are afflicting the world economy. Some Asian stock markets have suffered worse declines than the Wall Street crash of 1929 and in addition their currencies have also fallen to a fraction of what their value was when they were tied to the U.S. dollar . . . Russia has undergone a total financial meltdown. It . . . will have incalculable human and political consequences. The contagion has now also spread to Latin America."[7] Such an accusation of the current world financial system is being made not by the Communist Zyuganov, but by the capitalist Soros. His words can never be taken as Communist demagoguery. He deserves to be listened to.

In our country, all "Black Tuesdays" have been accompanied by a further redistribution of property along with contract murders and criminal terrorism.

The third criminologically significant problem is that of the substantial reduction of the capacities of national governments to govern society and fight crime. In late 2000, the World Bank published its twenty-second and most recent analysis.[8] As noted by J. Wolfensohn himself, the main problems covered in the report are globalization and localization, which today represent two contradictory global challenges for the world community.

Globalization dictates that national governments should strive to conclude agreements with other national governments and international organizations, including military entities, non-governmental organizations, and multinational corporations, the role of which is intensifying to an extraordinary degree. Corporations dictate the subjugation of national entities (not the United Nations, as a rule) and the limitation of the powers of national governments.

Localization or disintegration demands that national governments agree ("share") with regions and cities on matters regarding the division of responsibilities by subnational institutions. Here we see the decentralization of remaining power and sometimes even the breakup of countries, which might be seen as advantageous by supranational military and economic entities and thus supported by them (for example, Chechnya). It is expected that up to 500 states could be formed worldwide.

These two contradictory demands bring to mind he inviolability of borders and the right of nations to self-determination, which by the rules of double standards are advanced by supranational forces, depending on their interests. But force, as everyone knows, needs no justification.

Both globalization and disintegration carry with them substantial conditions for the growth of organized crime and its terrorist activity in a situation characterized by a harsh struggle for survival.

• • •

The list of criminological problems stemming from globalization could be continued. Along with economic and political globalization, there is the process of criminal globalization in the form of the intensive development of transnational organized crime. An analysis of five reviews of world crime trends on the basis of data collected by the United Nations since 1970 shows that each country has its own unique type of crime, based on criminal-legal definitions, rates, structure, dynamics, and other criminological characteristics.[9] The differences are great. However, along with existing national characteristics, there are more substantial common criminological characteristics in various countries and the world as a whole:

- Crime exists in all states.
- Its dominant motivation is the same everywhere.
- Its level is steadily increasing worldwide and in the absolute majority of countries.
- As a rule, crime is increasing at a rate several times higher than the rate of increase of the population.
- Crimes of greed predominate and are growing at a more intense rate than crimes of violence.
- Violent crime is becoming increasingly harsh and bloody.
- The most common victims of crime are men, especially young men. Meanwhile, the process of the feminization of crime has long been observed.
- Economic development in countries is not being accompanied by a reduction in the crime rate, as had been supposed.
- The criminal-legal struggle against crime is experiencing a profound crisis.
- Prisons do not reeducate.
- The death penalty does not keep the crime rate from increasing.

In addition, processes are under way that are leading to the unification of criminal actions, making criminals better organized, better armed, and better protected. Crime is becoming more transnational and international in scope. The above-mentioned characteristics represent the real marks of the globalization of crime and of the world as a whole.

•   •   •

Despite all the substantial variations in crime rates in various countries, the first and defining trend in the world is the absolute and relative growth of crime, with relative being understood in terms of population size, economic development, culture, and so forth. In the United States alone in 1994-1999, a reduction was noted in eight types of crime tracked statistically (the reduction totaled about 15% for the five-year period).[10] These notable successes cost the American taxpayer $30.2 billion. And this is due only to a law passed in 1994. The absolute majority of countries do not have that kind of money to fight crime.

There are sufficient grounds to assert that crime is now five times higher worldwide than it was a quarter of a century ago, relative to the size of the population. The highest levels of crime and the relatively high rates of increase regarding crime are registered in the richest and most developed democratic countries. Here one must take into account not only reported crime, but also latent crime as well as the objectivity of the records and record-keeping practices.

The lowest levels of crime are observed in countries with totalitarian regimes (fascist, religious-fundamentalist, communist, and other authoritarian forms), where the struggle against crime is often waged using methods common to crime itself. But such "effective" crime control is nothing other than a non-criminalized abuse of power by the authorities in such countries against their own people—state terror. The victims of such abuses pay many times over for the low level of criminally prosecuted crime.

Over the past century, mankind has driven itself into a criminal trap, the exit from which has yet to be found. Democracy is often powerless in the face of growing crime, acknowledging only brute force, while totalitarianism, capable of holding traditional crime somewhat in check, is itself criminal in its nature and therefore does not reduce the victimization of the people.

An optimal solution would appear to lie in firm social-legal democratic control over crime, based on laws passed democratically and carried out with strict observance of fundamental human rights. The world has suffered and will accept such a solution. But the forces pushing globalization propose another strategy: under the banner of the struggle for human rights and using double standards, they would impose their own supranational economic and military control over countries and territories within the orbit of their interests, which will only strengthen the determination of terrorists of various sorts, including the criminal variety.

A special danger is presented by transnational organized crime, which is terroristic, economic, and corrupting, parasitizing on the trade in drugs, weapons, people, and human organs. Growth rates for this sort of crime are higher than those for traditional criminal activities.

•   •   •

A second basic trend in the area of crime is the gradual lagging of social-legal controls over crime and its qualitative and quantitative tendencies. The reasons for this are numerous and varied. In the system defined as "crime and the fight against it," crime takes the first position. The fight against it is only the response of society and the state to its challenge, a response that is not always timely, adequate, expedient, or effective.

The trend toward the intensive growth of crime and the trend of the "lagging" of social-legal controls over it are linked together in a sort of vicious circle. This circle can be broken only by means of a limited combination of criminal-legal and criminological strategies of fighting crime, namely by controlling and preventing it on the national and transnational levels.

Based on current trends and basic laws of historical development, it is not hard to predict the future course of existing tendencies of national and transnational organized crime and its most dangerous forms—criminal terrorism under conditions of intensive globalization, the weakening of national governments, and an intensified struggle for survival—if human society does not come up with global and national measures to minimize such factors in a timely manner.

We continue to live in conditions marked by wars and armed conflicts; endless outbreaks of social, racial, national, and religious enmity; and an unprecedented onslaught of terrorism, violence, robbery, fraud, technological and ecological disasters, and other forms of modern crime.

•   •   •

Against this backdrop, other tendencies and characteristics of current Russian and, to a certain extent, world crime take on great significance.

1. The population is becoming accustomed to crime, and this is especially true of young people. About 20 years ago, we would have been profoundly shocked by the long list of incidents of bloody organized terrorism, massive seizures of hostages, trade in human beings, endless public contract killings, many millions of cases of fraud, and the open and unprecedented corruption of high-ranking state officials. Today we see this almost every day and take it as a given.

2. We see the bloody criminal everywhere in the virtual world of foreign movies and television programs. We are interested in this. In his book *Travels with Charley: In Search of America*, the American writer John Steinbeck writes that we love virtue, yet we take more interest not in the honest accountant, the faithful wife, or the serious scholar, but rather in the bum, the charlatan, the embezzler, the criminal, the bandit, the terrorist, et cetera. Increased demand intensifies the work of the industry turning out crime films.[11] Both becoming accustomed to crime and taking an interest in the criminal are no less dangerous trends.

3. The dominating motivation is pragmatic, utilitarian, and primitive—greed and other personal benefit. It has not changed since biblical times but has only intensified. The process of the "greedification" of social relations continues, not only in the economic field, but also in the political, moral, and even creative spheres. The hopes of mankind that progress based on economic development will lead to a universal softening and improvement of morals have not been fulfilled.

4. There are up to 500 million crimes registered in the world each year. Given that the world's population is 6 billion, that makes 8000 criminal acts per 100,000 people. Real levels of crime are at least twice as high, and in many countries including Russia the figures would be four or five times higher. In fact, up to 12 million to 15 million crimes are committed in Russia annually; 3 million crimes are officially registered along with 78 million administrative violations, based only

on data from the Ministry of Internal Affairs and the courts. Besides these, about 40 other agencies have administrative jurisdiction over various matters. The latency of administrative violations is an order of magnitude higher than the levels reported. Statistically, we have an even correlation of the number of lawbreakers with the number of people in the country, including children and the elderly.

5. Along with the real growth in crime, we are seeing an uninterrupted process in which an ever-increasing number of societally dangerous and socially harmful behaviors are being criminalized (legally classified as crimes) and "violation-ized" (classified as administrative violations). During the time that the last four Russian Criminal Codes have been in effect, more than 300 new actions were criminalized and about 100 were decriminalized. The individual changes and additions made to the code number in the thousands. There is an uninterrupted stream of proposals to increase the number of specific types of crimes in the Criminal Code. This process is natural. But when the trend toward criminalization is three or four times higher than that for decriminalization, the situation requires serious evaluation.

6. While the criminalization process is intensifying, it also frequently lags behind the pace of events in general. This lagging is linked with the condescending attitude of the ruling political elite toward many widespread and dangerous forms of organized criminal activity, factors that are especially important preconditions for crime. Meanwhile, until they are officially classified as crimes, deviations not affecting the interests of the elite occur practically freely.

7. Representatives of law enforcement agencies and research institutions mistakenly consider that the intensive expansion of the sphere of activity considered to be crime actually signifies a process of strengthening law and order. This long-time delusion is still accepted by many as an axiom. A concrete criminological analysis indicates the opposite. The criminal justice system is not coping with the truly enormous volume of crime. If it today registered, investigated, and tried even the majority of actions committed, it would collapse under the weight of the many millions of criminal cases that would result. The criminal justice system survives due to the fact that only a selected number of actions are charged, not all the guilty are ever identified or found, and only 10 percent of real lawbreakers are ever tried. Only two to five percent of those individuals who actually committed criminally punishable acts are condemned to real measures of punishment (generally imprisonment). But the penitentiary system cannot withstand even this. Annual mass amnesties provide some help.

8. Judging by the characteristics of those individuals who are arrested and tried, our criminal justice system is targeted mainly at the poor, low-level, poorly adapted, alcoholic, degraded, and marginal segments of society who have committed obvious traditional criminal acts and do not know how to defend themselves or buy their way out of trouble. Despite the declaration embedded in the consciousness of the masses that "all are equal before the law," such statistics have for centuries satisfied almost everyone—the government, the elite, law

enforcement agencies, the courts, the prisons, criminologists (who seemingly discovered the truth), and the majority of the population, except the segment that "fell" into crime. It is this segment of the population against which the basic force of the criminal justice system is today aimed. It is aimed selectively, as a means of survival for law enforcement agencies (since it is easier, simpler, and safer). Meanwhile, crimes of power, wealth, and intellect—that is, institutional organized and corrupting crime—remain practically untouched. All of this represents a serious causative agent behind criminal violence and terrorism.

9. Crimes are committed by all segments of society, including the rich; the educated; the high ranking; the ruling political, economic, and even scientific elites; presidents; prime ministers; ministers; and governors. The real crime rate among elite groups (expressed as a ratio of criminals from these groups compared with the total number of individuals in the given groups) is no lower (or not much lower) than the same rates for the low levels of the population. Crimes of power, wealth, and intellect almost never fall within the scope of the activities of law enforcement agencies. Nevertheless, it is in this sphere that colossal material, physical, and moral damage is done. Faith in democracy and in the economic and political reforms being carried out is destroyed. Trust in the authorities and the state is undermined. Bitterness grows in a significant portion of the population and, along with it, violence and criminal terrorism.

10. A situation has been created that has long been described in the literature: if you steal a loaf of bread, you go to prison, but if you steal a railroad, you will be a senator. And that is how it has always been. The first thing that those in power thought of after the death of the dictator Stalin was to obtain freedom from legal controls on the part of law enforcement agencies. They managed to achieve this, and their corruption even in Soviet times became almost universal. Since then, they have not relinquished this privilege (let us recall the recent fierce battle on the question of merely limiting [?] the immunity of deputies and "senators" in the State Duma and Federation Council). Such notorious indulgences do not exist in the so-called civilized countries. Our political and ruling elites easily adopt the declared rights and freedoms of European countries, but they regard democratic controls over their unseemly activities as a return to totalitarianism.

The above-mentioned trends and characteristics in the process of overall and criminal globalization against the backdrop of the intensive increase (far from just or well founded) in the gap between poor and rich countries and between wealth and poverty within countries could become uncontrollable by society or the state. The history of Russia and other countries shows that it is these factors that can serve as the basis for political, ethnic, and criminal terrorism.

International cooperation in the fight against crime will become a very important aspect in the fight against all types of terrorism and transnational organized crime.

Criminologically significant problems of globalization must be reckoned with in a timely manner both at the level of national crime fighting measures and at the level of international legal measures. Today it is becoming obvious that in the postwar period, crime became the main threat in our times. It is constantly changing, mimicking, and instantly filling unmonitored or poorly controlled niches.

The internationalization of modern life is accompanied by the internationalization of crime and by the spread of its typical characteristics, tendencies, and forms to other regions and countries. This demands an internationalization of the struggle against crime, inasmuch as controlling its transnational component has become practically impossible at the level of individual states acting alone.

The lack of measures to fight a particular type of criminal activity—for example, the laundering of "dirty" money, organized crime, drug trafficking, and terrorism—makes a country desirable not only to its own criminals, but also to those from other countries.

• • •

International cooperation in the fight against crime in turn requires the presence of legal, organizational, and scientific support structures. This is the set of problems that international cooperation must resolve in the process of ongoing globalization.

Globalization and transnational crime make the expansion of international cooperation in this area unavoidable. This can be done only with international coordinating organizations and international-legal resolutions. These functions have been undertaken by the United Nations, Interpol, Europol, and various nongovernmental organizations. It is important that they maintain and intensify their activities. However, there are symptoms of a weakening of the United Nations and its role.

The United Nations must continue to be the fundamental international body. However, its role is gradually being reduced, and it is being supplanted by other supranational agencies of leading countries of the world, by a "new type of hegemony," the "American global system"[12] in a unipolar world. Irving Kristol, one of the ideologists of this sort of world order, declares: "One fine day, the American people must recognize that they have already become the world's imperial nation."[13] The circle is closing. All of this has already occurred on a regional level in history. In this case, it is global totalitarianism with unavoidable state terror and other types of terrorism—political, nationalist, religious, and criminal. The world must not allow this. We shall also hope that it will not allow a return to the past either.

The process of globalization cannot be eliminated, but it must proceed along an evolutionary path in parallel with legal support from the United Nations and the entire international community in order to eliminate double standards, interstate forms of violence, and dictatorial methods from international relations.

NOTES

1. Modern Terrorism: Status and Prospects. 2000. Moscow, p. 74.

2. Uniform Crime Reporting Handbook. 1984. Washington, D.C.

3. Sourcebook of Federal Sentencing Statistics. 1999. P. 12.

4. Terrorism and Terrorists: A Handbook. 1999. Minsk, pp. 443-514.

5. Fyodorov, A.F. 2000. Russia's Prospects in the World System of Coordinates in the Twenty-First Century. Moscow, p. 34.

6. Martin, H.P., H. Schumann. 2001. The Global Trap: The Assault on Democracy and Prosperity. Moscow, p. 21.

7. Soros, G. The Crisis of Global Capitalism: Open Society Endangered. 1999. New York: Public Affairs, p. ix.

8. World Bank. 2000. Entering the Twenty-First Century: Report on World Development for 1999-2000. Moscow.

9. United Nations Office for Drug Control and Crime Prevention. 1999. Global Report on Crime and Justice. G. Newman, ed. New York: Oxford University Press.

10. Federal Bureau of Investigation. 1998. Crime in the United States: Uniform Crime Reports. Washington, D.C., p. 7.

11. Berkowitz, L. 1993. Aggression: Its Causes, Consequences, and Control. Boston: McGraw-Hill, Chapter 7.

12. Brzezinski, Z. 2000. The Grand Chessboard. Moscow, pp. 20-42.

13. Newsweek, April 26, 1999.

International and Domestic Terrorism

L. Paul Bremer III
MMC Enterprise Risk

The modern wave of international terrorism began 30 years ago with a group of spectacular attacks related to the Middle East situation. Much has changed in the world since then, but today's analysts ask themselves the same four questions they asked 30 years ago:

1. Who are the terrorists?
2. What are their motives?
3. How do they get their support?
4. How can we stop them?

Yet if the questions have stayed the same, the answers have changed. And it is this changing threat of terrorism that I want to address today.

TERRORISM AS A PUBLIC POLICY ISSUE

First, I would like to make a few general comments about the unique attributes of terrorism as a public policy issue. Terrorism is a highly emotional subject, especially in the wake of a terrorist incident. People are dead or wounded, property has been destroyed, lives have been upended, and safe places have been made insecure. Yet between incidents, the fight against terrorism rarely attracts much attention. Thus, political leaders are presented with a major dilemma: how to avoid the pitfalls of overly emotional responses while retaining enough attention to the problem to ensure adequate political support (i.e., money). In other words, political leaders must find an approach to the problem that is balanced and yet can be sustained for the long run. This is particularly difficult because successes in counterterrorism are rarely known to the public, and failures are very dramatic and visible.

Successes are made more difficult by two asymmetries particular to the fight against terrorism.

1. The offense has a huge advantage. In the fight against terrorism, defenders have to defend all their points of vulnerability around the world, while the terrorist has only to attack the weakest point.

2. The costs of defense are dramatically higher than the costs of attack. For example, defending an airport will require millions of euros, while a terrorist can do major damage with a single AK-47 machine gun or even a pipe bomb.

In sum, the fight against terrorism reverses conventional military wisdom, which holds that the offense needs at least a three-to-one advantage to overcome the defense.

Democracies are generally poor at planning ahead and are rarely proactive. When they do try to plan, democratic leaders tend to use words that simplify problems in ways that may actually complicate the search for effective policies, for example:

- Middle East: "problem"-"solution"
- Terrorism: "war"- "victory"

But the Middle East is really a "situation" to be managed, and terrorism is a "struggle" not a war.

There is a risk, particularly in the United States but also elsewhere, of over-personalizing the fight against terrorists—to search for a single terrorist who embodies all evil. We have had Gadhafi, Abu Nidal, and now bin Laden. There are two problems with this process. First, it builds up the villain in his own eyes and in the eyes of his followers. Thus, it paradoxically may make it easier for him to recruit new terrorists. Second, it suggests that if these individuals can be dealt with, the terrorist problem will be solved. But the problem does not go away; it evolves, as it has from Gadhafi to bin Laden.

Finally, it is important to avoid the Hamlet syndrome—in effect seeing only the arguments against actions to fight terrorism. Some or all of the following arguments are certain to be made about fighting terrorism:

- Diplomacy has its limits.
- Sanctions don't work.
- Covert actions are ineffective.
- There is a reluctance to use the military. "What good does it do? Won't they just strike back?"

- Law enforcement has its limits. "Don't we just create martyrs or a reason for other terrorists to seize hostages to get their colleagues released?"

Each of these arguments has some validity, but the total of all of them can easily lead to policy paralysis.

THE THREAT OF "OLD" TERRORISM

A careful analysis of terrorism as it existed when it first burst on the international stage 30 years ago shows that terrorists then had quite limited motives. These determined the mechanics of their attacks and the structure of their organizations.

- *Motives.* Terrorists had discrete political goals, for which they sought broad understanding and support. They wanted to win "a place at the table" to negotiate for specific objectives, such as the release of fellow terrorists.
- *Mechanics.* They killed enough people to bring attention to their cause, but not too many so as to risk alienating the broader public. Lots of people were watching, but not a lot of people were dead.
- *Structure.* Terrorists were often described as "crazy" or "irrational," but in fact they were often cold-blooded thinkers who also did not want to get caught or be killed. They exercised tight control over all aspects of the operation, not only as a security matter (to keep from being caught), but also to be sure that the attack served political goals. State sponsorship was important.

DEVELOPMENT OF A
WESTERN COUNTERTERRORIST STRATEGY

The West had some important successes in the fight against this "old-style" terrorism in the 1980s. Under U.S. leadership, the countries of the West developed a counterterrorist strategy based on three principles:

1. No concessions are granted to terrorists.
2. States that use or sponsor terrorism should be ostracized.
3. It is important to use the rule of law against terrorists. They are criminals.

European governments became serious about fighting and defeating their home-grown leftist terrorist groups—the Baader Meinhof, Red Brigades, Action Directe, and Cellules Communistes Combattantes. They did this by recognizing that the "good guys" should be at least as well organized as the criminals. So the Europeans greatly increased their mutual cooperation in intelligence gathering and law enforcement (largely through the so-called Trevi Group in the European Community).

With the constant (some might say "annoying") encouragement of the U.S. government, our friends in Europe came to support the position that states cannot legitimately use terrorism as an instrument of state policy. After our military response to Libyan terrorism in April 1986, Europeans joined the United States in putting pressure on Syria, another state sponsor, at the end of 1986. The reward was Syria's expulsion of Abu Nidal the following July, effectively marking the end of his activities. And most European states also came to agree that the Iranian revolutionary government's active use of terror was unacceptable.

However, past successes do not guarantee that the international community will be effective against the changing threat of terrorism.

THE NEW TERRORIST THREAT

The U.S. National Commission on Terrorism, which I was honored to chair, reached the important conclusion that the terrorists' motives, mechanics, and structure have all changed in the course of the past decade. This is a conclusion shared by all major European intelligence agencies.

- *Motive.* The motives of current terrorists are ideological, religious, ethnic, and apocalyptic in nature and are rooted in hatred and revenge.
- *Mechanics.* There is much less concern about numbers of casualties. Indeed, in some cases, the intention is to kill as many people as possible in a move from discriminate to indiscriminate violence. In the words of a former director of the Central Intelligence Agency, terrorists "no longer seek a place at the table— they want to overturn the table and kill everybody at it."
- *Structure.* States are still involved, but less so. Terrorist groups are less concerned about calibrating the level of violence carefully, and their structures can be looser and less hierarchical. This often means that good police and intelligence work can thwart attacks or at least catch perpetrators. However, terrorist groups are more difficult to penetrate and disrupt. They have become self-financing, using front organizations, companies, useful dupes, nongovernmental organizations, and drug and arms trafficking.

Facts bear out this analysis:

- During the 1990s, the number of international terrorist incidents declined, but the number of casualties rose.
- Today, a given terrorist attack is 20 percent more likely to result in deaths than was the case 20 years ago.
- In the United States, the 1993 attack on the World Trade Center killed "only" six people, but the terrorists' intention had been to topple one of the towers into the other, which would have resulted in thousands of deaths.

- Planned attacks on New York City's infrastructure were designed to kill thousands.
- Millennium attacks were planned.
- There is a steady increase in the number of terrorist attacks that are not claimed by any group, indicating that the motive often may be hatred or revenge.
- An increasing number of terrorists are not afraid to die in their attacks (East African embassy bombings, *USS Cole*, suicide bombings in Israel).

The "new terrorists" pose a policy dilemma. Their changed motives and willingness to inflict higher levels of casualties call into question the classic three-part strategy with which the West has fought terrorism.

1. There are no ambassadors to recall from a terrorist group.
2. There is no way to "embargo" a group's exports.
3. No diplomatic demarche, no matter how cleverly written by wise diplomats, will have an effect on these men.
4. There is no bargain to be made with them, so talking about not making concessions to such groups is irrelevant.

To take the most obvious example, bin Laden hates everything America and the West stand for, just as do his protectors the Taliban. There is nothing we can offer that would change his view of us. There is no deal to be made.

POSSIBILITY OF MASS CASUALTY TERRORISM INCREASING

Our commission concluded, as have three subsequent national studies in America, that there is a significant threat that terrorists will escalate their attacks by resorting to agents of mass destruction—chemical, biological, radiological, or nuclear. This is new and troubling.

During the 1970s and 1980s, counterterrorist experts concluded that there was little likelihood of terrorists turning to chemical, biological, radiological, or nuclear terrorism. Their analysis was as follows:

- Most terrorist groups in those years could accomplish their goals—attacks that would generate attention and publicity for their causes—more easily by using conventional means, namely bombs and machine guns.
- Escalating to higher levels of violence would risk alienating the public.
- Chemical, biological, radiological, and nuclear materials were not easy to acquire and were dangerous to handle.
- Negotiations would be asymmetrical since terrorist groups would not be able to formulate appropriate demands in return for not conducting a mass attack.

During the 1980s, this analysis seemed accurate. The first use of chemical materials was the attack by Aum Shinrikyo in the Tokyo subway system in 1995.

The Gulf War signaled a new threat environment. It showed that even a lavishly armed conventional military force—and Iraq at the time had the world's fifth-largest army—was no match for a modern military force. So terrorist states such as Iraq now understand the advantages of having force-multiplying chemical, biological, radiological, and nuclear weaponry to offset their conventional inferiority.

Five of the seven states identified by the U.S. government as state sponsors of terrorism have military programs to develop chemical, biological, and nuclear weapons, and they have ballistic missile programs to deliver the weapons.

Iraq poses the biggest danger. It is now known that before the Gulf War, Saddam Hussein had programs to develop nuclear, biological, and chemical weapons. Iraq had more than 100,000 people working on the nuclear program at a cost of over $20 billion. That is why UN Security Council Resolution 687 (April 3, 1991) at the end of the war explicitly required Iraq to accept the supervised destruction of all of these materials.

Iraq failed to comply with this resolution, and due to the feckless incompetence of the international community there have been no inspections in Iraq for more than two years. The German Intelligence Service recently concluded that Iraq could have nuclear bombs within three years and, by the year 2005, ballistic missiles with a range of 3000 km, more than enough to reach Europe.

Yet terrorist groups, too, can be attracted by chemical, biological, radiological, and nuclear weapons. Many such groups are no longer bound by concerns about creating massive casualties; indeed, that may be their goal.

Most experts consider biological agents to be the most tempting for terrorists. This was also the conclusion of my commission on terrorism.

• Biological agents often take days or weeks to become apparent, allowing the perpetrators time to escape.
• They produce a disproportionate psychological fear in the public at large.
• They could be used, as they have been in the past, in attacks on agriculture to cause economic and social damage. The recent reactions provoked by bovine spongiform encephalopathy and foot-and-mouth disease in Europe provide a glimpse of how devastating to public morale such attacks could be.

Western intelligence agencies know that some terrorist groups have tried to acquire agents of mass destruction. For example, three years ago, Osama bin Laden told reporters from *Time* magazine that it was the religious duty of good Muslims to kill Americans and to acquire any weapons possible for such attacks. Lest he be misunderstood, he repeated the threat two days later on American television. One of his top assistants was subsequently arrested in Germany trying to buy highly enriched uranium. And testimony last month at a trial in the United States revealed bin Laden's continuing efforts to acquire uranium in Sudan.

INTERNATIONAL COOPERATION IN THE FIGHT AGAINST TERRORISM

There is a useful but limited role for international cooperation in the fight against terrorism. Three issues limit cooperation:

1. The *definition* of what constitutes terrorism, based on the experience of the United Nations in the 1970s through 1990s;
2. The problem of *sharing intelligence*; and
3. The relative *importance of counterterrorism* in a country's national security policy.

PROBLEMS OF INTELLIGENCE

The first requirement for an effective counterterrorist strategy is good intelligence. After more than three decades in the foreign policy world, I can say that I know of no field in which intelligence is so vital to effective policy and yet so difficult to collect.

Thus, several of the Bremer Commission's key recommendations dealt with improving our capability to collect intelligence against terrorists. Since the goal of counterterrorism is to prevent attacks, good intelligence means knowing the terrorists' plans in advance. But the only sure way to get that information is to have a spy among the terrorists. This is difficult to accomplish, but it can be done.

Yet precisely because good counterterrorism intelligence is so hard and dangerous to collect, it is very difficult to share, even with close friends and allies. Most cooperation in this area tends to take place only bilaterally through special channels. Thus, there is little scope for making greater use of multilateral organizations, such as Interpol, in this area.

PRIORITY OF COUNTERTERRORISM

The relative priority a nation puts on the fight against terrorism depends on three factors:

1. The threat terrorism poses to the country;
2. The country's ability to respond to that terrorism on its own, with little help from other countries; and
3. The relative importance the country gives to the fight against terrorism as an aspect of the country's broader national security strategy.

As the world's number one target of terrorism, the United States has long placed a high priority on this fight. This is the reason successive American administrations of both political parties have placed so much emphasis on stopping state support for terrorism.

What then are the most promising areas for international cooperation, particularly from the point of view of U.S.-Russian cooperation?

• *Cooperation on the rule of law.* The United States has put considerable emphasis on mutual assistance agreements with other countries to help fight terrorist crime. Modernized extradition treaties are a good example. Information sharing among law enforcement agencies is also important.

• *Emphasis on enforcement of existing international treaties affecting terrorism.* There are now 12 UN treaties in effect that directly address terrorism. The United States is party to all of these. Regrettably, Russia has failed to sign five of these treaties, including several of the most important ones relating to aircraft hijacking. I hope the Russian government will show its commitment to the fight by signing and ratifying these remaining five treaties.

• *Mutual assistance in counterterrorist techniques.* Over the past 20 years, the United States has trained more than 20,000 law enforcement officials from over 100 countries in techniques such as hostage rescue, bomb detection, maritime and airport security, and crisis management.

• *Increased technical exchanges, such as this workshop.* Could our two countries, for example, cooperate on finding better ways to identify and control the specialized equipment needed to acquire, transport, and weaponize biological agents?

• *Continued exchanges of views on policy matters through bilateral and multilateral organs, such as the G-8 (Group of Eight).* Note particularly the useful coordination between Russia and the United States in supporting the UN Security Council resolution on Afghanistan.

However, we must admit that the United States and Russia have different views on how to deal with state sponsors. The most acute differences relate to Iraq, Iran, and Libya, all of which the U.S. government considers to be state sponsors of terrorism. Much of the U.S. rationale for establishing a national missile defense, broadly agreed by both our political parties, derives from this analysis.

Looking back over the past 30 years, it is fair to say that international cooperation has made a useful contribution to the fight against terrorism. Perhaps we can find new ways, through this workshop, to advance our common fight.

The Role of Internal Affairs Agencies in Efforts to Fight Terrorism Under High-Technology Conditions

Oleg A. Stepanov *
Academy of Administration, Russian Ministry of Internal Affairs

The problem of the role of internal affairs agencies in the life of society and the state today is insufficiently developed inasmuch as there is currently no generally accepted understanding of the concept of "internal affairs agencies." In the draft law "On Internal Affairs Agencies," the author of the bill provides the following definition: "Internal affairs agencies represent a system of state agencies of the Russian Federation that take countermeasures against illegal activities and ensure public and individual security on the basis of provisions of the Constitution of the Russian Federation and principles and norms of international law."

With this definition in mind, we may turn to one of the most complex aspects of the activities of internal affairs agencies, namely, that connected with the problem of combating terrorism under conditions characterized by the development of information-based high technologies. Within the scope of this problem, two pressing questions may be highlighted. The first concerns legal conditions for countering high-tech-oriented manifestations of terrorism. The second involves facilitation of the scientific-technical development of the country's population in a way that is proper from a legal standpoint.

In considering these questions, it should be noted that in Moscow alone in 1999-2000, five cases of successful attacks against very important information resources and potentially hazardous industries were detected and revealed. Meanwhile, the existing procedural and criminal legislation as well as the laws "On the Militia" and "On Operational Search Activities" do not allow for effective countermeasures against this phenomenon. Given conditions in the information-

---

* Translated from the Russian by Kelly Robbins.

based society, the text of at least six articles in the current Criminal-Procedural Code of the Russian Federation should be changed to ensure that the rights of citizens are guaranteed. Specifically, these include Articles 12, 69, 83, 84, 170, and 174.

It is proposed that Part 2 of Article 12, "Sanctity of the Home, the Protection of Personal Life, and Confidentiality of Correspondence," be amended as follows: "The personal lives of citizens and the confidentiality of correspondence, telephone conversations, and telegraph messages are protected by law. Citizens do not have the right to use communications channels, including telecommunications systems channels, for illegal purposes." The existing text would continue from there.

It is proposed that Part 1 of Article 69 be amended as follows: "Any factual data, including information stored by machine, computer, or computer system or network, may be used as evidence in a criminal case. On the basis of this information, organs of inquiry, investigators, and courts by legally-established procedures establish the existence or absence of socially dangerous actions and the guilt of the individual who took such action and make determinations on other circumstances having significance for the correct resolution of the case." The existing text would continue from there.

Article 83, "Material Evidence," should be amended as follows: "Material evidence is defined as objects that have served as tools of a crime, have retained traces of a crime, or have been the objects of the criminal activities of the accused, such as money and other valuables earned by criminal means as well as information stored by machine, computer, or computer system or network. Material evidence also includes all other items, including printouts of computer systems or network operation logs, that could serve as the means for uncovering a crime, establishing the factual circumstances of the case, or revealing the guilty, either in proving the truth of the accusation or in mitigating responsibility."

It is proposed that Part 1 of Article 84, "The Protection of Material Evidence," be amended as follows: "Material evidence must be described in detail in the inspection protocols and photographed if possible, or else transferred to information storage media (paper, machine-based, etc.) in a way that precludes the loss, intentional destruction, or modification of the information, including that taken from computers and computer systems and networks. This information shall be placed in the case file by special order of the individual conducting the inquiry, investigator, or prosecutor or by determination of the court. Material evidence must be preserved during the course of the criminal case." The existing text would continue from there.

It is proposed that Parts 2 and 3 of Article 170, "Procedures for Conducting Seizures and Searches," be amended as follows: "In making a seizure, after presenting the order the investigator requests that the items and documents subject to removal, including information stored by machine, computer, and computer systems and networks, be handed over. In the event this request is refused, he makes a forced seizure.

"In conducting a search, after presenting the order the investigator requests that the tools of the crime, items and valuables obtained by criminal means, and any other items or documents having possible significance to the case, including information stored by machine, computer, and computer systems and networks, be handed over. If they are handed over voluntarily, and there are no grounds for suspecting concealment of the target items, documents, and information stored by machine, computer, and computer systems and networks, the investigator has the right to limit himself to taking the items handed over and not making further searches." The existing text would continue from there.

Part 2 of Article 174, "The Seizure of Postal and Telegraphic Correspondence," should be amended as follows: "When it is necessary to intercept correspondence for the purpose of its review and seizure, the investigator shall submit an order providing justification. After authorization of the above order by the prosecutor or judge, the investigator forwards the order to the appropriate postal or telegraphic institution or to the organizations providing telecommunications services. He requests that correspondence be intercepted and provides information on the time of his arrival to review and seize the intercepted correspondence. The review and seizure are conducted in the presence of witnesses selected from among staff members at the postal-telegraphic institution or organization providing telecommunications services. The investigator has the right to call on the assistance of an appropriate specialist to participate when necessary in carrying out the seizure of postal or telegraphic correspondence or information from the electronic mail system." The existing text would continue from there.

Institution of all the above-proposed changes would facilitate the creation of a mechanism by which internal affairs agencies could combat acts of high-tech terrorism.

In this regard, it is important to focus attention on the need to make corresponding changes and additions in Articles 78 (Evidence), 85 (Material Evidence), 86 (Storage of Material Evidence), 185 (Procedures for Conducting Searches and Seizures), and 188 (Interception, Review, and Seizure of Postal and Telegraphic Correspondence) of the draft of the new Criminal-Procedural Code of the Russian Federation, which is currently being developed by the Legislation Committee of the State Duma of the Russian Federation.

In addition to the items noted above, a Part 8 with the following wording should also be added to Article 5 of the Federal Law "On the Militia:" "The storage of personal data in electronic form, as well as the giving of instructions to militia personnel to conduct automated processing of name-identified data, is carried out according to procedures established by legislation of the Russian Federation."

From the above-outlined standpoint on the problem of combating crimes of a terrorist nature, certain additions are also required in Chapter 28 of the Criminal Code of the Russian Federation, "Crimes in the Field of Computer Information." Specifically, Part 1 of Article 272 of the Criminal Code should be amended as follows: "Access to legally protected computer information—that is, information stored on machine, computer, or computer systems or networks—shall be considered unlawful if it results in the destruction, blocking, modification, or copying of information, disruption of the operation of computers or computer systems and networks, or even if it results in the disclosure of legally protected computer information. . . ." The existing text would continue from there.

Part 1 of Article 274 of the Criminal Code should be amended as follows: "Violation of the rules for operation of computers or computer systems or networks by persons having access to computers or computer systems or networks that result in (1) the destruction, blocking, or modification of legally protected information; (2) the blocking of access to computers or computer network resources; or (3) the disabling of computer security systems, if any such actions have caused significant damage. . . ." The existing text would continue from there.

Article 6 of the Federal Law "On Operational Search Activities" sets forth a list of operational search measures. In the interests of bringing it into accordance with fundamental principles for combating terrorism, an additional point should furthermore be inserted to allow agencies engaged in such activities to decode encrypted electronic information. This also requires the amendment of Part 6 of Article 8 of the above-mentioned law: "The conduct of operational tests, the decoding of encrypted electronic information . . ." and so on as in the current text.

The above-proposed changes will make it possible to bring the Federal Laws "On the Militia" and "On Operational Search Activities" and criminal and procedural legislation into accordance with the Federal Law "On Combating Terrorism." In addition, they will ensure the possibility of effective actions on the part of internal affairs agencies in the near term.

In connection with the problem under discussion, it must be noted that along with the development of computer technologies, genetic engineering and nanotechnologies provided society with more questions than answers in the last quarter of the twentieth century.

For instance, research on artificial intelligence and associated control procedures is being conducted at the University of Reading (Great Britain). Robots are being created that are capable of learning, interacting with one another, and reprogramming themselves independently. The main goal of the designers comes down to linking the human brain with the "brain" of the computer.

At U.S. universities such as Harvard, the University of California, and Princeton, research is being done on deciphering the codes of the nervous system in the aim of creating acceptable interfaces with the human brain. Furthermore, with the patronage of Congress and the White House, work is under way to develop biotechnical systems comparable in size to atoms and molecules that possess logic and the capability of self-reproduction. The development of such technologies could lead to the creation of previously unknown forms of artificial life, cultivated by man for the supposed benefit of mankind. However, along with the development of nanosystems aimed at previously discovered cancer cells in the human body or the delivery of medicinal preparations to an ailing organ, experiments are also being conducted to collect the simplest mechanisms from molecules. These mechanisms, guided by internal signals, must manipulate other molecules and create more complex mechanisms, even including biorobots.

In this regard, it is also appropriate to cite a statement by a top Pentagon official: "We are approaching a level of development where no one is a soldier, but everyone is a participant in military actions. The task now is not to destroy living forces, but rather to undermine the goals, views, and outlooks of the population—to destroy the society."

It is not by chance that I have cited these words, inasmuch as there have been reports in the media recently to the effect that the AIDS virus was also artificially created. According to these reports, it was developed in closed U.S. military laboratories, and as a result of an unsanctioned leak the virus spread around the planet.

High-tech inventions facilitate accurate diagnoses and the regulation of the mental and physical status of individuals, yet they also make it possible to evoke psychophysiological distress as a result of news of the latest research lab leak. There are no guarantees today that these inventions will not end up in the hands of terrorists of various types. Here it should be noted that the consequences of such a leak could be comparable to the results that would ensue if terrorists were to get their hands on a weapon of mass destruction.

For instance, U.S. laboratories are developing nanomechanisms the size of bees or even ants that can carry out any programmed functions from eavesdropping to shutting down electrical lines in response to commands transmitted from satellites or submarines.

There is also another point that cannot help but cause concern. The development of high-level computer technologies is at times linked with the relative simplicity and accessibility of preparing the means for possible terrorist actions. For example, one American inventor came up with the idea of an anticomputer cannon—a device that could disable computers, vehicles, medical equipment, and any other electronic devices from some distance away. The entire invention consists of a parabolic reflector, a horn-shaped antenna, and two automobile ignition coils, and it costs less than one hundred dollars. The cannon creates in its antenna a 20-MW burst of chaotic radio noise that is sufficient to change the normal operation of microcircuits. The impulse does not ruin a computer, but rather "freezes it up." The use of this device can produce chaos in electronic transactions systems, including in operation of integrated databases, a most valuable resource for internal affairs agencies.

It is completely possible to state that problems related to combating terrorism in the high-tech sphere are among the most complex and little studied issues today. It is also an indisputable fact that an effective struggle against manifestations of high-tech terrorism is possible only with the establishment of international coordination of the activities of law enforcement agencies. And if the first step in the right direction lies in gaining a clearer understanding of problems related to preventing the use of high-tech developments by terrorists, then the second step must lie in creating a mechanism that would make it possible to prevent the spread of terrorist acts of this nature.

In my opinion, at least two stages can be defined in the construction of such a mechanism. The first stage must be tied to the development of guiding legal principles providing for the prevention of high-tech terrorism. At this stage, the possibility of criminal punishment for the illegal development, distribution, and use of bio- and psycho-computer systems should also be stipulated in national legislation. Furthermore, concerning Russia, we could also discuss the insertion of the appropriate corrections in the law "On Combating Terrorism." In particular, the concept of "informational-electronic space" should be added to Article 3 of this law, which presents a list of objects included in the sphere for conducting counterterrorist operations. It would also be expedient to make the corresponding addition to Article 1 of the European Convention on the Suppression of Terrorism (1977).

The second stage of the above-mentioned mechanism is connected with developing a control and monitoring format that facilitates effective implementation of the first stage.

In particular, in carrying out this second stage, the Russian Ministry of Internal Affairs faces the problem of how it should efficiently focus its organizational development in the future. Even today, one must raise the question of creating within the Ministry of Internal Affairs structure a special control-analytical agency that would monitor the spread of bio- and psycho-information technologies in Russia and prevent cases of high-tech terrorism. This unit should focus special attention on participation in the development (in cooperation with foreign partners) of approaches to combating terrorist manifestations in the high-tech sphere. It should also be involved in the exchange of experience and information on ways of countering the most dangerous types of criminal activity.

The effectiveness of the work of the above-mentioned unit will be substantially greater if the appropriate interactions are established with such organizations as the Russian Foreign Intelligence Service (SVR) and the Federal Security Service (FSB).

A consideration of the problem of combating high-tech terrorism also presupposes recognition by the country's population of the consequences of the increased role of information technology in the life of society. The results of a survey conducted by the author of this paper in the city of Moscow speak to this fact. Specifically, the following results were obtained regarding a problem that is not directly linked with cases of high-tech terrorism but is to a certain degree characteristic of the level of legal consciousness among citizens. For instance, among survey respondents who were employees of organizations involved in computer hardware sales, a majority had a negative attitude toward the activities of the Microsoft branch office in Russia aimed at protecting the company's interests in the computer software market. In particular, about 90 percent of the respondents believed that Microsoft's activities are of the unceremonious nature of a monopolist dictating his own rules of the game. However, for some reason, no attention is paid to the fact that when selling licensed software, both the company representatives and the local dealer companies pay significant sums of money to the state in the form of taxes. When pirated software products are distributed, the state not only loses such an opportunity, but also in essence promotes the legalization of illegal actions in the high-tech sphere of societal activities. It is a well-known fact that terrorist manifestations become characteristic of those individuals who have previously gotten a taste for impunity. In the course of the survey, it was also established that approximately 30 percent of firms and organizations in this field of business have no interest in receiving information of a regulatory, legal, operational, or analytical character from law enforcement agencies through the agency for distribution of legal and criminal information that was recently created under the auspices of the joint publishing house of the Russian Ministry of Internal Affairs. Meanwhile, more 70 percent of respondents expressed their readiness to ensure the security of their own businesses (against racketeering, extortion, corruption, et cetera) over a network resource (the Internet) by means of establishing contacts with law enforcement agencies. Such figures should spur internal affairs agencies to step up activities in this direction, which could be viewed as promising in the sphere of preventing terrorism under information-based high-tech conditions.

In this regard, within the scope of this bilateral Russian-American seminar it is also of some interest to focus attention on the assessment made by internal affairs agency personnel of the abstract situation regarding criminal phenomena linked with the rising role of information technologies in the life of society. In response to a question concerning resolution of a case demanding a high degree of professionalism and restraint and offering opportunities for showing initiative in gaps in legislation, a case that is also contradictory and affects the lives of individuals, 45 percent of respondents (internal affairs agency personnel) chose the following behavior: do everything according to justice, both de jure and de facto. Furthermore, they felt that actions taken must not be hasty and must not transgress legal bounds. Another 20 percent preferred a skillful combination of the spirit and letter of the law in this situation, along with a striving to improve the legislation. Between 5 and 10 percent of the respondents preferred a flexible combination of the letter and spirit of the law in this case, without regard to conditions for implementing principles of humanity, justice, legality, and openness and without considering the need for the case to move through all of the procedural formalities, not to mention the sense of the unusualness of the factual content of legal relations. About the same percentage of respondents preferred to hide behind the law and observe it to the letter, being guided by considerations of their own personal benefit. Only 10 percent of the respondents expressed readiness to do anything to achieve a just outcome in the case, even to the point of exceeding the bounds of their authority and placing themselves in a difficult position.

In conclusion, it should be noted that it is very urgent and timely to analyze the problems of countering terrorism under high-tech conditions, with internal affairs agencies being among the key actors in this countering effort. Such an analysis will also promote overall improvement of the legislative base and will increase the effectiveness of the activities of the Russian Internal Affairs Ministry system as information technology becomes ever more important in society. This all takes on special significance as the international information space continues to expand. The problems that might arise as part of this process can at times take on the most unexpected forms. One example of this is the attempt to bring two Chelyabinsk hackers to punishment in the United States after the Federal Bureau of Investigation conducted an operation to lure them out of Russia. In the current situation, Russian and U.S. law enforcement agencies, as the main actors in countering terrorism, are called upon to improve the procedures and methods of their work under high-tech conditions. They must not allow events to develop along "Chelyabinsk" lines, a situation that has given rise to a number of questions of a legal and moral-ethical nature in relations between the United States and Russia.

From the Experience of the Intelligence Services of the Russian Empire in Combating Terrorists

Dmitry M. Aleksenko *

Commonwealth of Independent States Antiterrorist Center

The Latin word *terror,* meaning fear or horror, was known to residents of the Russian Empire as far back as the first half of the nineteenth century. But words arising from this root, such as *terrorism* and *terrorists*, have been applied differently in Russia in different historical eras.

In encyclopedias, dictionaries, and criminal codes, definitions of terrorism have appeared and continue to appear, varying in accordance with the demands of the time and in relation to which infringements of societal values evoke "fear" or "horror" in the majority of citizens. At first, these concepts included only the "sacred person of the sovereign emperor" and members of the imperial family. Later, they encompassed the concept of *power* (imperial, Soviet, state), and finally *man*, his rights and freedoms, which is recorded in the majority of the constitutions of members of the Commonwealth of Independent States (CIS).

Despite the fact the modern scholarship has not yet developed a universal internationally accepted definition of terrorism, the essence of such occurrences remains practically unchanged even after such a long period.

In the Commonwealth of Independent States, law enforcement agencies make almost no use of the experience that the intelligence services of the Russian Empire amassed in their struggle against terrorism up to 1917.

The scale of terrorism in those times was enormous. It bears recalling that during the prerevolutionary period in Russia, terrorists killed or wounded about 4500 government employees of various ranks. As for private citizens, terrorists killed 2180 and wounded 2530.

---
* Translated from the Russian by Kelly Robbins.

Today, there may be a certain value in the almost forgotten experience of the intelligence services of the Russian Empire in the struggle against the so-called bombers from among the ranks of the Socialist-Revolutionaries and anarchists.

The Socialist-Revolutionary Party began in late 1901, when various "neopopulist" groups both within Russia and outside its borders joined together in a unified organization. It was the only party that officially included terrorist tactics in its program and itself became the embodiment of terror.[1] The membership of the Socialist-Revolutionary (SR) Party varied at different times, but during the revolutionary uprising of 1917, it counted up to 700,000 members.[2]

Adhering to the opinion common at that time in radical circles regarding the need for professionalism in revolutionary and military activities, the Central Committee of the SR Party in late 1901 organized a special detachment for carrying out terrorist acts. It was known as the Combat Organization. This was a conspiratorial organization created on the basis of strong convictions, in which its members' loyalty to each other was valued more highly than their devotion to the party.

In the first terrorist acts carried out by members of the Combat Organization (the murder of Internal Affairs Minister Sipyagin on April 22, 1902, by Kiev University student S.V. Balmashev; the attempt on the life of Chief Procurator of the Holy Synod K.P. Pobedonostsev at Sipyagin's funeral; the attempt on the life of Kharkov Governor-General I.M. Obolensky on July 29, 1902; and others), the militants used firearms and targeted those specific Russian imperial officials whom the party's Central Committee felt were guilty of crimes against the people. This raised the authority of the SRs in revolutionary circles and created in the eyes of the common people an image of the "SR hero-terrorist, sacrificing his life in the struggle for the people's happiness." The word "terrorist" took on a positive aspect. Hundreds of young revolutionaries in Russia dreamed of becoming terrorists and joining the Combat Organization of the Socialist-Revolutionaries.

In their newspapers, brochures, and proclamations, SR theoreticians argued that the "crowd" was powerless against the autocracy. Against the "crowd," the autocracy could use the police and gendarmes, but against individual "uncatchable" terrorists, there was no force that could help.[3]

Terrorism in those years was for many simple and understandable, a most rational and even humane method, and terrorist revolution was more democratic and even humane. Indeed, if the choice were between thousands of victims of mass revolution, or a precisely inflicted strike on those individuals specifically responsible for the people's sufferings . . . .

At that time, the tsarist authorities focused serious attention on matters regarding the protection of gunpowder and other explosives produced in Russia, which practically ruled out the possibility of their theft from military facilities, plants, and laboratories. Therefore, foreign countries were the primary source from which terrorists could obtain explosives. But getting explosives across the border was extremely difficult, so terrorists began manufacturing the substances themselves. The membership of the Combat Organization began to include specialists in manufacturing dynamite bombs, such as Dora Brilliant, Aleksei Pokotilov, Maksimilian Shveitser, and others. However, their poor knowledge of chemistry and particularly of the fine points of the processes of nitration and chemical stabilization of nitroglycerine and nitrocellulose, the basic components of dynamite, made it impossible for the terrorists to make high-quality explosive devices. Sometimes, this even led to the deaths of the terrorists themselves.

> *Thus, on March 31, 1904, Aleksei Pokotilov was killed while making a bomb in the Northern Hotel in St. Petersburg. The same fate befell Maksimilian Shveitser on February 26, 1905, at the Bristol Hotel. In both cases, the destructive force of the explosions was enormous: the rooms in which the bomb makers were located were destroyed, along with the adjoining rooms, and the bodies of the terrorists were blown to pieces.*[4]

However, this did not stop the terrorists. In July 1904, they used a dynamite bomb in the assassination of Minister of Internal Affairs V. Plehve.

> *This terrorist act was planned under the direct leadership of Azef, who headed the Combat Organization after the arrest of Gershuni.*
>
> *Because of his policies, Plehve was universally hated by the revolutionaries, who scornfully called him "Cain" in their circles. He was accused of harshly suppressing peasant uprisings in Poltava and Kharkov provinces, imposing strict programs of Russification, and organizing pogroms against the Jews. On June 15, 1904, when Plehve was heading off for his latest audience with the Tsar, the militant Yegor Sazonov (known by the nickname "Avel") threw a bomb into the minister's carriage. Plehve and his driver were literally blown to pieces. Seven other people were injured in the blast, including guards, random passersby, and the terrorist himself.*[5]
>
> *In order to justify this barbaric act, the SR Central Committee issued several appeals in connection with Plehve's murder: "To All Workers," "July 15," "To the Entire Russian People," and "Eulogy for a Court Favorite." In these documents, the SRs attempted to justify the terror and viewed the acts as capable of inspiring revolutionary activity even among the less active elements of society.*

The next "big" terrorist act of the Combat Organization was the murder of the Governor-General of Moscow, Grand Duke Sergei Aleksandrovich, the uncle of Nicholas II.

> *The SRs decided to carry out this act as revenge against the governor for the so-called Khodyn disaster, at which 1389 people were killed and 1300 injured during the coronation of Nicholas II in 1896, and for the mass arrests, antisemitism, and persecution of the progressive press. The leaders of the SR Party's Central Committee understood that random casualties resulting from a terrorist act involving the use of explosive devices would reduce its political effect. However, the great destructive power of dynamite bombs guaranteed*

success and practically ruled out the possibility that the victims marked by the terrorists would receive only minor injuries. This therefore determined the selection of dynamite as the main weapon in the struggle for "democracy."

On February 2, 1905, the SR militant Ivan Kalyaev was standing in front of the Bolshoi Theater and already had his bomb in hand and his arm raised, ready to make the fatal throw into the Grand Duke's carriage. However, seeing that the Grand Duke was accompanied by his wife Elizabeth and children Maria and Dmitry, he decided to postpone the terrorist act. Two days later, at the Spassky Gates, he threw the bomb into the window of the Grand Duke's carriage, blowing up Sergei and seriously wounding the driver and Kalyaev himself. The terrorist was arrested, condemned, and on April 5, 1905, hung at the Schlusselberg Fortress. At his trial, Kalyaev spoke out with accusations against the government and declared that acts of terrorism "are history's judgment against you . . . ." Kalyaev's speech at the trial was widely distributed by the SRs for propaganda purposes.[6]

These two powerful explosions were in fact the last major successful acts by the Combat Organization of the Socialist-Revolutionary Party. They spurred the creation and activization of combat units in the Bialystok, Volyn, Dvinsk (Daugavpils), Vitebsk, Odessa, Gomel, Krasnoyarsk, Ufa, Nizhny Novgorod, Moscow, and Tbilisi committees of the Socialist-Revolutionary Party. These brigades became actively involved in the revolutionary uprisings that swept Russia in 1905, and they used dynamite bombs fairly frequently. According to police data, they carried out more than 30 terrorist acts during this period.[7]

Besides the Socialist-Revolutionaries, the widespread practice of using explosive devices was also observed among the anarchists, who advanced and put into practice the slogan "Death to the Bourgeoisie." The most famous instance in which this slogan was carried out occurred on December 17, 1905, in the city of Odessa, when anarchists threw bombs into the Libman Café, a place where, in their opinion, the bourgeoisie gathered. As a result, about a dozen people were killed, many were wounded, and the building itself suffered enormous damage. In 1905-1906, in the defense of workers' rights, anarchists made a practice of throwing bombs into streetcars and trains that were operating during strikes. They also blew up several merchant steamers and killed two captains whom the workers disliked.[8]

The use of explosive devices objectively led to the killings not only of those whom the revolutionaries had "condemned to death," but also of guards, adjutants, drivers, and random passersby, which was considered a grave sin even among the revolutionaries who believed in God. This gave the police both a moral and a religious basis for the recruitment and re-recruitment of God-fearing revolutionaries as secret agents.

In the struggle against the terrorist bombers, the police and gendarmes used all the resources of the state and its fundamental institutions. Their most important basic method was infiltration and the recruitment of agents within revolutionary organizations. According to incomplete calculations, there were about 6500 agents, provocateurs, and other political investigations specialists operating in various political parties and organizations in the Russian Empire at the start of the twentieth century. The difficult situation in which the intelligence services of the time found themselves was occasioned by the fact that the imperial ruling circles were not always able to define their political goals or the means of achieving them, even under the intensifying crisis conditions. Therefore, the police and gendarmes often set priorities themselves, at times even at the risk of the lives of high-ranking government officials and members of the imperial family. Matters concerning the security of the secret agents were of top priority, and maintaining the strong positions of agents within the terrorist organizations of the Socialist-Revolutionaries was considered more important than preventing assassinations, even against officials of the government.[9]

> One example of this was the case of the agent Evno Azef, who operated in revolutionary circles for about 15 years. From 1893 on, he was an agent of the police department. As a student in a German polytechnic school, he took the initiative of offering his services to the police department at the rate of 50 rubles per month, after which he attached himself to a foreign group calling itself the Union of Russian Socialist-Revolutionaries. He knew about the majority of terrorist acts being planned by the SRs, but he did not always report to his bosses about them. Nevertheless, the police paid him well for his services. In 1905, Azef's base salary from the police department totaled 600 rubles per month, and with "travel per diem" and "bonuses" the total exceeded 1000 rubles, which at that time was even higher than the salary of the governor. As a "professional" revolutionary, Azef received 120 rubles per month from the Socialist-Revolutionary Party. In this sense he could in all honesty be called a "professional agent" for the police, as he received almost ten times more per month from his job as an agent than from his "official source of income . . . ."
>
> After he was exposed as an agent in 1908, Azev fled to Germany, where he married a German woman and lived comfortably on the money he "earned" from the police and stole from the Combat Organization of the Socialist-Revolutionaries. He died there in Germany in 1918.[10]

Another method used in fighting the terrorists was the monitoring of the basic flow of information in the Russian Empire. The police department managed an efficiently operating system for inspecting the correspondence of foreigners and Russian subjects suspected of harboring antigovernment sentiments. Inspection of correspondence was one component in the fight against terrorism. So-called black offices, in which police personnel inspected letters, operated in the post offices of St. Petersburg, Moscow, Warsaw, Kiev, Odessa, Kharkov, Vilnius, Tbilisi, Tobolsk, Tomsk, and Irkutsk. On average, the police opened up to 380,000 envelopes per year in their search for operational information on the activities of revolutionary terrorists.[11]

Terrorist acts involving the use of explosive devices also spurred the tsarist authorities to apply radical legislative measures, which may be categorized as a third method in the fight against the terrorist bombers.

On August 12, 1906, an attempt was made on the life of Council of Ministers Chairman and Minister of Internal Affairs P. Stolypin, in which 25 people were killed (including even the terrorists) and 32 injured (including Stolypin's 3-year-old son and 14-year-old daughter) by the explosion of dynamite bombs thrown by terrorists into the drawing room of the minister's dacha. In the wake of this incident, the government took advantage of Article 87 in the Fundamental Laws, which permitted the issuance of urgent decrees in the absence of ratification by legislative organs (since the Second Duma had not yet been elected). Thus, on August 19, 1906, the government, with the tsar's approval, passed on an emergency basis a law making civilians subject to trial by military field courts.

According to this law, governors and military district commanders in areas under martial law or a state of emergency had the right to hold for military trial those individuals whose participation in such crimes as production, storage, or use of explosive devices, terrorist attacks and murders, armed attacks on government officials, or other acts of resistance was so obvious that it did not require detailed investigation.

> Each such military field court consisted of five officer-judges appointed by the local commander. Defendants had the right to call witnesses, but they did not have a right to legal assistance. Court sessions were held behind closed doors. Cases in such courts were heard within 24 hours from the time of arrest, sentences were handed down within 48 hours, there were no appeals, and sentences were carried out within 24 hours after verdicts were rendered. In the majority of cases, these courts issued sentences of either death or a long period of hard labor. In the eight months from the time this law was enacted until its validity was terminated in April 1907, over a thousand terrorists were shot or hung.

Along with the military field courts, the regular military and civilian courts continued to function. Although their sentences were lighter, especially in cases involving women and minors, they too, at Stolypin's order, instituted harsher trial procedures.

> The intensity of the struggle against revolutionary terrorism may be judged from the following data: in 1908 and 1909 in Russia, 16,440 civilians and military personnel were convicted for political crimes, including armed attacks, of whom 3682 were condemned to death and 4517 to hard labor.[12] The scale of the revolutionary terror that gripped the Russian Empire in the early twentieth century may be judged by the following data from the Police Department. From 1902 to 1911, revolutionaries carried out 263 terrorist acts. The victims of these acts were 2 ministers, 33 governors, governors-general, or vice-governors, 16 town governors, district division heads, police chiefs, public prosecutors, assistant prosecutors, or heads of police investigations divisions, 7 gener-

als or admirals, 15 colonels, 8 barristers, and 26 spies or provocateurs. Among the direct perpetrators of terrorist acts were 62 workers, 14 representatives of the intelligentsia, 9 peasants, and 18 high school or university students.

Placed in opposition to the terrorists by the police and gendarmes, this system of measures included both means of obtaining operational information and strengthening agents' positions in revolutionary circles (to break them down from the inside) as well as means for implementing legislative and judicial policies and practices merciless to terrorists. By 1910, it allowed the tsarist government to seriously break the wave of revolutionary terror and explosions that had gripped Russia at the start of the twentieth century.

The political results of the terror carried out by the Socialist-Revolutionaries turned out to be zero. The exposure of the agent Azev was an especially strong blow to the SR Party, after which it in fact broke apart into separate uncoordinated groups. After this, some of the SRs took up mysticism, engaging in "God-seeking" or "God-building."

In particular, this category included Azef's deputy in the Combat Organization of the Socialist-Revolutionary Party, B. Savinkov, who under the pseudonym V. Ropshin published a novel in Paris entitled Pale Horse. *In the book, he heaps scorn on the revolution and depicts the terrorists themselves in an unfavorable light. B. Savinkov took the name of the book from the Apocalypse, in which the description of the Last Judgment mentions the appearance of a "pale horse" whose rider will be death . . . .*[13]

NOTES

1. Geifman, op. cit., p. 75.
2. Razakov, F. 1997. Century of Terror. Moscow, p. 10.
3. Gusev, K.V. 1992. Knights of Terror. Moscow, p. 19.
4. Gusev, K.V. 1995. The SR Party from Petit Bourgeois Revolutionarism to Counterrevolution. Moscow, p. 59.
5. Geifman, op. cit., p. 192.
6. Kuras, L. 1998. Stories from the History of the State Security Agencies of the Republic of Buryatia. Ulan-Ude-Irkutsk, p. 19.
7. Aldanov, M.A. 1991. Collected Works. Moscow, Vol. 6, pp. 449-486.
8. Bolsheviks. Documents from the History of Bolshevism from 1903 to 1916 from the Former Moscow Police Department. 1990. Moscow, p. 8.
9. Geifman, op. cit., p. 317.
10. Gusev, K. V. 1995. The SR Party from Petit Bourgeois Revolutionarism to Counterrevolution. Moscow, p. 75.
11. Bolsheviks. Documents from the History of Bolshevism from 1903 to 1916 from the Former Moscow Police Department. 1990. Moscow, p. 8.
12. Geifman, op. cit., p. 317.
13. Gusev, K.V. 1995. The SR Party from Petit Bourgeois Revolutionarism to Counterrevolution. Moscow, p. 75.

On Historical Experience in Combating Terrorism

Oleg M. Khlobustov [*]
Regional Society Strategic Security Assistance Fund

In order to develop a modern strategy for countering terrorism and political extremism, it is very important to consider historical experience in combating these social phenomena. This consideration should include both domestic Russian historical experience and foreign experience. From this perspective, let us consider the problem of opposing terrorism under current conditions.

It should also be mentioned at the outset that a number of scholars of the phenomenon of modern terrorism are currently beginning to speak of new and nontraditional possible forms of terrorism in the twenty-first century (see, for example, O.V. Damaskin, 2000, "Terrorism Under Conditions of New Technologies," *Problems of Combating Terrorism: Materials from a Scientific-Practical Conference, March 21, 2000*, Moscow, pp. 83-86). However, in our opinion the same substantive characteristics of this criminal phenomenon that were used to describe political terrorism in the nineteenth and twentieth centuries still retain their significance. These characteristics include the presence of various ideological-theoretical conceptions (foundations for bringing like-minded individuals together), stage of development, and conditions for terrorist activity.

We proceed on the understanding that terrorism as a historical phenomenon represents the totality of individual actors and groups operating in a certain time period, recognizing terrorist means of political struggle, and developing concepts for the creation, justification, and tactical utilization of those means.

In our view, a study of the activities of a number of Russian (late nineteenth-early twentieth centuries) and foreign terrorist organizations from Europe, Asia, and Latin America makes it possible to identify a number of objective character-

---

[*] Translated from the Russian by Kelly Robbins.

istics of the organization, creation, and operational tactics of terrorists. These characteristics are very relevant to the organization of efforts to counter this threat in current conditions.

1. First of all, it should be noted that the appearance in society of terrorist groups, at times even uniting into larger terrorist organizations, is preceded by a certain preparatory incubation period. This period varies in length, sometimes lasting up to 10 years.

This period is characterized by the circulation of certain documents, either anonymous or "authorized" on behalf of some group of "like-minded individuals," containing incitements and calls to carry out terrorist actions. At the same time, radically opposition-oriented segments of the population are discussing the permissibility, expediency, and justifiability of beginning a terrorist "political struggle."

2. Many of these terrorist organizations not only are based on some fundamental ideological-political construct (a maximum program or "ideology"), but also often have legal political wings. Examples include Sinn Féin and the Irish Republic Army (IRA) in Ulster (Great Britain); Herri Batasuna and the Basque ETA (Spain); the Movement for Self-Determination and the Front for the National Liberation of Corsica (FLNC) in France; and others.

3. Despite the periodic blows inflicted on them by law enforcement agencies, some terrorist organizations continue to exist and operate for many years: the IRA in Northern Ireland since 1914, the Muslim Brotherhood in Egypt since 1928, ETA in Spain since 1959 (although it first announced itself only on June 7, 1968), the RAF (Red Army Faction) in the Federal Republic of Germany since the late 1960s, the Red Brigades in Italy since 1970, the Japanese Red Army (JRA) since the early 1970s, the Grey Wolves in Turkey since the mid-1970s, Direct Action in France since 1979, and Hamas since 1987.

It is this support on the part of the population that also ensures the "rebirth" of organizations and groups in cases of their destruction, as happened with the Executive Committee of *Narodnaya Volya* (People's Will) in the 1880s and with the RAF in the 1970s through 1990s.

4. Another characteristic feature of the functioning of terrorist groups and organizations is their increasing radicalization, at times leading to the splitting off of groups of especially "uncompromising" opponents of the existing social and governmental order.

5. Some of them are separatist organizations (IRA, ETA, FLNC). In others, their "ideology" combines nationalist and religious elements (IRA, Muslim Brotherhood, Grey Wolves, Hamas), which attests to the heightened survival capacity of organizations that rely on the sentiments and aspirations of significant segments of the population as a real social support base for their ideas. This circumstance is particularly important for predicting probable terrorist activities and organizing countermeasures against them.

6. In the 1970s and 1980s, contacts were established among various European organizations, the JRA, and Palestinian terrorists. At present, there are known ties between Muslim terrorist organizations (and their legal political wings) in Afghanistan, Turkey, Iran, and other countries with sympathizers in certain countries of the Commonwealth of Independent States, including Russia (Chechnya, Dagestan, and others).

7. Terrorist acts are sometimes carried out on the territory of other states, at times "under a foreign flag," including even cases where this is done with the consent of the true "bearers" of that flag.

8. As shown by the experience of foreign countries, when one form of terrorism (predominantly "left" or "right") becomes sufficiently widespread and persistent, its ideological antithesis can also appear: the Protestant Ulster Volunteer Force (since 1966) and the Ulster Freedom Fighters (since 1971) in Northern Ireland, the Ku Klux Klan in the United States and since the late 1960s the Black Panthers, which have in turn used terrorist methods as well. Other examples include the Farabundo Marti National Liberation Front and the death squads in El Salvador, and the Revolutionary Armed Forces, the White Hand, and the death squads in Guatemala.

This last circumstance should receive special consideration in organizing countermeasures against terrorism and political extremism, inasmuch as separatist extremism and terrorism can give rise to a "fundamentalist" response under the very popular slogan of "united and indivisible power."

It should also be noted that at times of their peak activity, terrorist organizations abroad are not mere groups of conspirators, fanatics, and ascetics, as had been typical until recently. Instead, they are full-fledged concerns with internal division of labor, workshops, warehouses, printing plants, laboratories, shelters, hospitals, and profit-making enterprises. They have turned bank robbery, racketeering, and the taking of hostages for ransom into a highly profitable sort of business. They have planted their agents in various segments of the government, industry, and finance (see, for example, V.V. Vityuk, 1993, "Terrorism in the Post-Perestroika Era," *Sotsis* [Sociological Studies] 7:45). In this way they have become especially dangerous and especially conspiratorial branches of organized crime.

We note here that in an article with the very significant title "Can Terrorists Be Stopped?" U.S. federal judge William Webster, who previously headed the Federal Bureau of Investigation (1978-1987) and the Central Intelligence Agency (1987-1991), also includes "criminal cartels" or organized crime under the heading of terrorism (*Reader's Digest* 3 [1997]:81, Moscow).

Adaptation and utilization of foreign experience in the fight against terrorism is associated with a number of questions. The following substantive questions may be drawn from a study of foreign experience in the fight against terrorism:

- The practice of legislative regulation of the fight against terrorism;

- The organization of countermeasures against terrorism (including principles and special characteristics of strategy and tactics combating terrorism, the distribution of function and authorities in this sphere of law enforcement activity, the organization of preventive measures against terrorism, et cetera); and
- Activities regarding the application of laws.

Based on published research, it is possible to highlight the following special characteristics of legislative regulation of the fight against terrorism. Its development is tied primarily with tendencies and features of the crime situation in a given country, the presence of political will among the country's leadership to combat terrorism, characteristics of the country's political traditions and culture, and the presence of certain circumstances related to international law that in turn must be implemented in the appropriate legislative acts.

At times, the development of an adequate system of measures for countering the terrorist threat requires a significant period of time, as well as flexible reaction to changes in the crime situation and operational circumstances. This reaction must be based on a study and consideration of both domestic and foreign experience.

For example, the experience of the Italian intelligence services in combating the terrorism of the Red Brigades, including the reduction in punishment for repentant terrorists and the strengthening of overall preventive work by law enforcement agencies, had an impact on changes in legislation in Great Britain and the Federal Republic of Germany.

The creative application of this experience, in our view, led in mid-1998 to consecutive declarations on halting terrorism made by the RAF in Germany, the IRA in Great Britain, and ETA in Spain (*Pravda*, December 3, 1999). (ETA later announced an end to the "cease-fire," and since January 2000 this organization has already carried out more than 30 terrorist acts.)

At the national level, the organization of efforts to combat terrorism are characterized as a rule by the following:

- The creation of an organ with special powers to fight this threat (the Coordinating Council on Combating Terrorism in 1991 in Germany, the Executive Committee on Ulster in 1991 in Great Britain);
- The improvement of administrative and preventive regimes; and
- The organization of international cooperation to combat terrorism.

On the whole, the UN-recommended and most commonly practiced forms of international cooperation in combating terrorism are the following:

- Facilitation of extradition, that is, the transfer to interested states of terrorists or other persons justifiably suspected of involvement in terrorism;
- Provision of assistance in criminal investigations;

• Development of regional and bilateral intergovernmental agreements on combating terrorism;
• Training of personnel for antiterrorist law enforcement units; and
• Pursuit of joint scientific research and exchanges of information on problems of fighting terrorism, including specific operational information.

All of these require painstaking study and analysis on the one hand and legal regulation on the other.

The topic of utilization of foreign experience would also include the development of new intergovernmental agreements or conventions countering the growth of terrorist phenomena in specific spheres, as well as certain recommendations adopted by the United Nations and its specialized institutions. In this regard, the utilization of favorably tested foreign experience includes the following:

• Its study and analysis, the identification of strong and weak points, and the development on this basis of direct recommendations for legislative and law enforcement activities;
• Its inclusion in various adapted forms in the systemic legal base for combating terrorism, that is, its incorporation into the nation's legal system;
• Its use in the training of law enforcement agency personnel, including the preparation of textbooks, monographs, and scholarly papers; and
• Its direct use in preventive antiterrorism measures. This practice has received its most widespread use in Israel, Great Britain (since 1973), and the United States (since 1996).

However, it cannot be said that foreign experience provides only positive examples. For example, despite all measures taken, for about 60 years now Great Britain has been unable to eliminate the Irish Republic Army, just as the German police have been unable to eliminate the RAF and the Spanish police have not liquidated ETA. More than a thousand operations carried out by Israeli special forces units aimed at physically liquidating terrorists still have not brought peace to the Middle East.

It should also be emphasized that as historical experience shows, the "slide" of a country and society into the realm of armed violence can occur relatively quickly, while getting rid of terrorism sometimes takes many years or even decades.

However, we believe that positive foreign experience is still not being fully utilized. Specifically, legislators and law enforcement officials have not paid attention to the participation of the mass media in efforts to fight terrorism. Meanwhile, certain press publications could be viewed as textbooks for potential terrorists.

Unfortunately, in the opinion of many analysts and experts, prospects for defeating terrorism are rather bleak, at least in the first decade of the twenty-first century. We shall note in this regard a novel factor on the international scene, namely, the appearance of history's first "terrorist international." I am referring here to the April 1998 formation of the so-called International Front for Jihad by extremist religious circles in a number of Islamic countries (Saudi Arabia, Pakistan, Egypt, Sudan, Afghanistan, and others). Many nations of Asia, Africa, Europe, Russia, and other members of the Commonwealth of Independent States have already become a staging ground for its activities. This organization is not an official union of states; rather, it involves the unification and organized cooperation of a number of religious and political organizations based in the above-mentioned states. Furthermore, several participants in this "front" are in their countries illegally.

In conclusion, it should be emphasized that the system of antiterrorist measures is constantly being improved and its effectiveness continually analyzed, both in Russia and abroad. Therefore, the study of foreign experience amassed in the battle of intelligence services against this national security threat must also be conducted in a constant, systematic, and planned manner.

What can and should be done to counter the threat of terrorism? In our view, all world experience indicates that the fight against terrorism is waged by law enforcement agencies, but it can be won, or more precisely "survived" or escaped, only by society itself.

The mass media also play a large part here, if they recognize their place and their role in this process. (For more on this topic, see O.M. Khlobustov, 2000, "The Mass Media and the Struggle Against Terrorism," *Contemporary Terrorism: Status and Prospects*, Moscow, pp. 176-180.)

It is impermissible not only for the mass media to carry any sort of justification of terrorism and terrorists, but also for them to repeat the statements that are at times heard to the effect that terrorism is a highly effective and relatively cheap means of achieving goals. The same applies to the slogan that "power comes from the barrel of a gun"!

The attention of society should be focused on the fact that terrorists have never managed to achieve victory at any time or in any place. The results and consequences of terrorism have been only its numerous senseless victims.

Thus, counterterrorist propaganda should be promoted under the slogan, "Let's leave terrorism in the nineteenth and twentieth centuries, in the past history of humanity!"

Along with the mass media, an effectively functioning system of public education, including the promotion of legal knowledge, is also highly significant in the cause of preventing and suppressing terrorism.

In our view, instilling a culture of peace among the population must be part of this process. As is generally known, the UN General Assembly at its fiftieth anniversary session on November 20, 1998, supported the UNESCO (United Nations Educational, Scientific, and Cultural Organization) resolution on proclaiming 2000 the International Year for a Culture of Peace and adopted a five-year Program on Education for a Culture of Peace.

The concept of a culture of peace includes all forms of behavior that respect the right to life, dignity, and human rights; reject violence in all its forms; and promote principles of peace, justice, solidarity, tolerance, and understanding among individuals, groups, and governments. It has been proposed to UN member states that they promote education

- In the spirit of a culture of peace, human rights, tolerance, and international understanding;
- In the spirit of protecting and respecting all human rights without discrimination;
- Promoting principles of democracy at all levels of societal development;
- Adding impetus to the fight against poverty and for progress and prosperity for all; and
- Ensuring for all citizens a quality of life appropriate to human dignity.

However, as history shows, contemporary world civilization still has a long way to go before the philosophy of a culture of peace truly becomes a reality.

Electromagnetic Terrorism

Yury V. Parfyonov *
Institute for High Energy Densities
Institute for High Temperatures

In the first two papers referenced below, specialists of the Russian Academy of Sciences carried out an analysis of the threat of electromagnetic terrorism.[1] It was noted that by using sources of powerful electromagnetic fields and specialized electrotechnical devices, the operations of electro-intensive targets may be disrupted. Distinct from nuclear, chemical, or biological terrorism, these actions leave no tracks; they do not require the terrorists to use means of individual protection. They may be accomplished at a distance from the target or by mobile means.

The problem of the vulnerability of radio-electronic information and control systems to the influence of electromagnetic radiation is an urgent one. Among the most powerful sources of such radiation are nuclear explosions, which, as is commonly known, are accompanied by the generation of an intense electromagnetic pulse. As a result of this pulse, massive failures of radio-electronic and electrotechnical systems occur over a considerable area, as observed in atmospheric nuclear weapons tests in the 1950s and early 1960s. Under current conditions, with microelectronics permeating all spheres of human life and fulfilling important functions, the influence of the electromagnetic pulse of a nuclear explosion would have global and, in a number of cases, catastrophic consequences. An understanding of this danger led to the creation in the late 1980s of Subcommittee SC77C under the auspices of the International Electrotechnical Commission (IEC). This subcommittee was assigned the task of working out a set of standards regulating methods and means for protecting civilian facilities from the electromagnetic pulse of a nuclear explosion. This work is nearing completion. The top-priority area for subsequent activities of the subcommittee will be

* Translated from the Russian by A. Chelsea Sharber.

the development of standards on preventing emergency situations in connection with the threat of unregulated use of nonnuclear sources of powerful electromagnetic radiation.

This decision by IEC is a consequence of the fact that a number of countries now have generators that can produce radiation comparable in intensity with the electromagnetic pulse of a nuclear explosion and would therefore have a more effective impact on radio-electronic systems. The high effectiveness of these generators is explained by the following factors:

1. They emit not a single pulse, as occurs in a nuclear explosion, but a series of pulses repeated with frequencies of up to several thousand hertz.

2. The radiation pulses are more broad-banded than the electromagnetic pulse of a nuclear explosion, and they cover the spectrum of sensitivity of most civilian infrastructure targets.

It should be specifically noted that the construction of super broad-band pulse generators is relatively simple. They may be manufactured in semiprimitive conditions with minimal expense. By this reasoning, analysts predict that these devices will fall into the hands of terrorists, common criminals, and hooligans.[2] In the opinion of specialists, the consequences of their ill-intentioned or careless use will be extremely serious. Such consequences could include aviation, automobile, and railway accidents; obstruction of radio communications over large areas; disruption of the operations of computer systems in major banks, supermarkets, and control centers; obstruction of technical security systems in major museums, art galleries, vaults containing valuables, and other secured facilities; breakdowns in the operations of the system for controlling electric power facilities; and so forth.

Of course, such predictions require serious examination and, if they are even partially confirmed, the implementation of serious measures to prevent acts of electromagnetic terrorism and to develop methods for eliminating the consequences of emergency situations in the event such acts are perpetrated. A limited study was conducted by specialists from the Institute of Thermophysics of Extreme States of the Russian Academy of Sciences. Two types of experiments were carried out, one investigating the action of super broad-band electromagnetic pulses on computers and the other studying the effect of these pulses on technical security systems. In the course of the experiments, it was established that the computers under investigation failed when exposed to electromagnetic pulses with an amplitude on the order of several hundred volts per meter. This confirmed the prediction about the danger of super broad-band periodic repeating electromagnetic pulses for computer hardware.

The experiments also showed that the following events occurred subject to the amplitude of electromagnetic pulses acting on technical security systems:

1. Failure of the elements of the security equipment;
2. False sensor readings, forcing security personnel to turn off the seemingly defective equipment; and
3. Temporary neutralization of security systems.

The last possibility calls for special concern, since it involves the likelihood that a criminal could get past the security system without sensors' making the appropriate signal to the central control station.

Apart from experiments utilizing the super broad-band electromagnetic pulse generator, the possibility of perpetrating terrorist acts using simpler and cheaper means was also investigated. One such means would be a high-voltage pulse generator. A set of theoretical and experimental investigations was carried out regarding the way in which this voltage permeates computer systems. The five-story building in which the institute is situated was chosen as the site of the investigation.

The goal of the work was to demonstrate the possibility of causing a considerable number of computers to fail by hitting them with pulses of current through the power supply and grounding circuits. Moreover, the points of entry for the pulses were located outside the building. According to the results of this work, it is possible to confirm that the electric power supply and grounding circuits represent an effective channel for the permeation of electrical pulses into the building, despite the presence of voltage limiters and filters. The test signals reached computers in the building practically without weakening, and in a number of cases the signals were even strengthened as a result of resonance phenomena. Estimations indicate that the failure of practically all the computers in the building could be caused by using a 10-100-kV pulse generator linked to the power supply and grounding circuits of the institute building.

In addition to the aforementioned experiments, the parameters of the grounding system in a major telecommunications center were also measured. A considerable imbalance was discovered in the parameters of the grounding devices of different receiving and transmitting stations. As a result, even at minimal (measured) levels of probing signals, failures were observed in the operations of the digital telecommunications system. There is no doubt that with a feed of pulses from 10-100 kV, these systems will fail.

Thus, it is possible to state that effective technical means of protection against electromagnetic terrorism must be developed. It may be necessary to review and enhance rules regarding grounding devices and the laying of power cable. In any case, research should continue, and immediate measures should be developed and implemented. Such efforts will be even more useful, given that they will increase the stability of electronic systems against any electromagnetic obstacles, including lightning discharges, discharges of static electricity, et cetera. Inasmuch as terrorism has taken on an international character in recent years, causing serious anxiety in all industrially developed countries, it would be expedient to take measures to facilitate international collaboration in this area. Among other possible efforts, it is necessary to organize a joint experiment on assessing the real danger of electromagnetic terrorism and developing means of protection.

NOTES

1. Fortov, V.E. 2000. About the potential possibility of commitment of large-scale terrorist acts by using electrotechnical devices. EUROEM 2000, Edinburgh, May 30-June 2, 2000.

Fortov, V.E. 2001. A computer code for estimating pulsed electromagnetic disturbances penetrating into building power and grounding circuits. 14th International Zurich Symposium on Electromagnetic Compatibility.

2. Schriner, D. 1998. The design and fabrication of a damage inflicting RF weapon by "back yard" methods. Statement before the United States Congress Joint Economic Committee, Wednesday, February 25, 1998.

BIOLOGICAL TERRORISM

Molecular Epidemiology as a New Approach in Detecting Terrorist Use of Infectious Agents

Sergey V. Netesov
Corresponding Member of the Russian Academy of Sciences,
Vector State Research Center for Virology and Biotechnology

The underlying basis for the casualty effect of bioterrorist weapons is formed by biological agents, namely, microorganisms and certain products of their live activities (toxins) as well as a number of pests and insects capable of transmitting infectious diseases. These biological agents are capable of causing disease in humans, animals, and plants, as well as producing widespread panic. Bioterrorist acts differ from other types of terrorist actions in that they may be open, announced, and demonstrative acts or hidden actions disguised as natural outbreaks or divine scourges. In the latter case, resources and procedures are required to investigate the episode, document its unconventional characteristics, and in the best possible outcome, prove that it is artificially created. It should be noted that according to available data, the majority of bioterrorist episodes up to now have been of a disguised and masked nature. In particular, this was reported in the presentation of Dr. H. McGeorge[1] at the World Congress on Chemical and Biological Terrorism in Dubrovnik, Croatia, in April 2001. Therefore, the problem of discriminating between natural and artificially created disease outbreaks is still a pressing one.

Let us begin by considering the list of possible infectious agents that may be used for bioterrorist purposes. Such lists usually include biological agents that might be used as biological weapons. Table 1, which presents only viral agents, consolidates five versions of such lists compiled at different times by different expert teams from different institutions.[2] It is evident that expert opinions differ considerably. Only variola virus, alphavirus chikungunya, yellow fever virus, and Rift Valley fever virus are present in all the lists. However, note that the World Health Organization (WHO) list was compiled in 1970, when Ebola and some other viruses were unknown. Note also that according to opinions of other

TABLE 1   Viruses Considered Potential Biological Warfare Agents by Various International or National Agencies

Viral Agents	Agency or Country				
	WHO, 1970	USA, AHSC, 1983	USA, BDRP, 1989	Australia and USA, 1992	Germany, 1990
Chikungunya virus	+	+	+	+	+
Crimean-Congo hemorrhagic fever virus		+	+	+	
Dengue virus	+	+		+	+
Eastern equine encephalitis virus		+	+	+	+
Ebola virus		+	+	+	+
Hantaan (HFRS) virus		+	+	+	
Influenza virus	+				+
Japanese encephalitis virus	+			+	
Junin (Argentine hemorrhagic fever) virus		+	+	+	+
Lassa fever virus		+	+	+	+
Lymphocytic choriomeningitis virus		+		+	
Machupo (Bolivian hemorrhagic fever) virus		+	+	+	+
Marburg virus		+		+	+
Monkeypox virus				+	+
Rift Valley fever virus	+	+	+	+	+
Smallpox virus	+	+	+	+	+
Tickborne encephalitis virus	+	+	+	+	
Venezuelan equine encephalitis virus	+	+	+	+	+
Western equine encephalitis virus		+	+	+	
Yellow fever virus	+	+	+	+	+

NOTE: AHSC—U.S. Army Health Services Command; BDRP—Biological Defense Research Program.

experts from our center as well as my own, this list is far from complete. In particular, it lacks hepatitis A virus, which causes a rather severe disease, especially in older people, and which is easily transmitted through the fecal-oral route. Furthermore, more than 60 percent of the population in the United States and Western Europe lacks immunity to it. On the other hand, it is not clear why this list contains tick-borne encephalitis virus yet lacks St. Louis encephalitis virus, since the diseases they cause are similar in their severity and transmission routes. It is illustrative in this connection that the German team omits tick-borne encephalitis, whose foci are common in Germany, and includes Venezuelan equine encephalomyelitis virus, which causes a considerably milder disease but is absent in that country.

Table 2 shows the list of biological agents selected by experts from the U.S. Centers for Disease Control and Prevention (CDC) as having the potential for terrorist use.[3] Interestingly, it contains virtually the same viral agents as Table 1. Again, hepatitis A virus is absent from the list. It is even more strange, given that the classic 1984 bioterrorist episode at the salad bar in Oregon, when more than 700 people were infected, involved the bacterium *Salmonella,* which displays

TABLE 2   Critical Biological Agents as Identified by the U.S. Centers for Disease Control and Prevention, 1998

Category A—Highest Priority

Variola major (smallpox)
Bacillus anthracis (anthrax)
Yersinia pestis (plague)
Clostridium botulinum toxin (botulism)
Francisella tularensis (tularemia)
Filoviruses
    Ebola hemorrhagic fever
    Marburg hemorrhagic fever
Arenaviruses
    Lassa (Lassa fever)
    Junin (Argentine hemorrhagic fever) and related viruses

Category B—Second-Highest Priority

Coxiella burnetti (Q fever)
Brucella species (brucellosis)
Burkholderia mallei (glanders)
Alphaviruses
    Venezuelan encephalomyelitis
    Eastern and Western equine encephalomyelitis
Ricin toxin from *Ricinus communis* (castor beans)
Epsilon toxin of *Clostridium perfringens*
Staphylococcus enterotoxin B
Salmonella species
Shigella dysenteriae
Escherichia coli O157:H7
Vibrio cholerae
Cryptosporidium parvum

Category C—Emerging Pathogens of Potential Future Use

Nipah virus
Hantaviruses
Tickborne hemorrhagic fever viruses
Yellow fever
Multidrug-resistant tuberculosis

the same transmission route as hepatitis A. In the Oregon case, the disease was first classified as a natural outbreak, and only after a year was it proven that extremists had added *Salmonella* to salads in order to disrupt local elections. However, this list contains *Salmonella,* although in category B. Generally, if we consider the biological agents listed in this table not from the standpoint of biological warfare (that is, the use of such agents by a state against another state) but as potential terrorist weapons, I believe that chances are not high that, for example, variola, Marburg, or Ebola viruses would be used for the following reasons:

- The high danger to the terrorists themselves;
- The great and hardly surmountable difficulties involved in obtaining the initial material for propagation—this is true at least for variola virus because its stocks in Atlanta and Novosibirsk are very well guarded, and the protection systems are constantly being improved; and
- The need for a high biosafety-level laboratory for propagation of these biological agents.

From this standpoint, it is more likely that terrorists would use more common pathogens that could be stolen from an average microbiological laboratory, easily produced, or isolated in considerable amounts—for instance, hepatitis A from sewage collection systems, since human feces would contain it in great amounts during an outbreak. In addition, such common pathogens are safe for vaccinated persons or only mildly hazardous for terrorists due to available means of emergency prophylaxis. With this in mind, the list should be supplemented with several viruses: the hepatitis A virus; rotavirus, which is transmitted via drinking water and food and causes severe diarrhea lasting several days; different variants of influenza virus, including old strains from the 1960s and 1970s; and rabies virus. The same is true for bacterial agents; among them, attention should be paid to *Salmonella,* enteropathogenic *Escherichia coli* O157:H7, ordinary diphtheria, and others.

Here, I would like to give you a hypothetical example of the possibility of using a biological agent of the hepatitis A virus type. A paper analyzing morbidity in the Russian armed forces during the first armed conflict in Chechnya was published in a Russian journal five years ago.[4] It is evident from Figure 1 that the majority (more than 90 percent) of infectious diseases within this contingent were anthroponoses with fecal-oral transmission routes. Figure 2 presents the infectious agents that caused these intestinal diseases and their rates. It is evident that the hepatitis A virus was the disease cause in more than 50 percent of the cases, with the dysentery-causing bacteria *Shigella* causing over 30 percent. The remaining cases were due to enterocolitis of different etiologies, including again those caused by *Salmonella.* Note that the hepatitis A morbidity rate in this contingent was essentially higher than in the other regions of Russia (Table 3).

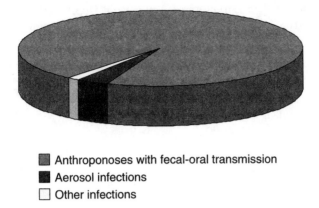

■ Anthroponoses with fecal-oral transmission
■ Aerosol infections
☐ Other infections

FIGURE 1   Prevalence of Various Infectious Diseases Among the Russian Military Contingent in Chechnya During the Conflict (February-December 1995)

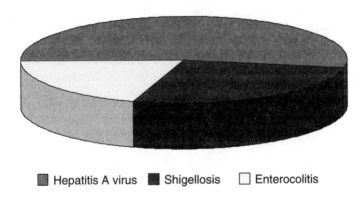

■ Hepatitis A virus   ■ Shigellosis   ☐ Enterocolitis

FIGURE 2   Prevalence of Various Etiological Agents Causing Enteric Infections in the Russian Military Contingents During the Chechnya Conflict (February-December 1995)

Unfortunately, the paper lacks the rate per 100,000 people; however, if we consider that the morbidity rate of hepatitis B and C is approximately equal in all three regions listed in Table 3, it is evident that the specific morbidity (per 100,000 people) of hepatitis A among Russian soldiers in Chechnya is about two times higher than the rates in military units located in other regions. The paper cited underlines this fact and indicates also that 82.4 percent of infection cases were found in recruits, and at times up to 20 percent of the contingent was hospitalized due to hepatitis A. This is the reason military hospitals in Chechnya were so overcrowded. A similar situation was recorded during the war in Af-

TABLE 3 Etiological Structure of Acute Viral Hepatitis Among Servicemen from Different Regions of Russia (Monoinfections, in Percent)

Nosological Forms and Serological Markers	Military Forces in Chechnya	Northwest Region (St. Petersburg Region and Baltic Fleet)	South Region (Black Sea Fleet)
Hepatitis A (anti-HAV IgM)	86.1	64.9	63.9
Hepatitis B (anti-HBc IgM)	4.3	14.9	8.2
Hepatitis C (anti-HCV)	0.5	2.0	1.6
Hepatitis E	0	0.9	0
Mixed hepatitis	1.0	13.7	16.5
Nondifferentiated hepatitis	8.1	3.6	9.8

ghanistan, when at times up to 40 percent of Russian soldiers were unfit for action due to hepatitis A.

Figure 3 illustrates the monthly morbidity plot from the same paper. It shows two waves of the disease: the first, in October-November, which is typical of this infection, and the second, in May-June, which is not typical and fails to coincide with the arrival of recruits. No correlations between the morbidity and type of dwelling (tents, houses, or trenches) were detected; however, there was a significant correlation with certain water sources, which were limited in number. Examination of water sources during the epidemic detected the viral antigen—that

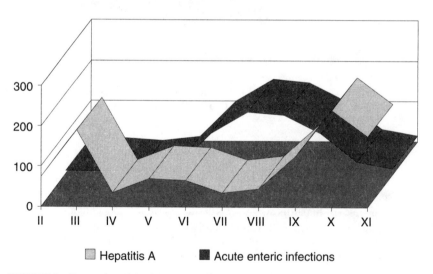

☐ Hepatitis A   ■ Acute enteric infections

FIGURE 3 Dynamics of the Incidence of Hepatitis Disease caused by Hepatitis A Virus during the Chechnya Conflict (February-December 1995)

is, the virus itself—in one water source. I am by no means saying that the hepatitis A virus was deliberately used as a weapon in this case. But if somebody infected several water sources with the virus during September-November, the resulting increase in the morbidity rate would hardly cause any suspicion regarding deliberate use of the virus as a weapon. It would, however, create considerable disorganization, require substantial additional expenses for hospitalization and treatment, and weaken or even temporarily halt military actions. Meanwhile, if such an outbreak occurred in the summer or in January-February, it would be very reasonable to suspect deliberate contamination of water sources.

It should be noted that the Russian publications also lack the list of biological agents that may be used in bioterrorist acts. However, there is one official document that indirectly indicates such a list: President Yeltsin's Decree No. 298-rp of June 14, 1994, which imposed controls over the export of pathogens.[5] The decree coincides completely with the Australia Group list presented in Table 1. It also lacks *Salmonella* and hepatitis A, which is reasonable for a list of this type (export control).

Summing up, I would like to underline that in my opinion, the above-mentioned lists on the whole pay appropriate attention to the most dangerous biological agents, and the special attention paid to corresponding protection systems is definitely reasonable. However, probably because of this special attention, it is the most common everyday pathogens that might now be being used and most likely will be used in the future.

Let us now turn to discussing already existing and potential capabilities for detecting the covert use of biological agents. I will dwell in detail on the detection of primary infection sources using standard epidemiological methods, since it is obvious that contamination not of an open water reservoir but rather of a closed vessel points in itself to deliberate contamination. Actually, if a water source is contaminated by a common pathogen and there is no direct evidence (a bottle labeled *Virus X*) or reliable information on deliberate infection, there is no way to categorize the incident as being of a deliberate nature using conventional methods. What other methods are capable of detecting a deliberate but disguised bioterrorist action? Before the sequencing era, different viral strains of a pathogen were characterized and differentiated only according to their phenotypic features: shape and size of plaques in cell culture, shape and size of viral particles, differences in pathogenesis in animal models, differences in their antigenic characteristics, and so forth. In several cases, these methods allowed distinctions to be made between strains within taxonomic genera and species. If such distinctions were absent, it was considered that there was no difference between the strains. Early efforts in genomic sequencing and comparative analysis of strains with weak or no phenotypic differences detected such distinctions and facilitated the development of reliable and sufficiently precise methods for differentiating between viral strains based on molecular characterization. This strategy was soon dubbed molecular epidemiology.

Here is one of the first examples of such research. Figure 4 shows a simplified phylogenetic tree of influenza virus subtype H1N1.[6] I would like to provide a few words on the history of this subtype. It is considered related to subtype H0N1, the famous Spanish flu. It spread during 1946-1947, causing mass epidemics all over the world, and circulated widely until 1956. The scale of its outbreaks then decreased considerably, and subtype H2N2 took its place. In the autumn of 1977, a mass outbreak of H1N1 influenza virus occurred among Russian sailors in the Far East, and it was widely discussed in the mass media and scientific publications. Some publications included speculations on the artificial nature of this virus and its accidental or deliberate release from laboratories. In the mid-1980s, the main genes of this strain were sequenced; moreover, the sequences of one of the genes were published independently by three laboratories during one year. In the figure, these data are shown as differences in amino acid sequences of hemagglutinin HA-1 subunits, together with sequencing data of several other strains. The relations between the strains were calculated using the method of maximal likelihood between closest neighbors. It is evident from the figure that the strains circulating in Russia and the strains circulating in Australia since 1978 should actually have a common ancestor. In addition, this ancestor is antigenically close to the strain of 1950 (not the 1956 or 1946 strains, since almost no substitutions occur in the antigenic determinants). However, very important substitutions are localized in the region of amino acids 253-258 of the first Russian branch and at positions 56 and 295 of the Australian branch. The overall data obtained indicate unambiguously that the new epidemic caused by this subtype did not start from a single test tube, but involved a heterogeneous material that differed considerably from the strain circulated in the world in 1950 and kept in cold storage thereafter. Thus, the viral genome sequencing data demonstrated that the hypothesis on the artificial origin of the new epidemic wave of the influenza virus H1N1 is rather unlikely. I have one more comment regarding the figure. It is evident that sequencing data on the strains A/USSR/90/77 obtained in the three different labs differ from one another. This is the result of both the imperfect sequencing technique of the time and actual distinctions between subclones of the same strain and does not affect the conclusions made. It is now becoming clear that this method is very sensitive and sometimes even allows detection of changes in the virus population that occurred during its three- to seven-day circulation in the body of a single patient.

It should be stated that hundreds of subsequent publications on the natural diversity of viruses and bacteria demonstrated that the genomes of these pathogens are far from stable and uniform. For example, Figure 5 is a dendrogram describing the main genotypes of the hepatitis A virus. As shown in this figure, the scale of differences in percentages shows that the range of distinctions is wide enough to provide a reliable differentiation. In fact, a study tracing transmission of this pathogen at a molecular level in a stepwise manner from one person to another during an outbreak was presented in 1999 at the International

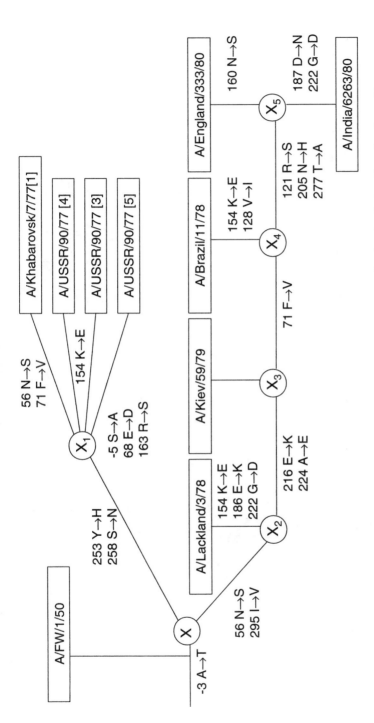

FIGURE 4 Evolutionary Relationships of Isolates of H1N1 Influenza Virus on the Base of Derived Amino Acid Sequences of its HA₁-Subunits (The amino acid numbers start from the first amino acid of the mature HA₁-subunit; the designation of the amino acid is presented as a one-letter code, as recommended by IUPAC-IUB.)

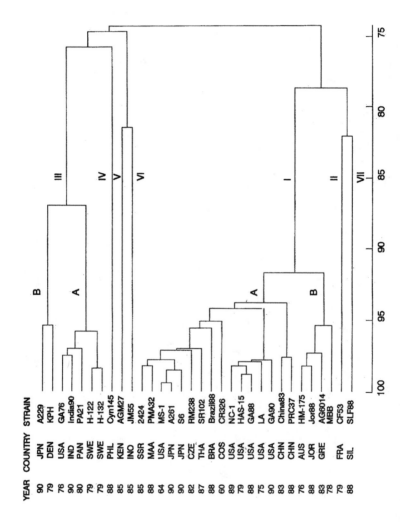

FIGURE 5 Dendrogram Demonstrating Differences in Nucleotide Sequences Among 32 Isolates of Hepatitis A Virus (The scale of identity is presented beneath the dendrogram in percent figures.)

Congress of Virology in Sydney.[7] Shown in Figure 6 is the dendrogram of M segment nucleotide sequences of HFRS (Hantaan) virus strains isolated in the Khabarovsk and Primorsky regions of Russia.[8] It shows a small group of strains with numbers 4290 and 4029 sitting apart. This group of strains occurs only in a small part of this territory, and it can be isolated only from local rodents *Apodemus peninsulae,* which makes it possible to predict the place of infection solely based on sequence data of the isolate taken from the patient. There are many examples of the use of the molecular epidemiology approach and not only for viruses. For instance, a study of the molecular diversity of meningococcus in Russia during 1969-1997 was published recently.[9] It provided the basis for a number of important predictions concerning this disease, including the hypothesis of the next serotypes that are expected to come soon to this territory. It is such methods that have led to the discovery of the source of the annual worldwide bacterial meningitis epidemics that result from the massive migration of Muslims to Medina and Mecca during the hajj. Another application of this approach is clarification of the sources of poliomyelitis cases, which are now rare in developed countries. As it turned out, these cases were the result of an extremely rare reversion of the live vaccine strain to the wild-type pathogenic virus.[10] Consequently, the worldwide program of poliomyelitis eradication now includes a five-year period when only inactivated vaccine will be used, and this step was included because of this finding.

Similar findings led to the recent proposal to organize the worldwide PulseNet network for molecular epidemiological surveillance of intestinal infections based on this approach.[11] Although these studies still entail substantial costs, they will form the basis of a new epidemiology, as the opportunities and advantages they provide expand global prospects for combating infectious diseases.[12] An outstanding recent example of the advantages of this approach is a molecular epidemiological study of a case of deliberate HIV infection. A medical employee of a U.S. hospital injected serum from an HIV-infected patient into his unwanted girlfriend, pretending it was a medication. It was the sequencing data and further analysis that unambiguously proved the origin of the strain[13] and helped to convict this person.

CONCLUSIONS

1. Existing lists of infectious agents with bioterrorist potential need to be expanded and should never be considered final.

2. The wide natural diversity of strains of infectious agents provides the principal possibility of investigating and differentiating between natural and artificial origins of an infectious disease outbreak.

3. A detailed genomic inventory of the diversity of the strains of infectious agents will allow natural and artificial outbreaks to be differentiated on a routine basis.

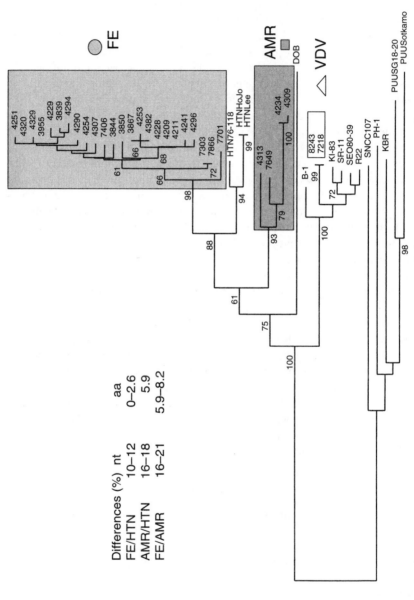

FIGURE 6   Phylogenetic Analysis of Nucleotide Sequence of M Segment of HFRS Isolates from the Russian Far East

NOTES

1. McGeorge, H. 2001. An analysis of 404 non-military incidents involving either chemical or biological agents. World Congress on Chemical and Biological Terrorism. Dubrovnik, Croatia, April 22-27, 2001. Abstract Book, p. 53.

2. Geissler, E. 1994. Arms control, health care and technology transfer under the vaccines for peace programme. Control of Dual Threat Agents: The Vaccine for Peace Programme. E. Geissler and J. P.Woodall, eds. SIPRI Chemical and Biological Warfare Studies 15:10-37 (see especially p. 29).

Anderson, W.C., III, King, J.M. 1983. Vaccine and antitoxin availability for defense against biological threat agents. U.S. Army Health Care Studies Division, Report No. 83-002. Fort Sam Houston, Tex.: U.S. Army Health Services Command.

3. Biological and Chemical Terrorism: Strategic Plan for Preparedness and Response. 2001. Recommendations of the CDC Strategic Planning Group. MMWR 49-#RR-4.

4. Ogarkov, P.I., V.V. Malishev, S.A. Tzutsiev, N.V. Mikhailov. 1996. The epidemiological characterization and laboratory diagnostics of viral hepatitis in the Russian federal military forces on the territory of the Chechen Republic. Voenno-Meditsinskii Zhurnal 8:48-55.

5. Russian Federation President's Directive No. 298-rp. June 14, 1994.

6. Beklemishev, A.B., V.M. Blinov, S.K. Vassilenko, S.Ya. Golovin, V.V. Gutorov, V.A. Karginov, L.V. Mamaev, N.N. Mikryukov, S.V. Netesov, N.A. Petrov, V.A. Petrenko, L.S. Sandakhchiev. 1984. Synthesis, cloning and primary structure determination of full-length DNA copy of hemagglutinin gene of H1N1-subtype influenza A virus. Bioorganicheskaya khimiya (in Russian) 10(11):1535-1543.

7. Robertson, B., H. Khopraset, O.V. Nainan, T. Cromeans, K. Krawczynski, H.S. Margolis, et al. 1996. Transmission, excretion and genetic variants of hepatitis A virus within a community-wide outbreak. X International Congress of Virology, Jerusalem, Israel. Abstracts, p. 42.

8. Yashina, L.N., N.A. Patrushev, L.I. Ivanov, R.A. Slonova, V.P. Mishin, G.G. Kompanez, N.I. Zdanovskaya, I.I. Kuzina, P.F. Safronov, V.E. Chizhikov, C. Schmaljohn, S.V. Netesov. 2000. Genetic diversity of hantaviruses associated with hemorrhagic fever with renal syndrome in the Far East of Russia. Virus Research 70:31-44.

9. Achtman, M., et al. 2001. Molecular epidemiology of serogroup A meningitis in Moscow, 1969 to 1997. EID 7(3).

10. Macadam, A.J., et al. 1989. Reversion of the attenuated and temperature-sensitive phenotypes of the Sabin type 3 strain of poliovirus in vaccines. Virology 172:408-414.

11. Swaminathan, B., et al. 2001. PulseNet: the molecular subtyping network for foodborne bacterial disease surveillance, United States. EID 7(3).

12. Pfaller, M.A. 2001. Molecular approaches to diagnosing and managing infectious diseases: practicality and costs. EID 7(2).

Centers for Disease Control. 2000. Preventing Emerging Infectious Diseases: A Strategy for the 21st Century.

13. Vogel, G. 1998. HIV strain analysis debuts in murder. Science 282(5390): 851-852.

Bioterrorism: Threat and Response

Michael L. Moodie
Chemical and Biological Arms Control Institute

Since the sarin gas attack by Aum Shinrikyo in the Tokyo subway in March 1995, the United States has been debating the dangers and risks posed by the potential use by terrorists of chemical and biological weapons. With respect to biological weapons in particular, a debate has ensued as to how serious those risks are. Some analysts argue that the threat has been "hyped." Others contend that it is severe—and imminent. However, neither argument, as publicly articulated, is all that helpful for decision makers who confront hard choices about planning, programming, and allocating resources to address the biological weapons threat.

Emphasizing the potential impact of biological agents that might be weaponized produces vulnerability assessments that suggest virtually limitless dangers. Focusing on only the most horrendous events, however, overwhelms any estimates of their likelihood. But the possibility of occurrence—the likelihood—is a critically important factor in planning efforts. It does little good to engage in elaborate preparations for an event that is not likely to happen to the exclusion of addressing those contingencies that are likely.

On the other hand, it is not necessarily the case that the future will resemble the past. The historical record, however, provides scant evidence on which to make hard judgments. Faced with a paucity of data, one cannot be confident that looking at history will alert us in advance to what will happen in the future.

A strong argument can be made that the threat of bioterrorism will increase. Several reasons account for this heightened concern. Interest in bioterrorism is increasing because it has become less expensive, it is highly destructive, and it is psychologically devastating.

Over the next several years, the world will witness incredibly rapid and profound changes in biology and biotechnology. These advances could have a major influence on prospects for bioterrorism. Biological weapons are based on a technology that is now almost 70 years old. Yet remaining obstacles are not trivial. Genetic modification, biomolecular engineering, and enhanced bioproduction technologies may make it easier for terrorists to overcome barriers that have inhibited acquisition of biological weapons in the past.

Terrorism of the future will be in response to broad trends such as globalization, accelerating interconnectedness, and population dynamics, but it is also likely to entail narrow psychological elements from marginalization to "technorage" to revenge for real or imagined wrongs. As motivations move away from the traditionally political, the special mindsets of terrorists become more important. A refined understanding of the threat of bioterrorism demands special attention to these distinctive mental topographies. Equally important is the requirement to understand how these unique psychologies interact with circumstances, capabilities, and opportunities to take potential terrorists down particular paths, including the one that leads to bioterrorism.

Classic terrorists used violence like a volume control knob (to use Brian Jenkins's term) to generate fear in order to extract political concessions. New terrorists do not calculate thresholds of pain and tolerance in society, or they seek to exceed them, uninhibited by the need to shape behavior, unmotivated to spare innocents. They are less interested in concrete political goals and more motivated to win an immediate reward—emotional or physical—or to achieve a long-term goal.

The structure of terrorist organizations is changing also. Today terrorist groups are more transnational, network-based entities, rather than traditional hierarchies.

Traditional arguments for methods of dealing with terrorism are insufficient. Neither the "laid-back" approach nor the one that hypes the threat is adequate. Both define the threat too narrowly by focusing on only a single factor. What is needed is a multifactor threat assessment.

Factors to consider are the actors, agents, operational requirements, and targets. Each of these categories is divided into many subcategories; for example, actors could be from traditional political groups, religious radical groups, individuals acting alone, or the right wing. Agents could include anthrax, plague, smallpox, and so forth. Some combinations of factors could produce dramatic results; others may produce no results at all. It is essential, therefore, to trace how the factors interrelate. Only by doing so can one make a determination of which outcomes are most and least likely. This focus on relationships and interactions of factors creates "plausible threat envelopes."

As a terrorist seeks higher casualties with biological weapons, fewer paths are available to achieve that objective. Those that remain are more difficult. Therefore, the degree of risk declines as the level of desired casualties increases, insofar as the threat becomes less likely.

Few terrorist organizations have the necessary combination of size, resources, skills, facilitative ethos (willingness to experiment and accept failure), or appropriate organizational capacity to achieve mass casualties. Traditional agents capable of inflicting mass casualties are difficult either to acquire, cultivate, and produce or to disseminate effectively. Likely targets do not necessarily facilitate mass casualty outcomes given the other requirements for conducting an effective attack against them, including technical knowledge (e.g., of airflows in large arenas) or operational skills (surveillance, finance, planning).

We do not know at what point the response system will become overburdened and stressed to the point of collapse. This point is probably not very difficult to reach. Therefore, while events that produce casualties in the tens of thousands are unlikely, lesser contingencies—even those with casualty levels in the hundreds—are likely to have major consequences, not least of which will be a severe psychological impact.

Terrorism analysis tends to exclude actors allied with foreign governments in times of conflict because such actions are considered acts of war. This is shortsighted for several reasons:

• The consequences are no different.
• State-sponsored entities are among the few actors who could assemble the requisite skills and materials to conduct a successful attack.
• A particular U.S. concern is pursuit of "asymmetric strategies" by hostile states.

Among the actors who now define contemporary terrorism, those who might be most attracted to use of biological weapons include the following:

• Non-state actors inspired by religious ideals,
• Groups from the extreme political right wing,
• Actors with millennial world views combined with notions of "cleansing" society through violence,
• Transnational networks less constrained by central authority, and
• Radical single-issue groups.

A bioterrorism attack could take an almost infinite variety of forms. Therefore, a "one-size-fits-all" approach to response will not work. Rather, an effective response must be built around a flexible package of capabilities that can be "mixed and matched" according to circumstances.

In dealing with bioterrorism, effective health responses are especially critical. This means, in particular, better disease surveillance, monitoring, reporting, and epidemiology.

Shaping an effective response to bioterrorism will be neither easy nor cheap. Many players must be integrated into a genuinely strategic approach that is based on a range of sometimes complex capabilities. An effective response requires demanding planning requirements, many actors from many agencies, ongoing training, complex communication capabilities, and organizational adaptability.

The Department of Justice Cities Program is intended to promote training in the 120 largest metropolitan areas in the United States. Its approach emphasizes "training the trainers." The program, however, tends to focus on law enforcement and emergency management, and it often stresses a chemical scenario rather than a biological one.

The Department of Defense support role takes many forms, including involvement from the U.S. Army Medical Research Institute of Infectious Diseases, Naval Medical Research Institute, Chemical/Biological Incident Response Force, and National Guard Weapons of Mass Destruction (WMD) Civil Support Teams. Some elements, however, are controversial. The plan to create National Guard WMD Civil Support Teams, for example, has prompted a debate about just what such units could contribute to response capabilities, particularly in a biological event.

As argued, the health dimension of a bioterrorism response capability is especially important. The United States has a number of its leading public health assets focused on enhancing capabilities in this area, such as the Department of Health and Human Services (National Medical Response Teams for WMD and the Metropolitan Medical Response Systems); the Centers for Disease Control and Prevention, with a focus on the Bioterrorism Preparedness and Response Program; and the National Institutes of Health (NIH).

Responding to bioterrorism has created the following policy lessons:

- Draconian measures are not warranted;
- U.S. budgets are generally moving in the right direction;
- Cataloging and covering vulnerabilities is a fool's errand; a better alternative is to set priorities and work incrementally;
- Choose things desirable to do anyway, particularly in terms of enhancing the public health infrastructure;
- Do things that make a difference in time of crisis; and
- Do not focus on a short-term fix; make long-term solutions a priority.

A constant dynamic exists between terrorists and those who fight them. The relationship is constantly in flux, and it is difficult to define precisely at any one point in time. There is certainty only if we do nothing, and it is the certainty that we will lose. Risk is unavoidable; the challenge is to reduce it to a manageable level.

Bioterrorism: A View from the Side

Oleg S. Morenkov *
Russian Academy of Sciences Institute of Cell Biophysics

I work as head of a group at the Russian Academy of Sciences Institute of Cell Biophysics in Pushchino, one of the leading biological research centers of Russia. My work there has been associated with the study of the regulation of monoclonal antibody synthesis by hybridized cells. I have a Ph.D. in molecular biology and a doctor of science degree in virology, and my dissertation focused on the antigen structure of the glycoproteins of the Aujeszky's disease (pseudorabies) virus and the development of serological methods for diagnosing this disease. The Aujeszky's disease virus is a porcine alphaherpesvirus and causes widespread disease in many types of animals, but not in humans. At present, my work is devoted to the study of molecular mechanisms of interaction of the Aujeszky's disease virus with cell plasma membranes.

My research work has never had and does not now have any relation to the development of biological weapons. I have never been involved in the problem of bioterrorism. Furthermore, I have not even taken an interest in this problem.

Recently I was invited to make a presentation at a Russian-American seminar on bioterrorism, to look at the threat of bioterrorism to Russia and the world from the viewpoint of a virologist who has never had any relation to the development of biological weapons, from the standpoint of a scientist living in Russia who is well acquainted with the current status of biology in Russia. I was invited to present my own subjective views on this problem, and I accepted.

Thus, the report that I am presenting is a view of bioterrorism from the side, the view of a nonspecialist in this field who has never been connected with

---

* Translated from the Russian by Kelly Robbins.

biological weapons, the view of a virologist living in Russia and possessing a certain amount of special knowledge.

Any scientific-technical progress leads to the development of not only positive, but also negative technologies. This leads to improvements not only in the means of supporting life, but also in the means of destroying it. The development of chemistry led to the creation of explosive and poisonous substances, of physics to nuclear weapons, and of biology to biological weapons.

Biological weapons will undoubtedly be very attractive to terrorists of the twenty-first century. In the opinion of specialists, it is already pointless to ask the question, Will terrorist acts be committed using biological weapons? Instead, we face the questions, When will it happen? How can the consequences of such terrorist acts be minimized? How can we reduce the probability that terrorists will use biological weapons?

It seems that bioterrorism is an evil we will have to encounter in the near future, and the entire world community will have to fight it with united efforts.

In my view, the attractiveness of biological weapons for modern terrorists is determined by the following points:

1. We are currently seeing the explosive development of biological science, medical biotechnology, and pharmacology. Increasing numbers of people are working in these fields, and they have the knowledge and qualifications necessary for developing and manufacturing bioweapons. There are also increasing numbers of laboratories and biological and pharmacological production facilities that have the conditions necessary for the production of biological weapons.

2. There is free access to information concerning the manufacture of bioweapons (the culture of viruses and microorganisms, the production of toxins, etc.). Access to this sort of information has become much simpler with the development of the Internet. Even with minimal specialized knowledge, such information is fairly easy to find.

3. The manufacture of biological weapons is relatively easy and cheap. If one has the appropriate strain of a pathogenic virus or microorganism, the pathogen can be cultivated in sufficient quantities without any particular problems in any laboratory possessing facilities for work under sterile conditions. Such conditions are easy enough to create, even at home.

4. The problem of obtaining a pathogenic strain of a microorganism or virus is also solvable, although it might appear to be one of the most difficult problems for bioterrorists. A pathogen might be obtained by bioterrorists by illegal means from laboratories or production facilities where these microorganisms or viruses are being studied or where the corresponding vaccines or test kits are being manufactured. A pathogenic viral or microbial strain could be transferred to bioterrorists by another terrorist group. The important point to remember is that at present, international borders are completely open for the movement of pathogenic strains of microorganisms and viruses. This could happen in the form of an

ordinary letter or sheet of paper containing a dried drop of a pathogenic strain. Viruses can be transported in the form of a dried nucleic acid, which presents absolutely no danger to the person transporting the virus. Once at the destination, cells are transfected with the nucleic acid, and the full-fledged virus multiplies. Thus, a pathogenic strain could be obtained in one place and biomass produced from it in somewhere else, even in another country. If bioterrorists were to develop their own strain using current molecular biological methods, it would require substantial expenditures, and at present I believe this to be unlikely, although possible.

5. Bioweapons are effective in very small doses. The ease of concealing the presence and use of bioweapons, the lack of external evidence at the moment of their use, and the relative ease of their production make it highly unlikely that they could be found and suppressed.

6. Biological weapons make it possible to carry out both individual terrorist acts and mass infections of people, animals, and plants.

7. In my view, the task facing bioterrorists is substantially easier than that faced by the developers of military bioweapons for use under battle conditions. An act of bioterrorism is unexpected. No one is taking countermeasures against it, and it is carried out openly, aimed at unprepared and unprotected people. I believe that the demands made of bioweapons by bioterrorists are significantly lower than the demands made of military bioweapons. Considered ineffective under battle conditions, bioweapons could be very attractive for bioterrorists. Bioterrorists have no need to resolve the problem of stabilizing biological agents or cultivating enormous quantities of them. Even "nonmilitarized" pathogens are sufficient for carrying out an act of bioterrorism.

8. At present, there is practically no technology for protecting against bio-weapons that would make it possible to detect and identify a pathogenic micro-organism or toxin before it began taking effect. Thus, the fact that an act of bioterrorism had been committed could be discovered only after the victims began to get sick and the illness was identified, which could take a fairly long time, during which a large number of people, animals, or plants could already have become infected.

9. A difficult point in uncovering a case of bioterrorism is the fact that after an outbreak of a certain disease is discovered, it is very hard to say anything about the etiology of the disease. Therefore, if the act of bioterrorism is not of a demonstrative nature and is not announced by the bioterrorists themselves, it is no simple matter to confirm that the premeditated spread of a pathogen has taken place. This is especially true with regard to the spread of diseases affecting animals and plants.

10. Society is neither technically nor psychologically ready for cases of bioterrorism.

Therefore, the relative simplicity of producing biological weapons, the practical invulnerability of the perpetrators, and the possibility of the spread of disease on a huge scale obviously make biological weapons one of the most attractive tools for terror in the twenty-first century.

All types of bioterrorism are dangerous, whether based on political, criminal, religious, or economic reasons or carried out by mentally ill people. In these various cases, the terrorists are pursuing different goals:

• Criminal bioterrorism will obviously be aimed at specific people or groups of people with the aim of eliminating or blackmailing them; that is, it will be of a localized nature.

• Religious fanatics, separatists, and mentally ill people could probably be attracted by the demonstrative aspect of bioterrorism. Bioterrorism of this type could obviously be of a localized nature or could take the form of a wide-scale terrorist act, which, with good planning on the part of the extremists and the necessary equipment and supplies, could lead to large numbers of victims.

• Bioterrorism could become a means of resolving political problems and destabilizing countries, especially those with already unstable political systems and economies. Terrorist acts involving the widespread release of dangerous human pathogens (smallpox, anthrax) in crowded areas could potentially lead to huge numbers of human casualties and enormous economic costs involved in dealing with the consequences, which could destabilize the situation in a country. This type of bioterrorism is technically the most difficult and requires the dispersion of pathogens in aerosol form. It is necessary to solve numerous technical problems to carry out such an act of terrorism (stabilization of the bioagents, development of a dispersal system, etc.), and it requires a long development period and large investments of money. In the opinion of a number of experts, such a wide-scale act of bioterrorism is unlikely in the near future, if it is not purposefully sponsored by a government that could provide terrorist groups with the finished technology for manufacturing bioweapons.

• Neither can one underestimate economic bioterrorism (the spread of diseases affecting animals and plants). This might serve as a means of waging a competitive economic struggle (including on a scale involving competition between countries). In such a case, certain agricultural sectors could suffer enormous losses, which could lead to destabilization of the countries affected. In the majority of cases, the very fact that such an act of bioterrorism had been carried out could go unnoticed if it is not announced by the terrorists themselves.

In my view, the main factor restraining the spread of bioterrorism is the lack up to now of a sufficiently wide-scale successful act of bioterrorism receiving worldwide attention. Two or three successful acts of bioterrorism, regardless of the country in which they occurred, could change the orientation of terrorists throughout the world and encourage them to actively seek capabilities for using biological weapons for criminal purposes.

What, in my view, are the special characteristics of the situation in Russia with regard to bioterrorism?

- In Russia, there are a large number of institutes and production facilities of a biological, medical, and pharmacological nature. Many of them are in a difficult financial position and sit half empty, rented out to private firms. The laboratory facilities of such institutes and plants could potentially be used by bioterrorist groups to cultivate pathogenic viruses and microorganisms.
- Russia has a large number of specialists—virologists, microbiologists, molecular biologists—with the skills sufficient to be used by bioterrorists for making and developing bioweapons. Some of these specialists are still working in their professional fields and often live on the verge of poverty. Some of them were retrained and now work in other sectors. Here I would like to emphasize that the majority of these specialists were never associated with the development of bioweapons under the old program and are (or were) working on basic or applied science.

Given the poor situation of many scientists working in biology, there is a potential danger that they will be used by criminal elements or terrorist organizations, including those from third countries, in the manufacture of bioweapons. A pathogen can be obtained from any country. There is a potential danger that these pathogens could also be acquired in Russia itself through people with access to pathogenic strains of microorganisms or viruses (for example, people involved in related scientific research or in the production of vaccines or diagnostic tests). For a certain amount of compensation, specialists could cultivate biomass, possibly without even guessing which microorganism or virus they were cultivating.

Russian biologists also could potentially be used by bioterrorists in the development of bioweapons. Despite the difficult situation in Russian science, biological scientists, especially those working in the area of basic science, continue to maintain their high status and to conduct world-class research. Take, for example, a recently published study by Australian researchers that attracted worldwide notice. These researchers cloned the interleukin-4 gene in mouse pox virus and, as a result, unexpectedly obtained a virus substantially more virulent than the initial strain. It is highly probable that cloning such a gene in human smallpox virus could lead to the appearance of a terrible bioweapon. In my view, it would be no particular problem to repeat this work or to insert the interleukin-4 gene in another virus. The work used standard molecular biology methods. Such work could be carried out in many Russian biological institutes, as well as in American universities. Terrorists might plan their work in such a way that one team of specialists clones the virus sequence and another the interleukin gene, a third group makes the recombinant virus, and a fourth tests the virus on animals. None of the researchers could even guess the aim of the work.

• The next important point concerns Russia's lack of modern detection equipment and the associated methodology, thus complicating the possibility of finding pathogenic agents before the moment of their use.

• Russian medical institutions are not prepared to work under conditions that would be produced by bioterrorist actions. Judging from the literature, this problem is also a concern in the United States. There are no specialists trained for such cases, no modern diagnostic methods or equipment for pathogen identification, and no stockpiles of the appropriate vaccines and antibiotics.

In this regard, however, it should be noted that an expert analysis of the current level of preparedness of other countries for acts of bioterrorism shows that, at present, not a single country in the world is fully prepared to take adequate actions in such a situation. A well-planned and successfully conducted wide-scale act of bioterrorism in any country would unavoidably lead to heavy casualties (or enormous damage to agriculture). The scope of the consequences will depend on the preparedness of the government, both technical and economic, for terrorist acts of this nature.

Given Russia's economic weakness and its poor technical preparedness for dealing with the consequences of bioterrorism, a wide-scale bioterrorist attack carried out on Russian soil would in high likelihood produce an unfavorable scenario that might lead to a large number of casualties, social tension, and a destabilization of the situation.

Thus, Russia finds itself in a situation characterized on the one hand by favorable conditions for terrorist groups to make or even develop bioweapons and on the other hand by a lack of preparedness to counter a bioterrorist act if it is committed. In taking all of this into account, it seems to me that Russia could potentially become one of the top places for the manufacture of bioweapons by terrorists (including bioterrorists from other countries). Russia could also become one of the main proving grounds for the testing of bioweapons in terrorist or criminal actions. This cannot be permitted. Having organized the production of bioweapons or having successfully carried out a bioterrorist act in Russia, where it is now easier to do, terrorists will move on to other countries as well.

Russia must become part of the international system for countering bioterrorism. Given Russia's economic problems, it needs help to create an effective system for combating bioterrorism. This is in the interests of the entire world community.

In order to fight bioterrorism, the international community needs to resolve a three-part problem:

1. Society must recognize the seriousness and reality of the problem of bioterrorism. Society has not yet recognized this fact. I fear that society will have to encounter bioterrorism face to face in order to recognize the scale of the danger fully. In this situation, scientists must play the role of experts, who must

convince governments and society as a whole of the need to take appropriate measures.

2. Society must build a system of barriers to block acts of bioterrorism and reduce the likelihood of their being carried out.

3. In case an act of bioterrorism is nevertheless carried out, society must build a system of effective measures that will make it possible to minimize the consequences of these terrorist acts. Since preventing terrorist acts is very difficult, it seems to me that minimizing their consequences should be a top priority.

I will not discuss issues pertaining to the organization of an international system for countering bioterrorism. This is a difficult and complex problem involving a number of fields in which I am not a specialist. I will convey a few more thoughts concerning the potential use by bioterrorists of individual Russian biologists in the manufacture or development of bioweapons on the orders of bioterrorists. It seems to me that the poverty of Russian biological science is the fundamental reason creating the preconditions for the potential use of Russian biologists by bioterrorists for criminal purposes. World-class specialists earn salaries of $50 to $100 per month. It is hard to maintain your dignity when you are poverty stricken. In order to earn money, scientists take various side jobs not connected with their basic scientific activities—cloning, sequencing, cultivating biomass, or obtaining recombinant viruses for those who pay them. In doing so, they often have no interest in exactly what they are doing or for what purpose or whom they are doing it. One of the many side jobs being done by Russian scientists could turn out to be an element of work to develop or manufacture a bioweapon. As I have already emphasized, specialists could carry out this work without even having a clue.

In my view, the most effective means of resolving this problem is support for Russian biology on the part of the world community, in particular the United States of America. I would like to stress that serious attention needs to be paid to support not only for military science, but also for peaceful biological science not associated with bioweapons. From the standpoint of potential involvement in the manufacture or development of bioweapons, civilian virologists or molecular biologists are even more attractive to bioterrorists than are military specialists, given the weak control and monitoring research work carried out in civilian biological institutes in comparison with military organizations. I believe that the substantial expansion of the system for grant support of Russian biological science, especially basic biology, and of the system for joint Russian-American projects in biology will be beneficial to both sides and would promote the integration of Russian biology into the world scientific community. In this regard, Russian-U.S. cooperation is possible in the area of basic biological research and in the joint development of means for detecting and diagnosing potential pathogens or toxins that could be used by bioterrorists, as well as means of preventing and treating diseases caused by these pathogens. The more active involvement of

Russian biologists in joint research projects would undoubtedly reduce the probability of their potential use by bioterrorists.

Without a doubt, the development of biological science and biotechnology that we are currently observing will lead in the near future to outstanding fundamental discoveries affecting our understanding of the functioning of certain genes in microorganisms, mechanisms of pathogenesis, and the interaction of viruses with the immune systems of animals. This will make it possible to combat human, animal, and plant diseases more effectively. On the other side of the coin, these discoveries will also lead unavoidably to the appearance of new artificially constructed microorganisms and viruses with greater virulence than the initial strains, pathogens not recognized by the immune system, modified toxins with a high degree of stability, and so forth. At present, bioterrorism based on the use of the latest achievements in molecular biology appears unlikely due to the need for large expenditures and highly skilled specialists associated with terrorist groups. However, within the next few years it could present a colossal problem for the modern world.

In conclusion, I would like to focus attention once again on certain statements included in my report:

1. The relative ease of making biological weapons, the practical invulnerability of the perpetrators, and the possibility of the outbreak of disease on a gigantic scale obviously make biological weapons one of the most attractive tools for terror in the twenty-first century.

2. In connection with the poverty-stricken position of Russian biology, Russia possesses favorable conditions for terrorist groups, including terrorist groups from third countries, to make or even develop biological weapons. In this regard, Russia could potentially become one of the top sites for the manufacture of biological weapons by terrorists. Active targeted support for Russian biological science by the world community, and primarily by the United States of America, would undoubtedly promote the elimination of these negative tendencies.

3. The main factor restraining the spread of bioterrorism is the lack up to now of a sufficiently wide-scale successful act of bioterrorism receiving worldwide attention, regardless of the country in which such an act might occur. An unfavorable situation has developed in Russia, and it might become one of the main proving grounds for the testing of bioweapons in terrorist or criminal actions. This cannot be permitted, because the successful staging of an act of bioterrorism on Russian soil might serve as the starting point for the further spread of bioterrorism. It is essential that an international system for countering bioterrorism be created and that Russia be actively involved in this system.

CHEMICAL TERRORISM

Chemical Terrorism:
Assessing Threats and Responses

Jonathan B. Tucker
Center for Nonproliferation Studies
Monterey Institute of International Studies

Efforts to enhance the nation's ability to prevent and respond to acts of chemical terrorism are warranted by the fact that hazardous chemicals are ubiquitous in modern industrial society and hence are more accessible to terrorists than either biological or fissile materials. Four possible types of chemical terrorism have been identified:

1. Release of a military-grade chemical warfare agent against a civilian target with the intent to inflict indiscriminate casualties;
2. Sabotage of a chemical manufacturing plant or storage facility (including a rail tank car) in which toxic materials are held in gaseous or liquid form, or as solids, which have the capability of reacting with air or water to release toxic gases or vapors;
3. Contamination of public water or food supplies with toxic agents; and
4. Targeted use of a chemical agent to assassinate specific individuals.

Terrorists intent on acquiring chemical weapons have two options: buying or stealing them from existing national stockpiles, or manufacturing them independently. Because the synthesis of military-grade agents entails significant technical hurdles and risks, the acquisition of toxic industrial chemicals is more likely. Although such chemicals are hundreds of times less lethal than nerve agents, they could still inflict significant casualties if released in an enclosed space or outdoors under optimal atmospheric conditions. This paper assesses the threat of chemical terrorism and examines strategies of prevention and response.

CHEMICAL THREAT AGENTS

Chemical warfare (CW) agents are poisonous, man-made gases, liquids, or powders that, when absorbed through the lungs or skin, have incapacitating or lethal effects on humans and animals. Although many CW agents are liquids, the explosion of a munition can transform a liquid agent into an aerosol (a fine mist of tiny droplets) and then a vapor. Most warfare agents fall into five broad categories: blister, nerve, choking, blood, and incapacitating. Beyond their differing physiological effects, CW agents vary in their persistency and volatility, or tendency to evaporate. Nonpersistent agents dissipate within a few hours and pose mainly an inhalation threat, whereas persistent agents remain hazardous for as long as a month when deposited on terrain, vegetation, or objects, and pose primarily a skin contamination threat.

Blister agents, such as sulfur mustard and lewisite, are liquids that cause chemical burns. When absorbed by direct contact with the skin or eyes or by inhalation of aerosol or vapor, sulfur mustard induces painful skin blisters, blindness, and severe damage to lung tissue after an asymptomatic "latent period" of from one to eight hours. Mustard exposure also has harmful effects on the blood-forming tissues of the bone marrow, the lining of the gastrointestinal tract, and the central nervous system. Lewisite causes skin blistering similar to that of mustard, but its effects are immediate rather than delayed. Historical evidence from World War I and the Iran-Iraq War suggests that blister agents can inflict large numbers of casualties, although less than 5 percent are generally fatal. No effective treatment is available.

Nerve agents, such as sarin and VX, are the most lethal chemical poisons known: they disrupt the functioning of the human nervous system and can kill within minutes. Sarin is the most volatile of the nerve agents, evaporating at about the same rate as water. In an enclosed space with poor ventilation, the evaporation of few liters of sarin can generate a lethal concentration in the air. Outdoors, however, much larger quantities are required to offset the dispersive effects of wind and air turbulence. VX is an oily liquid that persists in the environment for days or weeks, depending on ambient temperature, and acts primarily by penetrating the skin. The lethal dose is about 10 mg.

Because of the extreme hazards associated with handling and disseminating nerve agents, terrorists might seek to develop "binary" weapons, which are safer to produce, store, and transport. In a binary system, two relatively nontoxic ingredients are stored separately and mixed together before use to generate the lethal agent. Sarin, for example, can be produced in a binary system by reacting isopropanol (rubbing alcohol) with methylphosphonic difluoride (DF). Nevertheless, the synthesis of DF is complex and difficult. Terrorists would also have to mix the precursor chemicals manually before use—an extremely hazardous operation—or attempt to design a remote-controlled device that would carry out the mixing and dispersal steps, a task requiring considerable technical expertise.

Although nerve agents have by far the greatest lethality, terrorists might employ other classes of toxic chemicals effectively. For example, choking agents (e.g., chlorine, phosgene gas) and blood agents (hydrogen cyanide, cyanogen chloride) were used on a large scale during World War I. These chemicals dissipate rapidly outdoors, but they could potentially cause mass casualties if released by terrorists in an enclosed space, such as a subway station or an indoor sports arena.[1]

THE CASE OF AUM SHINRIKYO

Much of the current concern about chemical terrorism stems from the case of the Japanese cult Aum Shinrikyo, which conducted sarin attacks in Matsumoto in 1994 and Tokyo in 1995. Founded in 1987, the quasi-Buddhist sect attracted young intellectuals in their late twenties and thirties who were disillusioned with mainstream society. Aum had some 40,000 members by 1995, most of them in Japan and Russia. The cult ran a variety of legitimate businesses and also engaged in land fraud, drug dealing, and other criminal activities, enabling it to accumulate a net worth of about $1 billion.[2] Aum leader Shoko Asahara planned to use a large-scale chemical attack to trigger a major war between the United States and Japan that cult members would survive, enabling them to seize control of the Japanese government. In pursuit of this mad scheme, Aum aggressively recruited scientists and technicians from Japanese universities to work on the development and production of chemical weapons as part of a "chemical brigade" within the cult's "Ministry of Science and Technology."[3]

Aum chemists chose to manufacture sarin because of its relative ease of production compared with other nerve agents, its volatility, and the fact that the necessary ingredients could be obtained from commercial suppliers. The cult purchased a Swiss-made pilot plant with computerized process controls, normally used by industry to prototype chemicals. Installed at Aum's headquarters near Mount Fuji, this plant produced some 30 kg of sarin over a two-year period. Cult members successfully tested the nerve agent on sheep at a remote ranch that the cult had purchased in Western Australia.[4]

Asahara planned to acquire a stockpile of 70 tons of sarin and then employ a Russian military helicopter to spray the deadly agent over downtown Tokyo. On June 27, 1994, Aum staged a trial nerve gas attack in a residential area of Matsumoto, a city about 125 miles northwest of Tokyo. The primary targets were three judges who were about to reach a verdict against the cult in a fraud case brought by local landowners. Aum members drove to Matsumoto in a truck that was equipped with an electric hot plate, which they used to vaporize drops of sarin, and a fan and nozzle to vent the toxic fumes. Over a period of about 25 minutes, the team vaporized 3 liters of sarin, generating a toxic cloud that drifted downwind over a residential neighborhood. The Matsumoto attack killed seven and injured 144 others, including the three targeted judges. Initially, the police authorities did not suspect terrorism and blamed the incident on a local resident who was falsely accused of synthesizing pesticides in his backyard.

For the subsequent terrorist attack on the Tokyo subway on March 20, 1995, Aum chemists synthesized 24 liters of sarin on short notice. Asahara ordered the subway attack as a diversionary tactic in response to a tip from informants that the police were training for an imminent raid on Aum headquarters. Because the sarin was not distilled, it was only about 25 percent pure. The agent was also diluted with acetonitrile to reduce its volatility and thus give the perpetrators time to escape.[5] This solution was poured into 11 two-ply nylon-polyester bags, which were then heat-sealed.

During the morning rush hour on March 20, cult members boarded five different cars on three lines of the Tokyo subway system, carrying the sarin-filled plastic bags wrapped in newspapers. The trains were scheduled to arrive at the central Kasumigaseki Station within a few minutes of each other. At the appointed time, cult members placed the plastic bags on the floor, punctured them with sharpened umbrella tips, and quickly left the trains. The punctured bags released puddles of liquid sarin that slowly evaporated, generating toxic fumes. In addition to 12 fatalities, 17 victims were in critical condition requiring intensive care, 37 suffered from severe symptoms of nerve agent exposure such as miosis (pinpoint pupils), shortness of breath, muscular twitching, and gastrointestinal problems; and 984 had miosis only.[6] Had the sarin been purer and disseminated in aerosol form, the attack would have caused many more deaths.

A few weeks later, on May 5, 1995, Aum staged another chemical attack in a Tokyo subway station, this time using a crude binary weapon. The device consisted of two plastic pouches, one containing 2 kg of sodium cyanide crystals and the other filled with 1.5 liters of dilute sulfuric acid. A primitive fusing system ignited the sodium-cyanide pouch after a time delay. The two pouches were arranged so that as the flames from the first spread to the second, the cyanide crystals would react with the sulfuric acid to form deadly hydrogen cyanide gas. Cult members placed the jury-rigged chemical bomb in the men's room at Shinjuku subway station, Tokyo's busiest, but the device malfunctioned. Although four subway workers who doused the flames were overcome by toxic fumes and hospitalized briefly, the station was evacuated before anyone else was hurt.[7]

Aum also employed nerve agents as an assassination weapon. In late 1993, cult hit squads used sarin in two failed attempts on the life of the leader of a rival religious sect. Then, in December 1994 and January 1995, the cult reportedly carried out three assassination attempts with VX, one of which was successful. In each case, a small amount of liquid agent was sprayed with a hypodermic syringe in the victim's face. The targeted individuals included an anti-Aum attorney and an old man who had harbored an Aum defector.[8]

ASSESSING THE THREAT OF CHEMICAL TERRORISM

Other than Aum Shinrikyo, relatively few terrorist groups have engaged in chemical terrorism. According to a database compiled by the Monterey Institute's Center for Nonproliferation Studies, only 125 incidents were reported worldwide between January 1960 and May 2001 involving the politically or ideologically motivated use of toxic chemicals. Responsibility for these incidents was distributed among the following types of groups: nationalist-separatist (18); religious (16); single issue, such as antiabortion or animal rights (14); lone actor (9); left wing (10); and right wing (4). In the remaining 54 cases, press accounts did not identify the perpetrators. Of the 125 reported incidents, most were small scale: only 6 caused 10 or more fatalities, and 12 caused more than 10 injuries.[9]

One possible explanation for this historical pattern is that few terrorist organizations are motivated to inflict indiscriminate casualties, particularly with weapons that are widely viewed as abhorrent. Staging a chemical attack would alienate a terrorist group's political constituency and bring down on the perpetrators the full repressive wrath of the government authorities.[10] Nevertheless, terrorist groups lacking outside supporters, such as apocalyptic cults or religious fanatics who believe they are acting on divine commands, may be more inclined to employ indiscriminate weapons such as toxic chemicals. It is still too early to tell whether Aum Shinrikyo was a bizarre aberration or the harbinger of a new trend in terrorism. But Osama bin Laden has declared that it is his "religious duty" to acquire chemical and other nonconventional weapons for use against U.S. targets.

In addition to the motivational side of the equation, technical impediments to the acquisition of military-grade CW agents, such as sarin and VX, seem likely to prevent the large majority of terrorist groups from producing and employing these weapons. Synthesis of nerve agents requires the use of high temperatures and corrosive and dangerous chemicals, and would not be feasible for terrorists untrained in synthetic organic chemistry. Blister agents such as sulfur mustard could be produced more easily if the necessary ingredients were available, but ordering large quantities of a key precursor chemical such as thiodiglycol from a commercial supplier would arouse suspicion and might lead the requested company to notify law enforcement authorities.

In at least one known case, however, an individual with expertise in chemistry managed to produce blister agents and other powerful poisons in a clandestine laboratory. Valery Borzov, a 40-year-old Russian chemist, was arrested in Moscow on August 6, 1998, for attempting to sell a sample of nitrogen mustard to an undercover police officer. After having been fired from the Moscow Scientific Research Institute of Reagents in 1997, Borzov set up a sophisticated chemical laboratory in his apartment and synthesized mustard agent and other unspecified poisons for sale to the Russian mafia and other criminal buyers, charging his customers $1,500 a vial. After his arrest, a police search of his apartment uncovered chemical equipment, 50 liters of "strong poisons," 400 ml of mustard agent, and a thick notebook containing recipes for the manufacture of toxic substances. Borzov was found mentally incompetent to stand trial, diagnosed with schizophrenia, and committed to a treatment facility.[11]

Even if chemical warfare agents can be produced successfully, they are difficult and hazardous to handle and deliver. "Weaponization" of a toxic chemical includes the addition of stabilizers to extend its shelf-life and the development of a system for delivering the agent to the target population by mechanical, pneumatic, or explosive means. The most effective but technically challenging delivery system is an aerosol generator, which disperses the agent as tiny droplets that float in the air and are inhaled by the victims. According to a report by the General Accounting Office, an analytical agency of the U.S. Congress, CW agents "must be released effectively as a vapor, or aerosol, for inhalation exposure, or they need to be in a spray of large droplets or liquid for skin penetration. To serve as terrorist weapons, chemical agents require high toxicity and volatility . . . and need to maintain their strength during storage and release."[12] For example, introducing sarin into the air-handling system of a large building to kill those inside would require a leak-proof container that was small enough to be easily carried by one person yet could deliver a high enough concentration of agent in aerosol or vapor form to inflict widespread casualties. A device possessing such characteristics would be technically complex, probably exceeding the design and manufacturing capabilities of most terrorist groups, even those that managed to attract university-trained scientists.[13] These hurdles might be overcome, however, by a wealthy terrorist organization that recruited military scientists and engineers who had been formerly employed in a state-level chemical weapons program.

As an alternative to synthesizing military-grade CW agents, terrorists might acquire toxic household or industrial chemicals such as sulfur dioxide, ammonia, phosgene, arsenic compounds, hydrogen cyanide, or methyl isocyanate. Cyanides, for example, are employed in a wide variety of industrial applications including electroplating, mineral extraction, dyeing, printing, photography, agriculture, and the production of paper, textiles, and plastics. The United States alone produces 300,000 metric tons of cyanides a year for peaceful purposes.[14] In addition, tens of thousands of toxic organic chemicals are produced by the commercial chemical industry. According to one estimate, the number of organophosphate compounds—a category that includes nerve agents, pesticides, and fire retardants—exceeds 50,000.[15] Thus, toxic industrial chemicals are widely accessible in a way that the materials needed to produce military-grade CW agents are not.

The Monterey Institute database suggests that, historically, terrorists have tended to employ "off-the-shelf" chemicals that are readily available. Of the 125 chemical attacks reported worldwide between January 1960 and May 2001, the toxic weapon was identified in 86 cases. Of this total, only nine incidents—most of them linked to Aum Shinrikyo—involved the use of a military CW agent. Instead, the great majority of attacks were carried out with household or industrial chemicals, such as cyanides (22), butyric acid (21), tear gas (19), insecticide or pesticide (6), sulfuric acid (3), rat poison (2), mercury and mercury compounds (2), arsenic compounds (1), and weed killer (1).[16]

The delivery system, when known, was often equally low-tech: direct contact with the target (34 cases), spray or aerosol (24), contamination of food or drink (15), consumer product tampering (10), explosive device (8), contamination of the water supply (6), jug or jar (5), letter or package (4), injection or projectile (2), and insertion into a building ventilation system (1).[17] Using a toxic chemical to poison a large urban reservoir would be difficult, because it would take impractically large quantities of agent to overcome the effects of dilution and filtration. Food and drink, however, are potentially more vulnerable. In 1999, for example, chickens in Belgium were unintentionally given animal feed that had been contaminated with a dioxin, a cancer-causing chemical. Because the contamination was not discovered for months, dioxin was probably present in chicken meat and eggs sold in Europe in early 1999.[18] This experience suggests that other toxic chemicals could be used to poison the food supply, by way of either animal feed, a food-processing facility, or direct product tampering.

A terrorist incident involving the deliberate poisoning of a beverage took place in Dushanbe, the capital of the former Soviet republic of Tajikistan, on December 31, 1994. Six Russian peacekeeping soldiers, three civilians, and the wife of a Russian embassy worker died after drinking champagne that had been laced with a cyanide. The locally produced champagne had been sold at a kiosk near the Russian military compound. It is not known how many bottles were poisoned.[19]

Sabotage of Chemical Industry Plants

Another possible form of chemical terrorism is sabotage of a commercial industry plant engaged in the production, processing, or storage of a highly toxic chemical, causing its release and the exposure of a nearby populated area. Such an attack might involve penetration of the plant site by outside terrorists or an inside job by disgruntled plant workers. The deliberate release of a hazardous chemical could be brought about by detonating a conventional explosive to rupture a storage tank or, alternatively, by manipulating the manufacturing process to cause a runaway reaction. In the latter case, if no group claimed responsibility, it might be difficult for investigators to distinguish a terrorist attack from an industrial accident. Terrorists might also use an improvised explosive device to puncture a railroad tank car carrying a hazardous chemical.

According to an estimate by the U.S. Environmental Protection Agency (EPA), approximately 15,000 facilities in the United States, many of them in urban areas, produce or store hazardous or extremely hazardous chemicals.[20] Phosgene, for example, was used as a chemical warfare agent in World War I, yet today more than 1 billion pounds of phosgene are produced and consumed in the United States each year for the production of plastics.[21] Another highly toxic industrial chemical, methyl isocyanate (MIC), is an intermediate in pesticide production and was responsible for the 1984 accident at a Union Carbide plant in Bhopal, India, that caused more than 2,500 deaths. The Bhopal disaster, allegedly the result of sabotage by a disgruntled employee, occurred just after midnight on December 3, 1984. Over a period of a few hours, an estimated 30 to 40 metric tons of MIC in vapor and liquid form escaped from a holding tank at the plant, forming a toxic cloud that blanketed an area of more than 10 square miles, including densely populated shantytowns. An estimated 500 people died before getting treatment, 2000 more died within the first week, and roughly 60,000 people were seriously injured.[22]

An example of a toxic release in the United States resulting from deliberate sabotage took place on February 28, 2000, at a chemical plant near the town of Pleasant Hill, Missouri. At about 4:00 a.m., an unknown individual opened a valve in a storage tank, causing 200 gallons of anhydrous ammonia to leak out. The chemical formed a cloud of poisonous vapor that spread through the downtown area, forcing the evacuation of more than 250 residents. Although the perpetrator and motive remain unknown, the facility manager speculated that the individual might have wanted ammonia to produce methamphetamines.[23] According to the EPA, a toxic release from any of more than 2000 facilities in the United States could affect at least 100,000 people.

PREVENTING CHEMICAL TERRORISM

Government authorities can take a number of measures to reduce the risk of chemical terrorism. First, state and local emergency management officials should conduct vulnerability assessments of the chemical manufacturing plants within their jurisdictions and encourage the owners to improve security at sites that produce or store toxic chemicals. At the same time, the locations of these plants and the associated vulnerability assessments should not be made public because of the risk that such information could fall into the wrong hands.

Second, the federal government should tighten restrictions on the sale by commercial suppliers to private individuals (either U.S. citizens or foreigners) of dual-use chemicals that can serve as precursors for chemical warfare agents. Although the United States controls the export of 54 precursor chemicals to countries of proliferation concern, domestic sales of these chemicals are not currently regulated.

Third, federal law enforcement agencies such as the Federal Bureau of Investigation (FBI) and the Bureau of Alcohol, Tobacco, and Firearms (ATF) should enhance their cooperation with state and local law enforcement agencies.

To this end, the FBI and the ATF should reassess the balance between securing classified information about unconventional terrorism and sharing it with state and local agencies when it is relevant to preventing an incipient attack.

RESPONDING TO CHEMICAL TERRORISM

Unlike biological agents, which have an incubation period of days to weeks before clinical symptoms appear, chemical agents induce incapacitating or lethal symptoms within minutes after exposure—with the sole exception of sulfur mustard, whose clinical manifestations are delayed up to several hours. Whereas explosives generate instantaneous destructive forces that are difficult to defend against, the toxic effects of some classes of chemical agents can be reversed or mitigated through the prompt administration of antidotes and other drugs. Antidotes are available only for a few types of chemical agents, however, and the time window for effective treatment is limited. Although much of the historical experience with the emergency response to chemical terrorism derives from the 1995 Tokyo subway incident, one can also draw important lessons from industrial accidents involving toxic chemicals.

First Responders

During the Tokyo sarin incident, the city fire department received the first call about a medical emergency in the subway within minutes of the attack. Additional calls flowed in from 15 subway stations in rapid succession, yet it took more than an hour before emergency dispatchers realized that a single event was responsible rather than a series of unrelated incidents. As the crisis mounted, police, firefighters, 131 ambulances, and 1364 emergency medical technicians (EMTs) were dispatched to downtown subway stations on the three affected lines.[24] They arrived to find a chaotic scene. Critically injured casualties littered the sidewalks and subway entrances, vomiting or convulsing, and scores of less seriously affected commuters stumbled about, vision impaired and struggling to breathe. EMTs sought to triage the victims and offer some medical assistance, but they did not administer antidotes, intubate serious cases at the scene, or attempt to decontaminate the victims or even remove their sarin-saturated clothes.[25]

The Tokyo subway incident demonstrated that first responders to an incident of chemical terrorism who lack personal protective equipment (such as police, paramedics, and ordinary firefighters) are at considerable risk of becoming victims themselves.[26] Indeed, some observers have called police officers "blue canaries" because they would probably succumb to the toxic agent shortly after arriving on the scene. Because of this vulnerability, first responders lacking gas masks and protective clothing must resist the initial instinct to run to the rescue. Instead they must stand back, upwind and uphill of the spreading toxic cloud, and use loudspeakers and public address systems to direct the victims to safety. The first group to enter the danger zone should be members of the local hazardous material (Hazmat) team, who are equipped with personal protective equipment. Most fire departments in major U.S. cities have well-trained Hazmat teams with extensive experience in handling spills of toxic industrial chemicals, such as chlorine and organophosphate pesticides.

The first step in responding to an incident of chemical terrorism is for police and firefighters to establish a perimeter around the danger zone to prevent more people from becoming exposed. A complicating factor, however, is that the danger zone can move. Although volatile gases such as chlorine or phosgene dissipate rapidly, more persistent agents such as sarin can form clouds that last for hours, drifting with the breeze to form an elongated plume downwind from the point of release. In an urban environment, the air turbulence generated by tall buildings can redistribute the agent plume into zones of high and low concentration, creating "hot spots" in unexpected locations. Moreover, ventilation systems can spread a toxic gas throughout a building, and subway cars can force an agent cloud down tunnels, spreading it from one station to the next.

Rapid detection and identification of the toxic agent are crucial to ensure the prompt medical treatment of those who have been exposed and to reassure those who have not. Most fire departments, however, lack the specialized equipment needed to detect and analyze chemical warfare agents. Thus, a sample of the agent—itself highly toxic—would have to be collected and sent to a chemical laboratory for analysis. In a small, isolated U.S. city, several hours might elapse before the agent could be identified. To address this problem, scientists at the U.S. National Laboratories are developing handheld detectors that first responders could use to identify about a dozen different CW agents.[27] Until the toxic agent has been identified, medical practitioners should treat exposed persons according to the resulting clinical syndrome (cluster of symptoms), such as chemical burns, pulmonary edema, cardiorespiratory failure, neurological damage, or shock.[28]

At the same time that first responders are treating the casualties of a chemical attack, law enforcement officials will have to conduct a criminal investigation in order to identify and arrest the perpetrators. Careful coordination among the FBI, state and local police, and other agencies will be necessary to avoid destroying valuable forensic evidence while delivering urgently needed medical care. Another key task for state and local emergency responders is to inform the public and the news media immediately and continuously after a chemical incident has occurred, so as to prevent widespread confusion and panic. In particular, the authorities must be prepared to explain the cause of the disaster, what the victims should do, how long the crisis will last, where to obtain help, and how people can avoid exposure.

Decontamination

After the local Hazmat team is in place, the next challenge for emergency workers is to decontaminate the victims before they are evacuated for treatment. If people have come in contact with liquid agent or concentrated vapor, they will carry traces of the toxic substance on their clothes and bodies. Accordingly, decontamination is needed not only to prevent further absorption of the toxic agent through the skin or by inhalation of vapor, but also to prevent the victims from contaminating other people and the interior of cars and ambulances.

During the Tokyo subway incident, police were slow in establishing a perimeter around the affected zone and did not decontaminate victims on-site. As a result, many cases of secondary exposure resulted from the off-gassing of sarin from patients in cramped ambulances and poorly ventilated hospital rooms. Of a total of 1364 EMTs who transported victims to hospitals by ambulance, 135 (10 percent) developed symptoms of sarin exposure and had to receive treatment themselves. Moreover, although many patients were directed to a shower upon arrival at a hospital and their contaminated clothes were removed and sealed in plastic bags, 110 hospital staff members (23 percent) complained of symptoms of sarin poisoning in a follow-up questionnaire.[29]

In general, water is the best decontamination solution, with soap recommended for oily or otherwise adherent chemicals.[30] Decontaminating large crowds poses complex logistical challenges, however, and the various methods offer different strengths and weaknesses. The usual approach is to direct the victims to "decontamination corridors" where they strip off their outer clothing and shower. Even so, persuading a frightened and mixed-gender group of strangers—many of them scared, sick, blinded, or choking—to undress and leave their valuables behind could easily result in panic and chaos. Special decontamination trucks or trailers containing showers are commercially available, but this equipment is expensive and time-consuming to set up. Some cities plan to use ordinary fire hoses to spray victims, yet that approach would expose them to public view and, in winter, might cause hypothermia. Other approaches to decontamination problems include the use of protective tarpaulins, inflatable heated tents, and plans to commandeer the nearest large building equipped with showers, such as a high school or college.[31]

Medical Treatment

Medical treatment for victims of chemical terrorism varies depending on the type of toxic agent involved. In general, the prompt onset of symptoms after chemical exposure puts a premium on rapid response. If a nerve agent is used, the administration of antidotes within several minutes to an hour can save lives. Although those exposed to a massive dose would probably die before they could be treated, victims on the periphery of the attack who received sublethal doses would benefit from receiving antidotes. The U.S. Army's nerve agent antidote kit contains atropine and an oxime (2-PAM [praloxidime] chloride), plus diazepam to prevent seizures. Such drugs may be in short supply: most ambulances carry atropine for treating heart attacks, but only in doses less than a tenth of what a nerve gas victim requires. Thus, each major U.S. city should acquire and maintain a stockpile of nerve agent antidotes.

In the event of exposure to hydrogen cyanide, immediate treatment with antidotes that bind cyanide ions in the blood can accelerate detoxification. But no antidotes currently exist for exposure to choking or blister agents, which must be treated symptomatically. Inhalation of choking agents typically results in pulmonary edema, which can be managed by administering oxygen, cortisone, and a drug to widen the bronchial tubes. Mechanical ventilators may also be required to keep victims breathing while their damaged lungs recover, although such equipment is rare and expensive. Because the cost of stockpiling specialized antidotes and ventilators in quantities sufficient for a mass-casualty incident is too high for any city to bear, the U.S. Department of Health and Human Services has established a two-tiered stockpile system. At least in theory, enough materials for 5000 victims can be made ready within hours to be flown to the site of a terrorist attack, and more would be en route the following day.

In a serious incident of chemical terrorism, the only option may be triage: giving priority to patients who have the best chance of survival in view of the resources available to treat them. For this reason, ambulatory patients should be among the first to be decontaminated and evacuated.[32] If thousands of people are affected, rapid triage and holding sites may have to be established where patients are decontaminated and given initial treatment; seriously ill patients would then be evacuated to appropriate care facilities. Within the triage areas, medical staff would work in full protective clothing.

Hospital Care

The U.S. medical system is poorly equipped to treat the mass casualties that might arise from a chemical attack. In the age of "managed care," most urban hospitals are private-sector entities that are under strong pressure from insurance companies to contain costs and thus run at full or excess capacity even under normal conditions. As a result, they have little room to accept an influx of casualties from a terrorist attack. A survey of nearly 200 hospital emergency departments conducted by the U.S. Public Health Service found that less than 20 percent had plans or equipment for dealing with even 50 victims of a nerve agent attack, such as an isolated decontamination unit. Only 29 percent of the hospitals surveyed had adequate supplies of atropine to treat 50 patients, and just 6 percent had all of the "minimum recommended physical resources" to deal with a release of sarin by terrorists. Urban hospitals were three times more likely than rural hospitals to have a plan for responding to chemical terrorism.[33]

Given these statistics, it is likely that in the event of a major incident of chemical terrorism, the local supply of hospital beds would rapidly be exhausted. To avoid chaos and overcrowding, it is essential for cities to plan for satellite treatment areas in sports centers, schools, armories, and other public buildings equipped with central heating, hot and cold running water, and telephones. At these locations, medical personnel and equipment could be brought in and a large number of patients treated.[34] Another problem would be finding enough health care personnel to care for the injured. Some cities are creating databases of doctors or nurses who have retired, moved into administrative jobs, or changed careers but could be called up in an emergency. Such systems may not be rapid enough, however, to cope with a major incident of chemical terrorism.

To augment local medical response capabilities, the Metropolitan Medical Response System (MMRS) links federal emergency services with first responders, public health officials, and private hospitals into an integrated community disaster plan. As part of this program, the Department of Health and Human Services (HHS) has provided 97 U.S. cities with an average of $600,000 each in seed money, although the cities must expend their own resources to continue training and exercising people and to maintain equipment. Another federal program managed by HHS, the National Disaster Medical System (NDMS), would be activated after a major incident of chemical terrorism. More than 70 Disaster Medical Assistance Teams (DMATs), each consisting of up to 100 medical personnel, have volunteered to deploy to disasters ranging from earthquakes to terrorist attacks. These teams would probably take several hours to mobilize, however. NDMS can also transfer overflow patients, by medical airlift if necessary, to veterans' hospitals and 2000 participating private hospitals nationwide.

Psychosocial Impact

Another problem that will inevitably arise during an incident of chemical terrorism is that a large number of people will experience psychogenic symptoms or extreme anxiety and self-report to hospitals and doctors' offices for treatment. During the 1995 Tokyo subway incident, roughly 80 percent of the casualties who arrived at hospitals (about 4000 people) had no chemical injuries but still demanded medical attention. This influx of "worried well" swamped the available medical resources. Thus, after a major incident of chemical terrorism, physicians and other health care providers will have to distinguish real from psychogenic casualties so as to deliver priority treatment to those most urgently requiring it.

It is also clear that in the event of a large-scale chemical attack, survivors of and responders to the incident will experience extreme psychological trauma. For more than a week after the Tokyo subway incident, dozens of city residents continued to arrive at local hospitals complaining of various symptoms. Even months later, survivors sought treatment for posttraumatic stress disorder

(PTSD), including panic attacks and fear of riding the subway.[35] Thus, psychiatrists, clinical psychologists, and social workers will have to treat the widespread incidence of PTSD and other psychological sequelae.

ORGANIZATIONAL ISSUES

Because of the short time window available for medical response, the most cost-effective way to address the threat of chemical terrorism is to enhance local capabilities that can be brought to bear during the first critical minutes and hours after an attack. City and state governments have an institutional infrastructure for responding to chemical incidents, such as Hazmat teams and public health departments, that can be leveraged for enhanced domestic preparedness against terrorism. But although Hazmat specialists deal routinely with spills and accidental releases of toxic industrial chemicals, they require additional training to safely contain military-grade agents and to decontaminate and treat large crowds of victims.

The Defense Against Weapons of Mass Destruction Act of 1996, sponsored by Senators Sam Nunn, Richard Lugar, and Pete Domenici, tasked the Department of Defense (in conjunction with other federal agencies) with providing training, expert advice, and $300,000 worth of protective gear, detection, and decontamination equipment to emergency responders in the nation's 120 largest cities. This effort, known as the Domestic Preparedness Program, was designed to give each participating city a limited response capability and enable it to keep training after completion of the program. On October 1, 2000, lead responsibility was transferred from the Pentagon to the Department of Justice (DOJ), which has shifted the program's focus from the 120 cities to all 50 states. To be eligible for federal funds, each state must perform a comprehensive self-assessment to identify likely terrorist targets and threats, and must develop a three-year domestic preparedness plan. DOJ has also established a Center for Domestic Preparedness, based at the former U.S. Army chemical school in Anniston, Alabama, to give Hazmat specialists hands-on experience with military CW agents that might be used in a terrorist attack.

In recent years, however, spending priorities have drifted away from the original intent of the Nunn-Lugar-Domenici legislation. Of the $1.4 billion allocated to terrorism preparedness programs in fiscal year 2000, only about $315 million (22 percent) went to first responders in the form of training, equipment grants, and planning assistance.[36] With 46 different federal agencies seeking a piece of the counterterrorism pie, and eight congressional committees and seven subcommittees with jurisdiction over terrorism issues, the Domestic Preparedness Program has become a hodgepodge of overlapping and often duplicative programs. For example, a host of redundant federal response teams have been established, including the Marine Corps' Chemical/Biological Incident Response Force, the FBI's Hazardous Materials Response Unit, the Army's Chemical-

Biological Rapid Response Team, the EPA's Emergency Response Team, HHS's National Medical Response Team, and the National Guard's Weapons of Mass Destruction Civil Support Teams, among others.

Given the fact that most of these teams would take several hours to deploy to the scene of an incident of chemical terrorism in a small to medium-sized city, it makes little sense to invest a large proportion of domestic preparedness resources in such efforts.[37] Instead, the federal government should return to its original strategy of leveraging existing state and local assets by training and equipping first responders, while giving those agencies that have technical expertise in dealing with toxic chemicals, such as the U.S. Army and the EPA, a support role in the event of a massive attack.

CONCLUSIONS

The historical record indicates that most incidents of chemical terrorism have involved the use of household or industrial chemicals. Although such compounds are far less toxic than military-grade agents, the Bhopal disaster demonstrates the deadly potential that could result from the sabotage of a commercial chemical plant or a series of railroad tank cars. It therefore makes sense to devote more resources to addressing forms of chemical terrorism that would be less catastrophic but are more likely, such as industrial sabotage, rather than focusing exclusively on worst-case scenarios involving the large-scale release of a military nerve agent. Improving the security of chemical plants and the transportation infrastructure will require cooperative efforts by government and the private sector.

With respect to consequence management of a chemical terrorist attack, greater emphasis and funding should go to training and exercising local and state first responders, particularly Hazmat teams, and improving their capabilities for crowd decontamination, medical triage, and treatment of large numbers of casualties. At the same time, federal assets such as information hotlines, drug stockpiles, and rapid response teams should be better coordinated, rationalized, and streamlined, with the primary aim of providing support to state and local authorities.

NOTES

1. Sidell, Fred. 1996. Testimony in Proceedings of the Seminar on Responding to the Consequences of Chemical and Biological Terrorism, July 11-14, 1995, sponsored by the U.S. Public Health Service, Office of Emergency Preparedness. Washington, D.C.: U.S. Government Printing Office, pp. 1-66.

2　Kaplan, David E. Aum Shinrikyo. 2000. Toxic Terror: Assessing Terrorist Use of Chemical and Biological Weapons, Jonathan B. Tucker, ed. Cambridge, Mass.: MIT Press, pp. 208-210.

3. Murakami, Haruki. 2001. Underground: The Tokyo Gas Attack and the Japanese Psyche. New York: Vintage International, p. 118.

4. Kaplan, op. cit., p. 214.

5. Murakami, op. cit., p. 217.

6. Sidell testimony, p. 2-32.

7. U.S. Senate, October 21, 1995. Committee on Governmental Affairs, Permanent Subcommittee on Investigations. Staff Statement: Hearings on Global Proliferation of Weapons of Mass Destruction: A Case Study on Aum Shinrikyo.

8. Kaplan, op. cit., p. 222.

9. Monterey Institute of International Studies, Center for Nonproliferation Studies, WMD Terrorism Database, data as of May 7, 2001.

10. Tucker, Jonathan B. 2000. Chemical and biological terrorism: how real a threat? Current History 99(636):147-153.

11. Viktorov, Andrey, Stepan Krivosheyev. 1998. Moscow gangsters were preparing for chemical war: mad genius devoted lifetime to chemical warfare development. Moskva Segodnya (in Russian), September 11, 1998, p. 7; translated in FBIS document FTS19981001001057, October 1, 1998. See also Associated Press. September 11, 1998. Russian man arrested for manufacturing, selling chemical weapons.

12. U.S. General Accounting Office. 1999. Combating terrorism: observations on the threat of chemical and biological terrorism. Statement of Henry L. Hinton, Jr., Assistant Comptroller General, National Security and International Affairs Division Report No. GAO/T-NSIAD-00-50, October 20, 1999, p. 4.

13. Zilinskas, Raymond A. 1996. Aum Shinrikyo's chemical/biological terrorism as a paradigm? Politics and the Life Sciences15(2):238.

14. Schmid, Alex P. 2001. Chemical terrorism: precedents and prospects. OPCW Synthesis (Summer/June):12.

15. Mullen, Robert K. 1978. Mass destruction and terrorism. Journal of International Affairs 32(1):69.

16. Monterey Institute of International Studies, Center for Nonproliferation Studies, WMD Terrorism Database, data as of May 7, 2001.

17. Ibid.

18. U.S. Centers for Disease Control and Prevention, Strategic Planning Workgroup. 2000. Chemical and biological terrorism: strategic plan for preparedness and response. Morbidity and Mortality Weekly Report 49(April 21):1-14.

19. Los Angeles Times. January 3, 1995. Poisoned champagne kills 10 in Tajikistan, p. A18.

20. Begley, Sharon. 2001. Chemical plants: go well beyond "well prepared." Newsweek, p. 33.

21. National Research Council. 1999. Chemical and Biological Terrorism: Research and Development to Improve Civilian Medical Response. Washington, D.C.: National Academy Press, p. 127.

22. Jackson, Richard, M.D., M.P.H., Director, National Center for Environmental Health. Statement before the U.S. Senate Committee on Appropriations, Subcommittee on Labor, Health and Human Services, June 2, 1998.

23. Reuters. February 28, 2000. Dozens flee deliberate poison cloud.

24. Smithson, Amy E., and Leslie-Anne Levy. 2000. Ataxia: The Chemical and Biological Terrorism Threat and the U.S. Response. Washington: Henry L. Stimson Center, Report No. 35, pp. 91-102.

25. For vivid eyewitness descriptions of the Tokyo subway attack, see Murakami, op. cit.

26. U.S. Department of Health and Human Services. 1996. Planning Considerations for Health and Medical Services Response to Nuclear/Biological/Chemical Terrorism. Washington, D.C.: U.S. Department of Health and Human Services, p. 2.

27. U.S. Department of Energy, National Nuclear Security Administration, Office of Nonproliferation Research and Engineering. 2001. Chemical & Biological National Security Program, FY00 Annual Report DOE/NN-0015. Washington, D.C.: pp. 67-76.

28. U.S. Centers for Disease Control and Prevention, Strategic Planning Workgroup, op. cit.

29. National Research Council, op. cit., p. 102.

30. Ibid., p. 100.

31. Freedberg, Sidney J., Jr. 2001. Feds prepare state, local governments for terrorist attacks. National Journal, March 15, 2001. On-line at www.govexec.com/dailyfed/0301/031501nj/htm.

32. National Research Council, op. cit., p. 108.

33. American Journal of Public Health 91(May 2001):710-717. Cited in Reuters. May 1, 2001. Study: U.S. hospitals not prepared for bioterrorism.

34. Lorin, H.G., P.E.J. Kulling. 1986. The Bhopal tragedy—what has Swedish disaster medicine planning learned from it? Journal of Emergency Medicine 4:311-316.

35. Smithson and Levy, op. cit., p. 101.

36. Ibid., p. 289.

37. Green, Joshua. 2001. Weapons of mass confusion: how pork trumps preparedness in the fight against terrorism. Washington Monthly (May 2001):15-21.

NUCLEAR TERRORISM

Radiological Terrorism

Leonid Bolshov, Rafael Arutyunyan, and Oleg Pavlovsky[*]
Russian Academy of Sciences Nuclear Safety Institute

Like many countries in Western Europe, Russia has survived more than one wave of terrorism organized by people who often sincerely believed that the killing of crowned heads and high-ranking bureaucrats would facilitate a change in societal relations and bring everyone the joy of freedom and prosperity worthy of mankind. That being said, the terrorism of the late nineteenth century was of a focused nature and had limited consequences. Present-day terrorism, as a rule, is represented by fairly large organizations engaged in business or political activity, but having no aversion to achieving their goals by means of terrorist acts aimed against not only individuals but also groups of common and completely innocent people.

Current terrorist organizations have a fairly good understanding of a number of characteristic features of our times, among which one might point to the enormous influence of the mass media on the formation of public opinion in general, as well as the problems of "radiophobia" associated with the inadequate education of the public regarding the real consequences of nuclear accidents and incidents in particular.

In current practice, the possibility that nuclear, chemical, biological, and other components will be used in applications for terrorist purposes represents a very serious problem. A whole series of reports on chemical and biological terrorism has been presented at this seminar, so we would like to touch on the theme of nuclear or, more narrowly, radiological terrorism.

Terrorist acts using sources of radiation may be divided into three categories:

[*] Translated from the Russian by Kelly Robbins.

1. The detonation of (or threat to detonate) either a nuclear explosive device stolen from storage arsenals or a home-made nuclear bomb device using highly enriched uranium or plutonium;

2. The theft of radioactive waste materials and similar substances from nuclear facilities such as atomic power stations, research reactors, irradiated fuel processing plants, and storage facilities; and

3. The detonation of an ordinary explosive device including radioactive isotopes (^{60}Co, ^{90}Sr, ^{137}Cs, ^{239}Pu, etc.) as one of its components, with the aim of subsequently dispersing them over significant areas. This category would also include the possible addition of radioactive substances to water supplies.

Three years ago, at a seminar organized by the U.S. Federal Emergency Management Agency (FEMA), we presented a report on this same topic. Quite possibly, the lack of any sort of major progress, which we have yet to see in general since that time, is connected with the fact that such sensitive information is well protected and simply not visible to those of us in the Academy of Sciences. Perhaps the intelligence services have already taken all the necessary measures, and the representatives of these services hear reports of this sort with a smirk, as if the academicians don't know how life really is. If that is truly the case, then we shall be very glad. If that is not the case, then it is appropriate to ask the question, What needs to be done here and how should the top priorities be correctly identified? After all, we hear and say a great deal about enriched uranium and plutonium seized in customs during attempts to sell it illegally. These materials are closely related to nuclear weapons, to that which primarily concerns us. At the same time, we know that at the international level, the treaty on the nonproliferation of nuclear weapons was unable to prevent a whole series of countries from joining the nuclear club. Not being specialists in nuclear weapons, we do not wish to discuss this matter further and will limit ourselves to the problem of radiological weapons.

The authors of this report represent the Nuclear Safety Institute, which was created in the Russian Academy of Sciences after the Chernobyl accident so that the country would have a competent scientific organization, independent of the atomic power industry, that could conduct research on the safety of the power plants themselves as well as address issues concerning emergency and postemergency situations, the spread of radioactivity in the environment, and its impacts on human health. The experience of the Chernobyl accident has provided a great deal of factual material on the results of serious radiation contamination, and we would like to refer to this experience.

When we speak of radiation-related terrorism, it is necessary to keep in mind the important aspect of the intensification of public perceptions of the radiation factor, which is associated for well-known reasons with how society relates to nuclear weapons and atomic power in general. In Table 1, information on the real and exaggerated consequences of the Chernobyl accident in Russia is

TABLE 1   Differences in Assessments of the Radiological Consequences of the Accident at the Chernobyl Atomic Power Plant and in the Entire Nuclear Era

Author	Assessment of Radiological Consequences
A. Tsyb, member of the Russian Academy of Medical Sciences and director of the Medical Radiological Research Center, *Medical Consequences of the Chernobyl Accident*, Obninsk, 2001	"Among children in Bryansk Province, there have been 55 cases of thyroid cancer caused by ^{131}I irradiation. Among Chernobyl emergency clean-up workers, there have been 50 cases of leukemia and 12 cases of thyroid cancer caused by the radiation factor. The radiation risks of other cancers (tumors, leukemia) are at present so small that statistically they cannot be confirmed by factual data."
Ye. Masyuk, journalist. "Chernobyl: Tragedy and Business," NTV, 1999	" . . . In the past 13 years, 100,000 people have died from radiation sickness and another 200,000 from the consequences of the Chernobyl accident."
A. Yablokov, corresponding member of the Russian Academy of Sciences. *Human Health and the Environment as Victims of the Atomic Age.* Nuclear and Radiation Safety Program Bulletin No. 5-6, 2000. (Socio-Ecological Union)	"Thus, the total number of victims of cancer, genetic damage, and birth defects in the atomic age is 2 billion 337 million people. To these figures, we must add about 500 million miscarriages (spontaneous abortions) and stillbirths, 8-14 million infant deaths, and 5 million children with problems of delayed mental development."
"Nuclear Mythology of the Late 20th Century," *New World*, 1995	"A number of U.S. researchers have established that in the United States from May through August 1986 there were a significant rise in the total number of deaths among the population, an increase in infant mortality, and a lowered birth rate. The high correlation of these three groups of independent data with the concentration of radioactive iodine-131 from the Chernobyl cloud that covered the United States is so significant that there is no more than one one-thousandth chance that this link is coincidental. The number of deaths from pneumonia increased by 18.1 percent in comparison with 1985, the total mortality rate from various types of infectious diseases rose by 32.5 percent, and the death rate from AIDS increased by 60 percent."

presented in cumulative form, so to speak. As for the medical data, officially confirmed by 15 years of research, we have 55 cases of thyroid cancer caused by iodine among children in Bryansk Province (see the upper part of the table). Among the people who participated in emergency recovery and cleanup efforts at Chernobyl, a cohort of 116,000 individuals, there have been 50 cases of leukemia and 12 cases of thyroid cancer caused by radiation. All the other cancers in these cohorts cannot reliably be associated with radiation. And this is the factual side of the matter; that is, we have here dozens or hundreds of cases. Such is the order of magnitude of the medical data.

At the same time, if we look at materials presented in the mass media, for example, by the Russian television network NTV (see the middle part of the table), you will see assertions that 100,000 or 200,000 people died as a result of the Chernobyl accident. The factor of 10^4 in fact provides a fairly good reflection of the effect of the intensified impact of media reports on the population if it is announced that it wasn't just some sort of gas pipeline that exploded, but rather radiation. The very fact that radiation is present or even might be present quickly leads to the significant intensification of public interest in the problem and often to the hyperbolized assessment of the consequences of the event. We have not even mentioned certain members of the scientific community (see, for example, the materials in the lower part of the table) who allow themselves to make pronouncements that not only are antiscientific, but also contradict simple common sense, with millions and billions of victims. This, we think, is a reevaluation of the intensification factor that we are discussing, but nevertheless it is also a reflection of certain conceptions existing in society.

Moving directly to the question of the radiological factor, we would like to speak briefly about a second situation that we mentioned earlier. We have considered one of a multitude of possible versions, specifically the consequences of a terrorist action involving a research reactor. As is commonly known, any countries that are presently developing atomic power or conducting research in the nuclear field are devoting very serious attention to matters concerning physical protection and the creation of barriers to the access of terrorists or other persons (so-called unsanctioned access). Therefore, we do not wish to touch on this aspect, which is not appropriate for open discussion, but rather limit ourselves to purely balanced considerations.

Fuel assemblages that have been irradiated in research or power plant reactors could potentially be used to create different types of radiological weapons using various target delivery systems. The potential danger of radioisotopes being extracted from fuel assemblages and then dispersed over a target (the most vulnerable in this sense would be cities with a highly concentrated population) could be evaluated based on the hypothetical example of the use of fuel from a 5-MW water-cooled research reactor for such purposes (Table 2).

The amount of radiologically significant isotopes (cesium, strontium, plutonium) produced in this research reactor might total from 10 to 60 kCi for ^{137}Cs and from 10 to 50 kCi for ^{90}Sr. This reactor could also produce ^{239}Pu in amounts of 50 to 150 Ci. Dispersing radioactive substances from the reactor fuel assemblies by means of detonating a liquid or solid mixture at an altitude on the order of several hundred meters could lead to the wide-scale radioactive contamination

TABLE 2   Some Characteristics of a 5-MW Research Reactor

Type of reactor	Pool
Moderator	H_2O
Coolant	H_2O
Type of fuel	Uzr-Al
Enrichment	20%
Mass of fissile material	5.7 kg (^{235}U)
Maximum density of thermal neutron stream	3×10^{13} neutrons/(cm^2 • second)
Maximum density of fast neutron stream	1×10^{14} neutrons/(cm^2 • second)

of a population center. Estimates indicate that the area of urban territory where measures to protect the population would be needed (shelter, temporary evacuation) could reach 100-200 square kilometers.

This is the potential of one small research reactor. If we use the same criteria to discuss the situation with an atomic power station, the radiological potential for the discharge of the spent zone of one VVER-1000 type reactor would be two orders of magnitude higher. However, the weight of such a fuel assemblage (due to the fact that enrichment is substantially lower in commercial reactors) and the complexity of extracting active substances are so great that for the purposes of radiological terrorism it would obviously not make much sense to move from a research reactor to an atomic power plant and its irradiated fuel.

Let us now move on to the main theme of this report. Estimates indicate it would be relatively easy to make "fillings" for radiological weapons from industrial isotope sources such as cobalt, cesium, strontium, and plutonium, which are widely used worldwide in fault detection and sterilization systems, in self-contained power sources, and for medical purposes, among other uses (see Tables 3 and 4). These sources, in fact, were created by mankind for the very purpose of producing ionizing radiation. In contrast to the fuel for research reactors and atomic power plants, the fuel for these sources includes nothing extra, not ^{238}U and not a lot of construction materials. It is a highly concentrated radiation-producing product.

In view of the relatively weak controls over their use and storage, it would be significantly easier to use such sources to create radiological weapons. One could buy 100 to 1000 isotope sources operating on ^{60}Co, ^{90}Sr, or ^{137}Cs in a fairly legal fashion. The potential radiological weapons that could be created from such sources would be comparable to those from the enriched nuclear fuel from the discharge of one atomic power plant.

Judging from government reports published by agencies such as the Ministry for Environmental Protection and Gosatomnadzor (the Russian Federal Nuclear and Radiation Safety Authority), the situation in recent years has not been very favorable. For example, in 1998, more than 7000 enterprises, organizations,

TABLE 3   The Activity of Isotope Sources Produced Worldwide

Application	Radionuclide	Half-Life	Activity
Radiation therapy	^{60}Co	5.3 years	50-1000 TBq
	^{137}Cs	30 years	500 TBq
Industrial radiography	^{192}Ir	74 days	0.1-5 TBq
	^{60}Co	5.3 years	0.1-5 TBq
Sterilization	^{60}Co	5.3 years	0.1-400 PBq
	^{137}Cs	30 years	0.1-400 PBq
	^{90}Sr	29 years	50-1500 MBq
	^{103}Pd	17 days	50-1500 MBq
Well monitoring	^{137}Cs	30 years	1-100 GBq
	^{241}Am	432.2 years	1-800 GBq
	^{252}Cf	2.6 years	50 GBq
Level gauges, thickness gauges	^{137}Cs	30 years	10 GBq-1TBq
	^{60}Co	5.3 years	1-10 GBq
	^{241}Am	432.2 years	10-40 GBq
Density detectors	^{241}Am	432.2 years	0.1-2 GBq
	^{137}Cs	30 years	Up to 400 MBq
	^{226}Ra	1600 years	~ 1500 MBq
	^{252}Cf	2.6 years	3 GBq

SOURCE: Based on materials from the International Atomic Energy Agency General Conference, September 2000.

TABLE 4   Activity of Isotope Sources Produced in the Former USSR

Nuclide	Activity
^{60}Co	0.002-320 TBq
^{90}Sr	0.5-30 TBq
^{137}Cs	0.005-120 TBq
^{226}Ra	1.1 MBq
^{239}Pu	19-190 MBq

and institutions were working with atomic energy, with these locations having more than 18,000 facilities where radiation dangers were present. In 1999, only 2634 of these enterprises, having about 8000 radiation risk sites, had been licensed by Gosatomnadzor—less than half of the total. Gosatomnadzor has been actively functioning in Russia for the past 10 years. Despite the law on the use of atomic energy, which requires the licensing of any enterprise using a source of ionizing radiation, a large quantity of powerful radiation sources was also accumulated in medical institutions, industrial enterprises, and quarries during the long years of existence of the old system, which did not require Gosatomnadzor licensing. As is obvious from the figures presented above, a significant portion of these sources is not under official control. If an enterprise does not want to use a radiation source at a given moment, it either keeps it in storage, throws it out, or sells it in uncontrolled fashion. If we are referring to a new source, however, there is a Gosatomnadzor requirement covering both the seller and the buyer, who must obtain a permit to use the source.

Trends for radiation safety incidents at these enterprises for 1997-1999, based on data from the Russian Federation State Committee for Environmental Protection, are presented in Table 5.

The unfavorable situation with regard to control over the security and use of radioisotope sources in Russia is also demonstrated by the following facts. During 1980-1995, 80 areas of localized radioactive contamination with an open-field gamma radiation dose exceeding 1 R per hour were found on Russian territory. The nuclide content of the contamination was primarily found to be spent sources of ^{137}Cs (38 cases), ^{226}Ra (21 cases), ^{60}Co (10 cases), and others (11 cases).

A 1999 report of the Russian State Committee for Environmental Protection notes that "sources of ionizing radiation based on ^{90}Sr used in radioisotope thermoelectric generators (RTGs) used as heat sources (RIT-90) present" a serious radiation hazard. At the time of manufacture, these sources contain from 30 to 180 kCi (1100-6600 TBq) of ^{90}Sr, and the gamma radiation dose they create reaches 400-800 R per hour at a distance of 0.5 meter. According to data from the State Hydrographic Enterprise of the Russian Ministry of Transportation, along the Northern Sea corridor there are 381 RTGs in use, located in unpopulated hard-to-reach areas of the Arctic tundra and used as self-contained sources of electricity for naval navigational systems. No measures have been taken for the physical protection of these units, since, when they were installed, no thought was given to the possibility of damage inflicted on them by environmental or

TABLE 5   Trends for Radiation Safety Incidents Involving Ionizing Radiation Sources at Russian Enterprises (Not Including Minatom Facilities) for 1997-1999

Type of Incident	1997	1998	1999
Source failure (depressurization)	8	3	13
Theft of source	13	22	3
Discovery of unaccounted sources	14	16	5
Breaking off of source apparatus in well shaft during geophysical work	9	10	14
Loss of source during shipment	1	5	4
Intentional depressurization of source	1	2	n/a

NOTE: n/a = data unavailable.

TABLE 6   Certain Characteristics of Isotope Sources

Nuclide	Half-Life (years)	Type of Radiation	Mass of 1 TBq (grams)
^{60}Co	5.271	Gamma	0.024
^{90}Sr	29.12	Beta	0.20
^{137}Cs	30	Gamma	0.31
^{226}Ra	1,600	Alpha, Gamma	27
^{239}Pu	24,065	Alpha	435

anthropogenic factors. The report emphasizes that "due to a practical lack of accounting and control over these units by the organizations operating them, certain RTGs could be lost or forgotten." The operational life spans of the majority of RTGs (more than 80 percent) have already run out (State Report, 2000).

These very sources of ionizing radiation are connected with the most recent incident in which several people were irradiated, which occurred near the city of Kandalaksha in May 2001. The desire to remove the lead protective covering from an unprotected navigational beacon in order to sell it at a non-ferrous metal recycling center led to the destruction of an RTG, the loss of two of its three ^{90}Sr sources, radioactive contamination of the surrounding area, and high doses of radiation to the participants in this operation. This incident showed that there are very poor controls over such units, which are extremely dangerous from a radiological standpoint, and that the use of the radiation sources contained in them for terrorist purposes is highly possible.

For the following analysis of possible radiological consequences of terrorist acts involving the use of radioisotope sources, we decided to select five radionuclides, including examples of those most commonly used in the economy and those having very high potential danger to human health (Table 6).

Calculations were made with the help of the software packages "TRACE" and "NOSTRADAMUS" developed at the Russian Academy of Sciences Nuclear Safety Institute (Bolshov et al., 1995; Arutyunyan et al., 1999b).

The TRACE system is based on a fast integrated computer code utilizing a Gaussian model of atmospheric transport. In numerical, tabular, and cartographic form (both in summary and for individual isotopes), it provides predictions of contamination density, open-field gamma radiation dose level, and the effective dose for internal and external radiation over the whole body and for specific organs (thyroid, gonads, lungs, red marrow, etc.) for various age groups. It typically takes just a few seconds to receive results on modern personal computers using the mapping option.

The NOSTRADAMUS system is intended to support decision making with regard to reducing the impact on the environment and the population in the initial urgent phase of a radiation accident. The system has been used to prepare scenarios and conduct training games and exercises both in Russia and abroad.

This software package makes it possible to analyze accidents that vary in scale from the local (lasting a few hours and affecting a few dozen square kilometers) to the relatively serious (involving several days of emissions or dispersal with an affected zone encompassing up to 1000-2000 square kilometers).

The system uses the Lagrange trajectory model for the transport of elements in the atmosphere. In this feature it differs from the now widely used normative methodologies, which are based on Gaussian models. It also contains a model of the atmospheric boundary layer, which is necessary for supplying the vertical profile of the wind speed as well as for determining the category of atmospheric stability based on synoptic data. In order to determine the turbulence exchange coefficients, the system uses tabularized data based on many years of observations of the vertical profile of diffusion coefficients made by the Typhoon Research and Production Association. Trajectory modeling capabilities make it possible to calculate the transport of the contaminant over a distance of hundreds of kilometers and take into account the space-time heterogeneity of the wind field, the impact of the local land relief (orography), and the type and intensity of precipitation on the dispersion process.

One of the special modules in the NOSTRADAMUS system (the "Orography" module) is intended for adaptation of the wind field to the local topography. The algorithm is based on determination of the nondivergent wind field closest to the starting point and coordinated with the topography. The dosimetric module of the NOSTRADAMUS package includes a model for calculating the dose from an end cloud and a quick algorithm for calculating the radioactive decay chain. The results of the modeling (doses and dose levels, internal and external, effective and by organ, total and by nuclide, concentrations and fallout, duration of cloud presence, and levels of countermeasures) in the calculation process are depicted against the backdrop of a map of the local area (with the ability to change the levels of resolution, transparency, colors, etc.). The presentation includes either contour lines or colored areas showing the various levels. Also included are various types of output files—text documents, Microsoft Excel workbooks (with a time line of the situation broken down by population center or radiological monitoring point), and others that can be independently worked on with the help of standard software products. The NOSTRADAMUS package was used to consider the radiological consequences of accidents at the Chernobyl Atomic Power Plant and a hypothetical terrorist act involving the detonation of an explosive device with an isotope source in an urban environment.

In order to evaluate the scale of the possible consequences of such a terrorist act on the territory of a large city, it was decided to use as a threshold value the magnitude of the radiation dose level received by individual members of the population. Here, as per International Atomic Energy Agency (IAEA) recommendations, the possibility that individuals might take protective measures, such as seeking shelter, was taken into account. The concentration integral data for radionuclides in the near-ground air layer corresponding to these dose limits

TABLE 7   Airborne Radionuclide Concentration Integrals for Situations in Which It Becomes Advisable to Alert the Population to Seek Shelter

Nuclide	Concentration integral (MBq × second/m³)	Threshold dose (mSv)	Critical Factor of Effect
^{60}Co	120	5	Gamma radiation from soil surface
^{90}Sr	75	50	Inhalation
^{137}Cs	470	5	Gamma radiation from soil surface
^{226}Ra	13	50	Inhalation
^{239}Pu	0.26	50	Inhalation

are presented in Table 7. As evident from the data in this table, for ^{60}Co and ^{137}Cs the critical factor was the dose of radiation received by people from local radionuclide fallout during the first 10 days. Meanwhile, normalization for doses from internal radiation due to inhalation had a greater impact for ^{90}Sr, ^{226}Ra, and ^{239}Pu.

These calculations were made using the imitation Monte Carlo method for an urban area. Preliminary calculations indicated that depending on the orientation of buildings relative to the trajectory of the movement of the emission cloud and on the formation of stagnant zones and tunnel effects, the radionuclide concentration integral in the near-ground air layer in the urban environment can differ from its open-field value by one order of magnitude in either direction. For each possible variation in weather conditions, effective altitude of the emission cloud, and initial activity level of the radioisotope source, we calculated concentration integrals for 10,000 arbitrarily selected points in a 10- by 5-km rectangle. The emission source was located in a lower corner of this rectangle. Next, we evaluated the amount of radioactive material in the detonated device, after the explosion of which the radionuclide concentration integral values given in Table 7 would be exceeded at a distance of more than 100 meters or over an urban area of more than 1 square kilometer. The results of such calculations for a situation

TABLE 8   Amount of Dispersed Radionuclides (in Grams) Requiring the Population to Take Shelter at Distances of No Less Than 0.1 km from the Emission Source

Weather Category	^{60}Co	^{90}Sr	^{137}Cs	^{226}Ra	^{239}Pu
A	0.020	0.11	1.0	2.6	0.82
D	0.052	0.28	2.8	6.9	2.2
F	0.021	0.11	1.0	2.8	0.88

TABLE 9   Amount of Dispersed Radionuclides (in Grams) Requiring the Population to Take Shelter over an Area of at Least 1 Square Kilometer

Weather Category	^{60}Co	^{90}Sr	^{137}Cs	^{226}Ra	^{239}Pu
A	2.5	14	140	340	110
D	1.1	6.1	60	150	47
F	0.10	0.55	5.5	14	4.3

involving the detonation of a charge equal in power to 50 kg of TNT are presented in Tables 8 and 9.

From the material in these tables, it follows that the mass of radionuclides to be added to an explosive device could be very small. Therefore, there are no technical problems in producing such types of radiological weapons, at least those using beta- and alpha-emitters as radioisotopic filling. Unfortunately, it should also be noted that the illegal weapons market in Russia is currently very widespread, so that obtaining the necessary amount of explosive material or a ready-to-use explosive device is not an insurmountable obstacle. The events in Chechnya and adjoining regions also shows that Chechen terrorists have begun making a widespread practice of using condemned prisoners to carry out terrorist acts. One cannot rule out the possibility that in order to raise the morale of their fighters they may also find individuals wishing to explode a "radiological bomb" in the name of the struggle against the "infidel" and for the glory of Allah. Let us recall that after a container of ^{137}Cs was found in Moscow's Izmailovsky Park in November 1995, there followed a declaration by Dzhokhar Dudayev, who said that "what we have demonstrated in Izmailovsky Park to the entire world community and to Moscow is just a meager portion of the radioactive substances that we possess." It is entirely possible that this was simple bravado; however, we must not forget that one of the largest radioactive waste storage facilities in the region is located in the territory of Chechnya. No one can undertake to guarantee that nothing has disappeared from this facility in all the years of military actions.

This is an important result, from which very serious conclusions should be drawn from the standpoint of the need to observe the strictest controls both over the use and security of radioisotopes and over the creation of effective technical means for monitoring the transport of isotope-containing products within the country and across its borders. The increasingly frequent reports in the mass media and from official agencies regarding thefts of and subsequent attempts to sell radioactive substances speak to the fact that the criminal world is taking an ever more active interest in such types of products. It is entirely possible that we shall soon witness a case in which nuclear and radioactive materials are used as a means of terror or a tool of blackmail. A serious intensification of controls is also needed regarding the black market in conventional arms and explosive devices.

In conclusion, it should be emphasized once again that despite the seriousness of the possible unfavorable radiological consequences of such a terrorist act for the population, its sociopsychological and economic consequences for a given city, a region, or even an entire country could turn out to be simply catastrophic.

REFERENCES

Arutyunyan, R., I. Linge, O. Pavlovski, et al. 1999a. Experience of preparation of exercises and practical games on emergency preparedness and response in case of radiation accidents. Proceedings of the Seventh Topical Meeting on Emergency Preparedness and Response. Santa Fe, N.M., September 14-17, 1999, p. 62-A.

Arutyunyan, R., V. Belikov, V. Goloviznin, V. Kiselev, et al. 1999b. Models for the distribution of radioactive contamination in the environment. News of the Russian Academy of Sciences, Energy, first edition, pp. 61-76.

Bolshov L., R. Arutunyan, M. Kanevskiy, V. Kiselev et al. 1995. Development of specialized software for the analysis of consequences of large-scale radiological accidents. Proceedings of Ninth Annual Symposium on Geographic Information Systems in Natural Resources Management, Vancouver, Canada, Vol. 1, pp. 314-318.

State Committee of the Russian Federation on Environmental Protection. 2000. State Report on the Natural Environment in the Russian Federation in 1999. Moscow: State Center for Ecological Programs, 580 pp.

Nuclear Terrorism

Siegfried S. Hecker
Los Alamos National Laboratory

INTRODUCTION

As pointed out by several speakers, the level of violence and destruction in terrorist attacks has increased significantly during the past decade. Fortunately, few have involved weapons of mass destruction, and none have achieved mass casualties. The Aum Shinrikyo release of lethal nerve agent, sarin, in the Tokyo subway on March 20, 1995, clearly broke new ground by crossing the threshold in attempting mass casualties with chemical weapons. However, of all weapons of mass destruction, nuclear weapons still represent the most frightening threat to humankind.

Nuclear weapons possess an enormous destructive force. The immediacy and scale of destruction are unmatched. In addition to destruction, terrorism also aims to create fear among the public and governments. Here also, nuclear weapons are unmatched. The public's fear of nuclear weapons—or, for that matter, of all radioactivity—is intense. To some extent, this fear arises from a sense of unlimited vulnerability. That is, radioactivity is seen as unbounded in three dimensions: distance—it is viewed as having unlimited reach; quantity—it is viewed as having deadly consequences in the smallest doses (the public is often told—incorrectly, of course—that one atom of plutonium will kill); and time—if it does not kill you immediately, then it will cause cancer decades hence.

Fred Iklé[1] recently stated that "the morning after . . . a nuclear weapon has been used, the rules of warfare throughout the world will be profoundly transformed." He added, "Democracy cannot survive if a nuclear bomb can be detonated in Paris or Manhattan." Democracy would be even more vulnerable if nuclear weapons were exploded in democracies with shallower roots, such as those in Russia or India, for example. Hence, the consequences of a nuclear explosion almost anywhere on Earth would seriously impact the affairs of all nations.

POTENTIAL FORMS OF NUCLEAR TERRORISM

A nuclear weapon delivered by a missile, plane, boat, or van produces the gravest consequences of all forms of nuclear terrorism. Fortunately, the key ingredients for making a weapon, the fissile materials plutonium or highly enriched uranium, are difficult to make and the facilities to make them have quite visible signatures. A second form of nuclear terrorism that is much less devastating, but much more likely, is radiological terrorism, that is, the dispersal of radioactive materials. These so-called radiological dispersal devices (RDDs) can be made by packaging radioactive materials with chemical explosives and detonating such devices in high-value surroundings. A third form of nuclear terrorism is sabotage of nuclear facilities.

All of these forms of nuclear terrorism are old problems—with concerns first being expressed a few years after World War II. However, the world has changed significantly since then. As already mentioned, there is a strong proclivity toward greater levels of violence. Yet, the public today has a much lower tolerance for risk. There is also considerably greater technological sophistication today and there is much more information available to the public, especially on the Internet. The greatest change, however, since the early days of nuclear weapons and nuclear power is that terrorists have easier access to nuclear and radioactive materials.

Nuclear Weapons

Although nuclear weapons are complicated technological devices, it is generally agreed that a determined, well-trained subnational group could in time build a crude nuclear device with yields on the order of a few to tens of kilotons. The atomic bombs dropped on Hiroshima and Nagasaki were less than 20 kilotons. They devastated these cities and caused several hundred thousand deaths. The most difficult part of building such bombs is acquiring on the order of the tens of kilograms of highly enriched uranium or plutonium required to build them. The difficulties that a determined adversary such as Saddam Hussein experienced despite the expenditure of billions of dollars is a good case in point.

However, the dissolution of the Soviet Union with the consequent loss of order and central government control, especially in the early 1990s, raised the specter of theft or diversion of nuclear weapons or weapons-usable materials from the nuclear complex of the former Soviet Union. Although the "loose-nukes" concern received much play in the American media, it appears overblown. There is no evidence that Russia has lost control of any weapons in its nuclear arsenal. Unfortunately, we do not have similar confidence about the potential loss of weapons-usable nuclear materials. In fact, several high-visibility cases in the middle 1990s demonstrated that weapons-usable plutonium or highly enriched uranium were trafficked illicitly from Russia and other states of the former Soviet Union. These incidents provided a "wake-up" call for Russia. Since that time, Russia has greatly enhanced the security of its weapons-usable materials with much of the effort being financed by the U.S. government.

Although, the quickest way to deliver a nuclear weapon is by missiles, that remains an unlikely probability for a decade or more. Crude nuclear devices would be most easily transported to the desired site by boat, plane, or van. Although nuclear devices have a distinct radioactive signature that can be detected by sophisticated sensors, this signature is attenuated significantly by distance and by shielding. Moreover, the number of entry points into the United States or other states that have a significant U.S. presence is overwhelming. Hence, today we must assume that if a group possesses a nuclear device, there is a very high probability that such a device could be delivered to a place where it could cause unacceptable damage. Hence, our government must remain ever vigilant to prevent nuclear weapons or weapons-usable materials from falling into the wrong hands.

Radiological Terrorism

The human consequences of radiological devices detonated in high-value places are orders of magnitude less than those of a nuclear detonation. The immediate effects are principally those of the chemical explosive used to detonate the RDD. Dispersing the radioactive materials limits their immediate lethality. Furthermore, the lethality depends strongly on the nature of the radioactive material. Plutonium and highly enriched uranium, which are most feared by the public, are unlikely to result in a large number, if any, of immediate deaths because they do not emit highly penetrating radiation. Even the long-term cancer potential of their dispersal may not be terribly great.

However, radioactive materials with intensely penetrating radiation may cause significant casualties. Such materials result from the burning of uranium in nuclear reactors (that is, their spent fuel or nuclear waste from reprocessing of spent fuel) or from medical or industrial radiation sources used to generate intense radiation. Fortunately, the more lethal a terrorist's choice of radioactive material, the less likely it is for a terrorist to be able to fashion it into an RDD without first killing the terrorist. Moreover, it would be easier to detect such a device unless it is heavily shielded.

Hence, it is generally agreed that the greatest consequences of an RDD are public fear and the potentially enormous cleanup costs along with the consequent economic losses. Unfortunately, there is essentially no barrier to terrorists' acquiring a wide range of radioactive materials. By far the most vulnerable are medical and industrial radiation sources. There are currently more than 135,000 licensees of medical and industrial radiation sources in the United States, with more than 1.8 million sources in use.[2] Even in the United States, which has rather stringent regulations for the use and disposition of radioisotopes, approximately 200 sources are reported lost, stolen, or abandoned annually. Around the world, more than 110 states have no minimum infrastructure to properly control radiation sources.[3] In Russia, there were 500 reported incidents involving unlawful movements of materials with elevated levels of ionizing radiation in the year 2000 alone. The International Atomic Energy Agency (IAEA) has reported that since 1993 there have been 175 cases of trafficking in nuclear material and 201 cases of trafficking in other radiation sources. Fortunately, only 18 of these cases have actually involved small amounts of highly enriched uranium or plutonium. It is somewhat reassuring that historically there have been surprisingly few incidents of the theft or smuggling of radioactive materials for malevolent purposes. However, the increased proclivity toward greater violence in terrorist acts gives one much reason for concern.

Nuclear Sabotage

Blowing up a nuclear facility constitutes another form of potential nuclear terrorism. The much more than 1000 nuclear facilities around the world constitute a target-rich environment. Although nuclear power reactors are typically well guarded and some are designed to withstand a significant external insult, the radioactive source terms at such facilities have the potential to cause massive casualties. These power reactors, like other critical facilities such as dams and chemical plants, pose potentially serious hazards for nearby populations. The potential damages resulting from terrorist attacks on nuclear power plants depend on inherent design features and on local protective measures, which in turn vary widely from country to country. The IAEA reports that there are 438 nuclear power reactors in operation worldwide (with 103 of these in the United States). Since the Oklahoma City bombing, the U.S. Nuclear Regulatory Commission has overseen a significant safety enhancement of U.S. nuclear power reactors against the truck bomb threat.

The situation for storage sites housing spent fuel or high-level waste resulting from reprocessing is similar to that for nuclear reactors. The radiation source terms are potentially enormous. In addition, there are 651 research reactors (only 284 are currently in operation) and 250 fuel cycle plants around the world, including uranium mills and plants that convert, enrich, and store nuclear materials. These nuclear facilities represent a much smaller source term, but are also typically much less secure.

Although sabotage of some power reactors may cause Chernobyl-like damages, most sabotage attempts would most likely result in the dispersal of some radioactive materials without mass casualties, but with enormous public fear and economic losses. In addition to these consequences, any successful act of nuclear terrorism would also most likely set back any expansion of nuclear power or other peaceful uses of the atom for decades.

HOW TO DEAL WITH THE THREAT OF NUCLEAR TERRORISM?

Much has been written over the years about the nature of the threat. During the past four years, the U.S. Defense Science Board has twice focused on the nuclear terrorism threat during its summer studies. The principal recommendation from these studies is to develop a comprehensive architecture to counter all aspects of nuclear terrorism. Such an architecture should include the following:

- Information and intelligence
- Security
- Detection
- Disablement
- Mitigation
- Attribution

Some aspects of nuclear terrorism, such as the dispersal of radiation sources, have low consequences but virtually no barriers. Others, such as a nuclear detonation have unacceptable consequences but significant barriers. Hence, information and intelligence about potential terrorist activities is paramount to provide as much early warning as possible. Keeping radioactive materials secure—that is, protected, controlled, and accounted for—is very important, especially for weapons-usable plutonium and highly enriched uranium. Security of radiation sources is most problematical. A major worldwide effort is necessary to have every country with such sources develop a proper regulatory framework and system of control. The threat of nuclear sabotage calls for extending tight security requirements to all nuclear facilities.

Unlike biological and chemical agents, nuclear materials and radioisotopes have a distinct radioactive signature that can be detected at a distance. Unfortunately, this signature is attenuated by distance and by shielding, which makes it more difficult to detect some of these materials in a sea of cosmic background radiation. For example, plutonium's 7×10^7 gammas per second per kilogram are attenuated by a factor of 1 million by 1 km in air and a factor of 1000 by 1 inch of lead shielding. Detecting radiation at a distance continues to be one of the most important technological challenges in nuclear terrorism.

Disabling a nuclear device is extremely difficult but possible if one can gain access and render the device safe. The U.S. nuclear weapons laboratories have over the years developed several potential approaches. Any knowledge of the type of device or its country of origin would prove very helpful in attempting to render the device safe. If a device is actually detonated, then treating the casualties promptly and effectively becomes crucial. Likewise, rapid and effective cleanup of contaminated areas will help to limit the economic damages. Again, the United States has significant training experience with the Department of Energy's Accident Response Group (ARG) and its Nuclear Emergency Search Teams (NEST). Likewise, there is a substantial body of expertise for decontamination and cleanup based on experience with decommissioning nuclear facilities and cleaning up nuclear dispersal accidents. Lastly, a comprehensive architecture must include attribution. Forensics must be developed to determine the identity of the perpetrators, both for the purpose of retaliation and to guard against a potential repeat attack.

One additional critical dimension of an integrated architecture to respond to terrorism is education of the public along with the role of mass media. This is especially important for nuclear terrorism because of the public's lack of understanding of radiation and the great fear that accompanies this lack of understanding. For example, the likelihood of radiological terrorism in the near future is quite high—the necessary materials are readily available. However, it is important for the public to understand that the threat to human life is very limited from most such devices. The economic consequences from contamination, disruption, and cleanup, however, can be severe. Radiological sabotage represents a considerably greater threat to human life in the vicinity of nuclear facilities. However, there are immediate actions, including well-established medical treatments, that can reduce the threat to human life. Even a nuclear explosion with its enormous destructive power has a limited range of lethality. Mass media can play an important role in helping to educate the public on the real nature of the various nuclear threats.

I believe that any integrated architecture would also benefit substantially from U.S.-Russian cooperation on a wide front of activities designed to deal with nuclear terrorism. The first cooperative agreement between the United States and Russia to combat terrorism in general dates back to September 1993, with a memorandum of understanding between the U.S. Department of Defense and the Russian Federation Ministry of Defense. Although not much activity has occurred under this agreement, recent statements made by President Bush and Russian Minister Ivanov underscore the importance of this problem.

Specifically, I believe that cooperation between the Russian Academy of Sciences and the U.S. National Academies would be very beneficial. I believe that since this problem has so many dimensions, it should be viewed from as many different points of view as possible, including those of scientists and engineers. There are many areas in which specialists can help with the science and technology dimensions of nuclear terrorism. The U.S. National Academies have a long record of involvement in the counterterrorism arena. Working jointly with the Russian Academy of Sciences would prove very beneficial to both countries. Also, often the informal dialogue resulting from the discussion of specialists under the umbrella of the Russian and U.S. Academies can help to catalyze necessary government actions.

NOTES

1. Iklé, F.C. 1996. The second coming of the nuclear age. Foreign Affairs 75 (January-February):119.

2. Lubenau, J.O. 1999. A century's challenges: historical overview of radiation sources in the USA. IAEA Bulletin 41(3):2.

3. González, A.J. 1999. Strengthening the safety of radiation sources and the security of radioactive materials: timely action. IAEA Bulletin 41(3):2.

Could Terrorists Produce Low-Yield Nuclear Weapons?

Stanislav Rodionov *
Russian Academy of Sciences Space Research Institute

Quite recently, most specialists have implied that terrorists would try to produce nuclear weapons using existing scientific knowledge and technical potential. For example, the Committee on International Security and Arms Control (CISAC) of the U.S. National Academy of Sciences came to the following conclusions concerning the unauthorized use of plutonium:[1]

• Possible proliferators could produce nuclear explosive devices even from reactor-grade plutonium; a simple design (i.e., implosive systems) would provide a yield from one to a few kilotons, while a more modern design could provide a higher yield.
• In assessing security threats, it is necessary to understand who is trying to acquire and misuse plutonium. Terrorists might care little about the differences between reactor-grade and weapons-grade plutonium. Small nations would be likely to care more, in the sense of preferring to make weapons from weapons-grade plutonium, if everything else were equal.

I would like to focus on the fact that the situation might be much simpler. Indeed, although terrorism in general is an unpredictable and uncontrolled phenomenon, nuclear terrorism itself may have some specific features.

First, it might be dangerous and risky to keep stolen nuclear explosives for a long time. In this case, one could not spend the extra time needed to develop (not to mention, test) a reliable nuclear bomb. It is highly probable that terrorists

---

* Translated from the Russian by Kelly Robbins.

would need just an explosive device—and a very simple device at that—to carry out a single action.

Second, the explosion itself might be the most effective factor in achieving the terrorists' objectives, rather than the nuclear blast yield. Moreover, an enormous number of victims could have a negative effect on that part of the international community that adopts a positive or neutral attitude toward terrorists.

Therefore, low-yield nuclear explosive devices might be rather attractive for terrorists, barring any serious technical barriers to their construction. We shall see later that under some conditions this problem may have a solution.

Let us consider two approaches to lowering the yield of a nuclear explosion. The first is based on extremely high compression of a fissile material. It is well known that its critical mass is inversely proportional to the square of its density. For example, plutonium density in modern weapons designs is three to four times higher as a result of implosion.[2] At higher compressions, there is no limit on the minimum amount of fissile material required to construct a nuclear explosive. One can imagine micronuclear explosives with yields in the ton range, requiring fissile materials on the order of hundreds or even tens of grams. But what can actually be achieved along this line of development is limited only by available implosion technologies. Thus, it does not seem that this straightforward approach could be used by terrorists, because it requires a very high degree of technical expertise.

The other approach is connected to the so-called fizzle effect, which really is a preinitiation of a nuclear chain reaction in a fissile material in a supercritical state (due to the occurrence of "accidental" neutrons). As a result, the yield of the explosion is reduced in comparison with its nominal value. It should be noted that all types of nuclear weapons have a nonzero fizzle probability. One can categorize all types of nuclear weapons as either fast (implosive systems) or slow (gun-type assemblies) depending on the "waiting time" between the start of criticality and the moment of optimal condition. The fizzle effect is more probable in slow systems and for fissile materials with a high level of neutron self-emission (due mostly to the process of spontaneous fission). Therefore, nuclear terrorists could be very interested in a gun-type nuclear device with reactor-grade or weapons-grade plutonium.

Estimates of the fizzle yield were made by Dr. Carson Mark, former Theoretical Division Leader of Los Alamos National Laboratory.[3] He considered "as a purely hypothetical example" a weapons-grade plutonium assembly of the implosion type used at Trinity (the first American nuclear test, July 16, 1945), with the nominal yield of 20 kilotons. The fizzle yield in this case might be 0.5 kiloton. A similar assembly in a gun-type system would produce a fizzle yield of some 10-20 tons.

The fizzle phenomenon is of a statistical nature where the main parameter would be the moment of neutron occurrence during the waiting period. The fizzle could be managed to some extent, but management of this kind requires some extra technical complications that might be unacceptable for terrorists. Therefore, the "natural" fizzle seems to be more attractive for them. The above-mentioned natural-fizzle yield value of 10-20 tons was estimated for a rather high speed of bringing together two subcritical masses of plutonium (about 300 m/s). A yield about five times lower would be expected at a relative speed of 100 m/s. The corresponding yield value (a few tons) seems to be quite acceptable for terrorists.

Let us assume that the mass of a single plutonium piece would be, say, 5 kg. In this case, its kinetic energy (at a speed of 100 m/s) would be equal to 25 kJ. Such energy may be provided either by high explosives (the explosive energy of TNT is about 4 MJ/kg) or by some source of stored mechanical energy (a compressed spring, for example).

For systems with natural fizzle, the idea of testing makes no sense since every subsequent result can, in principle, differ from the preceding one.

The yield value of few tons is comparable with the explosive energy release in some instances where terrorists used chemical high explosives (as in the Oklahoma City case, for instance). So, a natural question arises, What could be the advantages of a low-yield nuclear device compared to a few-ton blast produced by chemical high explosives? In fact, one could identify certain advantages.

First of all, it would be a direct demonstration of the fact that terrorists do posses a nuclear explosive. From the psychological point of view, this action might produce the most important effect on public opinion.

Second, the nuclear explosion is characterized by higher effective temperatures. This results in a more powerful shockwave and thermal effects. One can estimate the "kill range" of a 2-ton nuclear blast using corresponding scaling laws and reference data about the consequences of the nuclear explosions in Hiroshima and Nagasaki. Such an estimated value will hardly exceed 100 meters.

Third, the nuclear explosion inherently produces radioactive contamination by fission products (not to mention radioactivity induced by fast neutrons). The yield of 2 tons would correspond to total fissioning of only 0.1 gram of plutonium. As a result, about 0.3 Ci of cesium-137 and 0.1 Ci of strontium-90 (the most abundant long-lived fission products) would be generated. The initial activity of short-lived fission products (which decay mostly within a few months after the explosion) would be greater by nearly two orders of magnitude (about 20-30 Ci). Plutonium itself is a toxic material as well, especially in the form of plutonium oxide aerosol, which is produced by a high-temperature blast. This aerosol could disperse over larger distances and be dangerous to the population.[4]

However, these low-yield nuclear devices cannot be "invisible." It has been shown that neutron emission from an ordinary plutonium warhead can be detected at distances of 50-70 meters.[5] The corresponding detection range would be two to three times greater for devices using reactor-grade plutonium. It is important to note that the detection range and kill range of a low-yield device are comparable. This makes it possible to protect some very important targets from terrorist nuclear attacks.

In conclusion, potential nuclear terrorists would encounter no serious technical problems in constructing a simple low-yield (in the order of few tons of TNT equivalent) and low-weight (in the order of a hundred kilograms) gun-type nuclear explosive device using weapons-grade or reactor-grade plutonium. A device of this kind would have destructive and thermal kill ranges of about 100 meters. Moreover, it would produce radioactive fallout with a total intensity of a few tens of curies as well as a cloud containing a few kilograms of plutonium oxide aerosol. The "threshold" amount of plutonium for such a device might exceed to some extent the mass of plutonium for an ordinary nuclear warhead.

This hypothetical example emphasizes the vital importance of very strict control over nonproliferation of any amounts of plutonium (both weapons-grade and reactor-grade material of any isotope composition). It also emphasizes the potential importance of very sensitive neutron detectors.

NOTES

1. Committee on International Security and Arms Control, National Academy of Sciences. 1995. Management and Disposition of Excess Weapons Plutonium: Reactor-Related Options. Washington, D.C.: National Academy Press, p. 44.

2. Cochran, T.B., C.E. Paine. 1995. Nuclear Weapons Databook: The Role of Hydronuclear Tests and Other Low-Yield Nuclear Explosions and Their Status Under a Comprehensive Test Ban. New York: Natural Resources Defense Council, p. 6.

3. Mark, J.C. 1993. Explosive properties of reactor-grade plutonium. Science and Global Security 4(1):111-124.

4. Fetter, S., F. von Hippel. 1990. The hazard from plutonium dispersal by nuclear-warhead accident. Science and Global Security 2(1):21-41.

5. Occasional Report. 1990. The Black Sea Experiment. Science and Global Security 1(3-4):323-333.

Problems of Preventing Acts of Nuclear and Radiological Terrorism

Vladimir M. Kutsenko *
Department of Protection of Information, Nuclear Materials, and Facilities
Ministry of Atomic Energy

A.P. Morozov
Interagency Group on Combating Nuclear Terrorism and
the Illegal Trade in Nuclear Materials and Radioactive Substances

The concept of the national security of the Russian Federation includes the possibility that a threat such as terrorism may occur in practically any sphere of activity in the country. The threat of nuclear or radiological terrorism is therefore viewed as part of the overall problem of ensuring national security.

The Federal Anti-terrorism Commission has been established under the federal law on combating terrorism. As part of this commission and under the auspices of the Russian Ministry of Atomic Energy (Minatom), a working group has been created to address issues of countering nuclear terrorism and the illegal trade in nuclear materials and radioactive substances. In conjunction with the State Commission on Nuclear Weapons at the federal and regional levels, this commission coordinates the activities of executive branch agencies of the federal government and of Russian Federation subjects involved in preventing and suppressing nuclear terrorism and eliminating (localizing) its effects. A federal system for reacting to terrorist incidents has also been instituted.

Minatom has itself carried out significant work aimed at preventing nuclear and radiological terrorism at industrial facilities. Such efforts include the following:

- Step-by-step upgrades to bring the system for physical protection of facilities up to the necessary standard;
- Improvement of the state system of control and accountability for nuclear and radioactive materials; and
- Coordination of the efforts of federal executive branch agencies aimed at preventing and suppressing possible acts of nuclear terrorism.

---

* Translated from the Russian by Kelly Robbins.

These efforts and other measures are essential, but the current world situation shows that they may not be sufficient. The potential for the occurrence of nuclear and radiological terrorism, one of the most dangerous varieties of high-tech terrorism, is ever intensifying, taking on an international, global character. Current reviews, publications, and expert assessments indicate that the problem of nuclear and radiological terrorism could become a reality at any moment. Understanding this threat and its consequences with a sufficient sense of responsibility requires that all possible aspects of this phenomenon be considered in detail.

Of the greatest concern is the possibility of terrorism involving nuclear weapons, which could take on an international character. Such terrorism could involve illegally obtained nuclear weapons or nuclear materials used in making such weapons. Terrorists might also use "dirty methods," that is, highly radioactive materials detonated using ordinary explosive substances. Problems connected with fighting this sort of terrorism must be resolved by maximally coordinated efforts aimed at creating an appropriate system of measures in Russia, the United States, and other states possessing nuclear technologies. It should also be noted that this type of terrorism as a phenomenon of modern life appeared relatively recently and is a rather broad, complex, and multifaceted concept.

The reliable physical protection of nuclear materials undoubtedly plays an exceptionally important role in the interests of preventing and suppressing possible acts of nuclear and radiological terrorism. In this connection, full support should be given to the efforts of the Office of Physical Protection and Materials Security of the International Atomic Energy Agency (IAEA) Department of Safeguards to strengthen the regime for physical protection of nuclear materials worldwide.

However, it is obvious that the problem of combating instances of nuclear and radiological terrorism cannot be resolved solely with measures of physical protection. The current situation creates a need for developing bilateral and multilateral international relations to coordinate measures for preventing and suppressing cases of nuclear and radiological terrorism.

These recommendations represent a systematic synthesis of the results of research on the problem carried out by scientists from the Federal Nuclear Centers (the All-Russia Research Institute of Experimental Physics and the Institute of Technical Physics) and the Institute of Physics and Power Engineering. They are aimed at developing a program for creating an international system to counter and react to cases of nuclear and radiological terrorism. In this regard, the main difficulty in resolving the problem lies in the creation of national systems.

Given all that has been stated above, we believe that it is essential to submit for discussion by this esteemed gathering a number of recommendations and suggestions aimed at the coordination of efforts to resolve this multifaceted problem.

1. The joint development of a dictionary of terminology on nuclear and radiological terrorism. This particularly concerns the conceptual definitions of nuclear and radiological terrorism. In the end, a clear conceptual characterization of this type of terrorism as a sociolegal phenomenon must serve as the basis for the definition of the issues as well as the legal, organizational, and resource-related aspects of the fight against terrorism.

2. The joint development of a list of threats and a basic model of the terrorist in the interests of forming a conceptual framework for the organization of countermeasures. It is proposed that the threats must include a list of goals and motives of cases of terrorism, while the model of a terrorist would include a list of features that would allow him to be classified as nuclear or radiological in orientation.

3. The creation by common efforts of a model for national systems for countering nuclear and radiological terrorism. Its open component would undoubtedly involve interaction and coordination of efforts.

National systems for reacting to threats of terrorism should be created as a unified informational and logical whole along with the system for combating the illegal trade in nuclear materials and radioactive substances. The concept of the national system for combating nuclear and radiological terrorism should include coordinated actions by federal executive branch agencies with functional responsibilities involving the prevention of acts of nuclear terrorism and the detection of and reaction to the illegal trade in nuclear materials and radioactive substances. The system should have a central competent organ to make decisions on assessing the level of the possible threat and to take preventive measures. This will facilitate further coordination of the work of these systems at the international level. At the first stage, this task is particularly urgent for states possessing nuclear weapons technologies.

4. Coordination of efforts by the international community. The international community must coordinate its activities in the fight against the illegal trade in nuclear materials and radioactive substances, since this trade carries with it the danger of nuclear or radiological terrorism.

This task is very complex. In the matter of preventing nuclear smuggling, the current actions of the Office of Physical Protection and Materials Security of the IAEA Department of Safeguards headed by Mrs. A. Nilsson are absolutely insufficient, as are the actions being taken by the international technical working group (ITWG) established at the initiative of the United States and the countries of the European Community. Furthermore, Mrs. Nilsson has frequently mentioned the need for closer coordination of this work.

In particular, Mrs. Nilsson has noted that expanded cooperation between the IAEA and the ITWG has been proposed. Such cooperation could include the establishment of an IAEA database on the illegal trade in nuclear materials and radioactive substances, an analysis of unknown materials that might be produced both in IAEA labs and in the labs of ITWG member states, assistance in identifying nuclear materials and radioactive substances, coordination of efforts to suppress the illegal trade in nuclear materials and radioactive substances, and broad efforts to inform IAEA member states about the results of ITWG activities. IAEA also counts on making use of the services of experts participating in the ITWG. In the opinion of IAEA, cooperation in these areas could be particularly important and worthy of support.

When the need for more coordinated interactions on these issues by national intelligence services and customs agencies is added to the above, it appears that overall coordination of these efforts can hardly be accomplished by IAEA staff alone.

Minatom is working to develop the conceptual model and the basic systems technology foundations for improving the State System for Preventing and Suppressing Illegal Trade in Nuclear Materials and Radioactive Substances. Work is under way to ensure the informational and logical unity of the data structures compiled and used in addressing matters of physical protection, accountability, and control of nuclear materials and in countering nuclear terrorism. In the course of these efforts, basic areas of activity and issues of cooperation among federal executive branch agencies are being defined.

The main goal of improving the State System lies in ensuring comprehensive control over the movement of nuclear materials and radioactive substances, the transport of spent nuclear materials and radioactive substances to temporary storage facilities, and the provision of temporary storage pending decisions on permanent disposition or recycling. To address this need, a unified information center that will be part of the State System is being created under the auspices of Minatom. Existing technologies and communications will be used to the maximum extent for cooperation with federal executive organs.

It should be noted that the illegal trade in nuclear materials and radioactive substances represents a serious threat to the international community. It must be combated jointly, using all cost-effective methods and means.

5. *The formation of an international database on the given problem* (unquestionably, on a voluntary basis). The international exchange of information among the appropriate national agencies regarding questions of the nonproliferation of nuclear weapons and the countering of the illegal trade in nuclear materials and radioactive substances can be conducted on the basis of bilateral and multilateral agreements. In the early stages, it would seem useful to establish cooperation among states possessing nuclear weapons.

It is important to determine the scope of this database, which presupposes the integration of existing information systems of national law enforcement agencies, competent agencies in the area of atomic energy utilization, and power agencies that collect information regarding the struggle against nuclear terrorism and the illegal trade in nuclear materials and radioactive substances. This integration should be defined along the following lines:

• Modernization of the database on the illegal trade in nuclear materials and radioactive substances according to an agreed-upon scale of gradations of such cases;

- Creation of a database on international criminal organizations oriented toward nuclear and radiological terrorism;
- Creation of a warning system regarding preparations for or attempts to carry out acts of nuclear terrorism; and
- Establishment of communications networks including the appropriate contact persons.

6. *National legislation in the area of preventing and suppressing acts of nuclear terrorism.* Such needs to be developed and improved. At the first stage, it would seem useful to develop international legal norms in this area. Voluntary agreement of states to include these norms in the appropriate legislation would facilitate the gradual formation of a legal basis for the international community in the fight against this threat.

7. *Providing law enforcement agencies with the necessary technology.* It is important to add impetus to efforts to resolve the problem of providing law enforcement agencies (customs, border guards, internal affairs agencies, et cetera) with the technology they need to detect nuclear materials and radioactive substances. This is an important problem to resolve mainly in the states possessing nuclear technologies. Minatom is prepared to supply mass-produced instruments and radiation control systems.

8. *Ensuring information security.* This problem cannot be ignored. Specifically, publications on technologies for manufacturing explosive-action nuclear devices and information on locations where weapons and nuclear materials are stored can serve as a stimulus for the threat of nuclear terrorism.

A reduction of the threat of terrorism and the illegal trade in nuclear materials and radioactive substances can be achieved only as a result of a comprehensive set of political, organizational, and technical measures. At the first stage, these measures would include the following:

- Preparatory work aimed at completing the Convention on the Suppression of Nuclear Terrorism (a draft has been submitted to the United Nations by the Russian Federation); and
- Improvement of coordinating measures under UN auspices to combat the illegal trade in nuclear materials and radioactive substances.

EXPLOSIVES TERRORISM

Selected Technologies and Procedures Intended to Restrict Unauthorized Access to Explosives

Bronislav V. Matseevich [*]
Federal State-Owned Unitary Enterprise
Krasnoarmeisk Scientific Research Institute of Mechanization

I represent the Federal State-Owned Unitary Enterprise Red Army Scientific Research Institute of Mechanization [KNIIM], which works on issues connected with the production and use of civilian explosives, as well as questions pertaining to the dismantling and recycling of munitions.

As noted here earlier in another report, explosions and their sources, explosive substances, are the cheapest and most effective weapons of terrorists. The list of explosive substances now includes more than 2500 items, from the simplest mechanical mixtures of saltpeter with diesel fuel, oil, and so forth, to those for which the manufacturing cycle lasts tens or even hundreds of hours. Explosives today are the bread that feeds industry. Suffice it to say that it takes 500-800 grams of explosives to mine one ton of iron ore, 1000-1200 grams for one ton of coal, and so on. The United States currently produces and consumes more than 3 million tons of civilian explosives annually, more than the amount used during the entire course of World War II by all countries on both sides. In the Soviet Union, the figures reached 2.3 million tons, with the portion lost to theft amounting to less than one-millionth of the total production volume. Today, Russia uses more than 600,000 tons annually. This multimillion-ton genie has been let out of the bottle, and there is no way of putting it back. It would seem that getting hold of 0.01 or 0.001 percent of this amount would not present any difficulty. Nevertheless, even these percentages would amount to tons, and furthermore, terrorists' manuals have long included methods for producing simple explosives themselves.

However, we must keep in mind that on the one hand, the simplest explo-

---

[*] Translated from the Russian by Kelly Robbins.

sives are less powerful. On the other hand, using them also requires a detonation intensifier, a so-called intermediate detonator or booster, in the mechanism of the explosive device. Such boosters must be made from powerful explosives such as TNT, hexogen, octogen, and others.

This is necessary because the detonating fuse or blasting cap simply will not detonate the simplest explosives due to their low sensitivity. Therefore, terrorists use powerful explosives such as TNT, hexogen, and plastic explosives in order to achieve a compact and reliably functioning charge.

Thus, the first measures that would help to restrict their uncontrolled spread could be taken right at the factory. I will cite several examples of such possibilities:

1. One such example in Russia is the system for placing serial numbers on cartridges and other products including civilian explosives such as TNT with saltpeter 6ZhV, 79/31, and others.

The mining industry uses about a billion such cartridges annually in 32-, 36-, 45-, 60-, and 90-mm diameters. To limit the uncontrolled spread of these cartridges and related products, each cartridge is assigned an individual number and each blaster must sign for the cartridges he receives, with the numbers being recorded. Thus, if a numbered cartridge is found anywhere, its path can be traced along the entire "producer-consumer" chain, from its manufacture at a plant to a specific mine, warehouse, shift, and individual blaster. All potential sources of losses can therefore be discovered and eliminated.

To put this system into place, 32 special cartridge numbering and packing lines with a capacity of 200 cartridges per minute each were designed, manufactured, and put into operation. All Russian plants producing civilian explosives are equipped with such lines. This is an expensive undertaking, since it entails major costs, detailed accounting, and so forth. But with the introduction of this system in the 1980s, losses and thefts of explosives were reduced to a level of 10^{-6} of total output. Serial numbers are also placed on explosive blocks, boosters, et cetera.

2. A nationwide audit is also conducted regularly regarding the production and consumption of civilian explosives and associated detonating mechanisms. The audit begins with comparing orders from customer firms with inventory logs at the producing plants regarding shipments and utilization of these explosives.

Without a special permit issued on the basis of such an audit, these substances cannot be shipped to customers, stored, or used. The system stipulates strict accountability on the part of producers and consumers. Those providing incorrect information can be held legally responsible, and violations of these rules will lead to loss of licensure by consumers and producers alike.

3. One effective means of limiting the use of powerful explosives in mining is the shift to ammonia nitrate emulsion civilian explosives, which are manufactured at the place of use. This has become a basic method worldwide over the

past decade and should remain so in coming years. Reducing shipment distances by tens of times and shifting to less sensitive explosives significantly limit the base for terrorism. For this purpose, the majority of mining enterprises use domestic- and foreign-designed stationary units for manufacturing explosives.

For this same purpose, Russia also manufactures four types of mixer-loader vehicles, one of which is the so-called factory on wheels, a vehicle in which all basic explosive manufacturing operations are carried out at the blast site during the charge loading process.

4. We attach extraordinary importance to current efforts to add markers or taggants to detect various types of plastic explosives, which are very difficult to detect during shipment inspections.

5. For shipments in dangerous regions, a vehicle has been designed with armored sides to protect against gunfire. The vehicle also has fire-extinguishing features.

6. At present, special attention is being devoted in Russia to matters regarding the circulation of military explosives obtained during the dismantling of decommissioned and obsolete munitions. To this end, a number of efforts have been and continue to be carried out in the Russian Federation based on the fundamental principle that the extraction of high-energy materials from munitions and their reprocessing into civilian explosives must be conducted at special enterprises using special equipment. In this process, powerful military explosives are turned into less sensitive materials by being mixed with additives.

For this purpose, a number of industrial plants and arsenals of the Ministry of Defense have been outfitted with special equipment based on methods developed by Russian specialists. One of these methods is the fundamentally new method of washing TNT-containing explosives with hot organic liquids, for example, paraffin. This causes a significant "phlegmatization" of the resulting recycled explosives, increases the safety of the recycling process, and reduces the sensitivity of the recycled substances. The safety and reliability of the process on the whole has made it possible to create a number of mobile self-powered units mounted in large shipping containers.

An example of such a unit is the modular-container complex for extracting TNT from 76–152-mm artillery shells and recovering TNT fragments at munitions storage facilities. The module consists of three or four 20-foot shipping containers, which can be moved by any means of transport and assembled in the course of 48 working hours. It runs on electricity either by connecting to the local power system or on a 100-kW diesel generator. The TNT output of the complex is 120 kg per hour.

Another example is the modular-container complex for dismantling land mines. It is mounted in three standard 20-foot 1SS or UUK-20 containers. Its TNT output is 240 kg per hour, and from 12 to 20 mines can be processed at once. It can be set up in 40 hours.

The existence of such equipment and its deployment at munitions storage sites facilitate the additional establishment not only of production controls, but also of controls on the part of the army.

Stationary units have also been developed and put into use for processing munitions with powerful mixed smeltable explosives. One example is a complex for dismantling large munitions, for example, aerial bombs weighing from 250 kg to 9 tons each. The complex has attained product output of up to 500 kg per hour. For this same reason, another complex has been built to dismantle large munitions filled with mixed explosives (for example, torpedo warheads, marine mines, missiles, depth charges, etc.).

The recycling process in all these examples is directly tied to the powerful desensitization of these explosives; that is, it requires 400 grams to 1 kg of powerful boosters to detonate them. Therefore, these substances become ill suited for use in terrorist acts.

To involve specialists and coordinate work in this field, five conferences have been held in the past eight years. Three of the conferences were international, and all of them had representatives from more than 100 organizations.

7. The comprehensive work carried out by KNIIM and a number of Russian organizations has shown the possibility of extracting nonfusible explosives from munitions by the method of hydrocutting and washing with a high-pressure stream of water. Experiments have been done on carrying out this process at pressures ranging from 100 to several thousand atmospheres. On the whole, the setup consists of a pumping unit, the washing unit itself, and a water purification system.

We have drawn some important conclusions regarding the safety of this process. They indicate that there exists a rather broad range of technological parameters for this process, within which hydrocutting and hydrowashing are advantageous for practically all types of powerful high explosives. This also makes possible the radical application of this process in various modified forms for the destruction of explosive packages and various terrorist-produced items in mobile units.

On the whole, we feel that applying various methods and procedures for limiting the uncontrolled spread of powerful explosives by various means—design related, substance compounding related, organizational, technological, and legislative—is an effective though far from comprehensive way of resolving the common problem. Therefore, the domestic policy of high-tech countries must support firms that are working to ensure accountability regarding explosives and related products, organizing product markings that would identify the manufacturer, mothballing explosive capacities in mine blasting zones, and creating less sensitive explosive substances and rapid, lightweight detectors for both explosives and narcotics. Other more reliable methods remain to be created.

Terrorism: Explosives Threat

Ronald L. Simmons
Naval Surface Warfare Center

INTRODUCTION

Material presented at this workshop is based on two previous National Research Council (NRC) and National Academy of Sciences (NAS) committee studies on bombings. The first study was devoted to explosive materials (excluding smokeless and black powders) in 1997, prompted by two mass bombings: the World Trade Center and the Oklahoma City Federal Building.[1] The second study, released in 1998, was devoted specifically to smokeless and black powder, which are commonly used in pipe bombs and small improvised explosive devices.[2] Further insight into terrorist attacks abroad has been provided by the Bremer Commission report, which was issued in 2000.[3]

Description of Explosive Threat

While it is recognized that the attacks of September 11, 2001, are attributed to terrorists, this paper is limited to a discussion of threats from explosives.

Within the United States. The explosive threat by terrorist groups has been rare within the United States. There have been only two bombings in the country that can be attributed to terrorist groups—the mass bombings referred to above. The first targeted the World Trade Center in New York City on February 26, 1993, leaving 6 people dead and approximately 700 injured. The terrorist group was Muslim extremists, and the explosive used was homemade nitrated urea. The amount of explosive involved is unknown but is believed to have been at least 100 kg.

The second mass bombing in the United States occurred at the Oklahoma City Federal Building on April 19, 1995, and produced 168 fatalities and a large number of injuries. This action has been attributed to a small group of domestic terrorists (fewer than four individuals) who used approximately 2200 kg of home-made ammonium nitrate fuel oil (ANFO) explosive.

On July 20, 1996, during the summer Olympic Games, an individual planted a pipe bomb (actually three bombs taped together) in Centennial Park, Atlanta, Georgia. Although the bomb was discovered, it was inadvertently detonated before it could be disarmed. There was one fatality—resulting from a heart attack, not directly from the explosion, and approximately 110 injuries. This bombing has not been attributed to a terrorist group. The amount of explosive involved is estimated to be about 1 kg.

Outside the United States. All known bombings occurring outside the United States and directed against U.S. citizens have been by terrorist groups. The most recent case was the attack against the *USS Cole* in the Port of Aden, Yemen, on October 12, 2000. There were 17 fatalities and approximately 36 injured. It is believed the attack was carried out by a terrorist group of Muslims using approximately 300 kg of Comp C4 high explosive.

Previous bombings outside the United States include the Planet Hollywood restaurant in Cape Town, South Africa, on August 25, 1998, where there were 2 fatalities and 25 injured. The bombing has also been tentatively attributed to a Muslim group of terrorists. The amount of explosive used is unknown but estimated to be around 50 kg.

On August 7, 1998, there were two almost simultaneous explosions at the U.S. Embassies in Nairobi, Kenya, and Dar Es Salaam, Tanzania. Both have been tied to Muslim terrorist groups. The total number of fatalities in the two Embassy bombings has been estimated to be 224, with more than 4600 injured. The amount and nature of the explosives used are unknown but believed to have been at least 100 kg.

Earlier notable mass bombings against U.S. citizens abroad include the following:

• On December 21, 1988, an explosion destroyed PanAm Flight 103 over Lockerbie, Scotland, killing 270 as a result of the explosion of a bomb containing less than a kilogram of high explosive believed to be Semtex. The incident has been attributed to a terrorist Muslim group.

• On October 23, 1983, an explosion demolished the U.S. Marines barracks in Beirut, Lebanon, killing approximately 240. The explosion was believed to have been caused by compressed flammable gas, not high explosives. The incident was attributed to a terrorist Muslim group.

• On April 18, 1983, there was an explosion at the U.S. Embassy in Beirut,

Lebanon, killing 63. This incident, like the previous terrorist incidents, was attributed to a terrorist Muslim group.

BOMBINGS: DESCRIPTION

Nature of Explosives Used. Aside from the bombings outside the United States, and neglecting the two mass bombings at the World Trade Center and Oklahoma City as aberrations, according to statistics kept by the Bureau of Alcohol, Tobacco, and Firearms (ATF) and the Federal Bureau of Investigation (FBI), the explosive materials used in bombings in the United States (in the decade before 1997) could be defined or categorized as follows:

- 32 percent of the bombings used smokeless or black powder;
- 29 percent used simple chemical mixtures (defined as simple gas-producing chemicals confined in a container capable of withstanding some pressure before bursting);
- 16 percent were commercial fireworks or pyrotechnic compositions similar to those used in fireworks;
- 3 percent were high explosives or ammonium nitrate (AN) blasting agents;
- 1 percent were improvised explosive mixtures;
- 14 percent could not be identified; and
- the remaining 5 percent were not reported.

The bombs that were either homemade or of undetermined origin totaled 49 percent, while 33 percent were smokeless, black powder, high explosives, or AN blasting agents. The remaining 16 percent used fireworks or similar pyrotechnic mixtures (other than black powder).

There are several likely sources of explosives used in illegal bombings. They can be made from commonly available chemicals, meaning that a homemade bomb could be derived from a number of possible chemicals. The explosives could also be bought on the open market, which means they most likely will be commercial explosives used for legal purposes such as mining. In addition, the materials could be stolen from either commercial or military sources, provided by a friend (or friendly country), or obtained from materials removed from demilitarized warheads or other munitions.

Nature of Bombings. Bombings in the United States can generally be described as a large number of small bombs causing little damage, punctuated by infrequent large-scale bombings causing serious consequences and galvanizing public concern. With the exception of the two large bombings (World Trade Center and Oklahoma City), bombings in the United States have been largely confined to attacks on individuals. Exceptions are churches, public places, abortion clinics, and transportation (aircraft). The amount of explosive contained in a bomb is small, usually less than 1 kg. Alhough the total number of these small bombings (usually referred to as pipe bombs) averages about 2000 per year, most are of the nuisance-type firecracker-in-a-mailbox variety. The number of "significant" bombings (defined as capable of causing serious injury, death, or more than $1,000 worth of damage) averages about 300 per year, resulting in about 10 fatalities per year. Of these fatalities, 60 percent are the bomb makers themselves.

Two federal agencies gather statistics on bombings—the Treasury Department through the ATF and the Justice Department through the FBI. Each maintains separate statistics by means of distributing separate reporting forms to local law enforcement agencies, who in turn fill out the forms on a voluntary basis. Discrepancies exist between the two sources of information, and the previous NRC-NAS committee studies in 1997 and 1998 recommended better coordination between the two agencies.

Bomb Makers. In a typical year (excluding the two large-scale bombings), in 76% of the cases where the bomb maker could be identified, the perpetrators were juveniles. For bombs containing simple chemical mixtures, juveniles were implicated in 92% of the cases. For bombs containing high explosives, 41% were made by juveniles, indicating that the explosives were most likely stolen. The remaining perpetrators were for the most part acquaintances, neighbors, and domestic partners.

Commercial Explosives. The annual production of high explosives (and ammonium nitrate) made for legal commercial uses is estimated to be 3×10^9 kg. In addition, another 10×10^6 kg of smokeless and black powder and 5×10^6 kg of energetic chemicals and fuels are produced in the United States. By comparison, the amount used in illegal bombings is extremely small, and policy measures to address this illegal use impinge on the substantially larger legitimate use of these materials in everyday commerce. The disruptive effect on this everyday commerce would have to be addressed.

THREAT PREVENTION

To control the illegal use of explosives and reduce (or prevent) the threat, the two previous NRC-NAS committee studies focused on four areas:

1. Detecting bombs or explosives and preventing explosions;
2. Identifying the source of the explosives to prosecute offenders and discourage other potential bomb makers;
3. Employing additives to render explosives or explosive precursors inert; and

4. Imposing stricter regulatory controls on explosives and explosive precursors to make it more difficult to obtain or make illegal explosives.

Detection. Likely scenarios for detecting explosives/bombs include the following:

1. *Portal scenario, in which people and packages pass through a well-monitored checkpoint.* In such a case, the bomb must be detected with a high degree of reliability and with a very low false alarm rate. Also, such portal monitoring strongly discourages would-be bomb makers, since they know that it will be virtually impossible to pass through undetected.

2. *Suspicious package scenario, in which a suspicious package is discovered that may or may not contain a bomb.* The problem here is to quickly detect whether or not a bomb is present.

3. *Bomb threat scenario, in which there is reason to believe a bomb exists somewhere within a large expanse.* This problem is the most difficult largely due to the very short time and very large expanse in which the bomb must be found before it is likely to explode.

Bombs and explosives can be detected by exploiting properties of both the explosive and the container. In the case of explosives that do not detonate, they must be packaged in a container that acts as a pressure vessel, rupturing only after a certain pressure has been developed. Such containers are usually heavy-wall metal pipes, which may be covered with fragmenting materials such as nails and tacks. Thus, the container provides certain characteristics that make it susceptible to detection.

Current x-ray systems can detect bombs at a portal, entryway, or passageway, but they are not suitable for large numbers of packages, large-area searches, or in situations where the location of the bomb is unknown.

Canines. Some explosives—for example, nitroglycerin dynamites—contain volatile components that are detectable by dogs. These volatile components represent a wide bouquet of odors, and it is not known specifically what it is that the dogs sniff. Canines are most successful and reliable in detecting explosive materials, according to the U.S. Secret Service. Both canine and human search is the only viable means of conducting large-area searches for hidden bombs. Unfortunately, circumstances exist in which there is chemical interference with canine detection, and the interference is not well understood.

Chemical Markers. It has been noted that chemical markers could assist in the detection of explosives or bombs, especially in large-area searches, suspicious packages, and rapid and routine screening of large numbers of packages, and they would enhance canine sniffing capability.

Chemical markers have been found to be very effective in plastic and sheet explosives that detonate in small diameters and thicknesses. Such explosives are CompC4 and Semtex. In 1995, the International Civil Aviation Organization (ICAO) adopted 2,3-dimethyl-2,3-dinitrobutane (DMNB) for these plastic and sheet explosives. DMNB has a low vapor pressure and, thus, a reasonably long shelf life, yet it has sufficient vapor pressure to allow reliable detection. At 25°C, DMNB has a vapor pressure of 2.1×10^{-3} torr, while the solid explosive RDX has a vapor pressure of 1.4×10^{-9} torr, and another solid explosive pentaerythritol tetranitrate (PETN) has a vapor pressure of 3.8×10^{-10} torr. By comparison, nitroglycerin (NG) has a vapor pressure of 2.3×10^{-4} torr. Thus, DMNB is much more easily detected than the neat explosive itself. Other chemical markers were evaluated (e.g., ethylene glycol dinitrate [EGDN] and ortho- and para-mononitrotoluene), but they were rejected in favor of DMNB because of their higher volatility and hence shorter shelf life.

DMNB is used at a concentration of 1.0% and costs about $0.40 per pound. Since Comp C4 costs between $11 and $20 per pound, the addition of DMNB does not add substantially to the cost of manufacture. On the other hand, the addition of DMNB to ammonium nitrate (which costs about $0.10 per pound) increases the cost of AN about 20%, not to mention the problems resulting from wide distribution of the chemical marker in the environment and the consequent false alarm rate. The use of AN blasting agents is several orders of magnitude greater than for plastic and sheet explosives.

The use of DMNB or a similar chemical marker in smokeless and black powder is not feasible at this time because of concerns of chemical compatibility, thermal stability, shelf life, and growing ineffectiveness through widespread usage. The legal use of millions of pounds of chemically marked smokeless and black powder would contaminate the environment and with time increase the false positive detection rate. Research has been recommended by the National Academy of Sciences to find suitable chemical markers in the event that their use in smokeless and black powder is warranted by increased threat levels.

ID Tagging. Unfortunately, more than 90 percent of the deaths and 80 percent of the injuries from bombs occur in locations with no security screening—that is, no portal screening exists. Fortunately today, forensic evidence from partially consumed explosives at the bomb scene can usually permit identification not only of the type of explosive, but also of the manufacturer of that explosive. However, it is impossible to determine details such as the date of manufacture and/or lot number. Existing databases of information on smokeless and black powder are incomplete, although both the ATF and the FBI have about 100 different types and grades of these powders in their databases.

Taggants added to explosive powders could assist a bombing investigation. The ideal taggant would have the following characteristics:

- No real or perceived health risks;
- Wide forensic applicability for law enforcement;
- No physical and chemical incompatibility with smokeless or black powder;
- No adverse impact on the environment;
- Low cost to commercial products;
- No viable countermeasures; and
- Unique information that is easy to read.

No successful taggant system has been demonstrated to date. All have inherent limitations. The current record-keeping system does not permit tracing specific lots or batches of explosive materials from the manufacturer through the complex distribution system to the final retailer and buyer. Unfortunately, increased record keeping may increase the number of lawsuits against the manufacturers of legal explosives and related industries. At this time, the costs outweigh implementation of taggants, and both NRC committees that studied this problem have recommended more research into taggants, in the event that the threat level increases.

Rendering the Explosive Inert. Ideally, an inerting substance is capable of preventing an explosion when intimately mixed with other materials chosen to provide the correct reaction stoichiometry. For example, it may be possible to mix substance "A" with substance "B" to prevent the use of "B" as an explosive. It must also prevent detonation in large diameters even when initiated by a large explosive booster.

In a 1968 U.S. patent, S.J. Porter[4] claimed that 10 percent ammonium phosphate added to fertilizer-grade AN will produce a non-detonatable mixture when used in ANFO mixtures. Following the 1995 Oklahoma City bombing, tests showed that non-detonatable Porter mixtures would actually detonate in charges where the diameter was ≥150 cm or when the charge weight was ≥36 kg. Tests also showed that the dilution of AN with 20 percent limestone does *not* achieve the desired inerting.

It was concluded that although there are a large number of common chemicals that could be used in bombings, the most likely material is AN. Despite much research in the United States and abroad, no practical method for inerting AN has yet been found. Furthermore, no widely accepted test exists for determining a priori the detonatability of a bulk, improvised AN explosive, such as the one used in the Oklahoma City bombing.

Limiting Access to Explosives. A very large number of chemicals can be used to make effective bombs. These are not listed explicitly as explosive materials, nor are they regulated by federal law. Some of these chemicals are molecular explosives, which can be used neat, or in mixtures with other reactive materials, or are non-explosive compounds (e.g., oxidizers and fuels), which can be combined to produce explosive compositions. For explosive purposes, these are known as precursors. Although the list of possibilities can be quite long, a short list of most likely precursors for explosive use is as follows:

Explosive Chemicals
Ammonium nitrate
Nitromethane

Oxidizers
Sodium nitrate
Potassium nitrate
Sodium chlorate
Potassium chlorate
Potassium perchlorate
Ammonium perchlorate

Reactant Chemicals
Nitric acid (concentrated)
Hydrogen peroxide (concentrated)
Urea

Inert precursors that can be reacted to produce explosives in one or two steps include acetone, ammonia, cellulose, glycerin, ethylene glycol, and hexamine.

It is recognized that given the proper expertise and equipment, explosive compounds can be synthesized from many starting materials, including many not listed above.[5]

SUMMARY

Both previous NRC committees that studied the explosive threat problem came to the following conclusions:

• Compared to many countries, the United States has relatively lax federal controls on the purchase of explosive materials.
• Many explosives used in bombings are stolen.
• Effective bombs can be made from readily available chemicals.
• It is not feasible to control all possible chemical precursors.
• Criminal access to explosives can be made more difficult through legislative actions.
• It is not realistic to expect to prevent or deter all illegal bombings.
• A more realistic goal is to make it more difficult for would-be bomb makers to operate and increase the chances that they will be caught.
• The current level of threat does not warrant additional controls.
• A major escalation of terrorism might merit emergency controls as a suitable response.
• At a lower level of threat, the use of such controls would have a severely disruptive effect on legitimate commercial industries and would be costly.
• Impacted industries include chemicals, explosives, and mining.

- Bomb makers have demonstrated that they can change tactics in response to shifts in controls or availability of chemical precursors.
- The level of sophistication of bomb makers will likely increase.

U.S. policy makers determine what constitutes a specific level of threat. Basic to a workable U.S. national strategy regarding the threat from the illegal use of explosives, smokeless powder, and black powder is the importance of maintaining a flexible approach to detection markers, identification taggants, and the regulation of explosives and chemical precursors.

DISCLAIMER

Although the author is employed by the U.S. Navy at the Naval Surface Warfare Center, Indian Head, Maryland, participation in this workshop is not under the auspices of the U.S. Navy. The material presented in this workshop is based on the author's experience in industry and with the National Academy of Sciences and does not reflect official Navy policy.

NOTES

1. Committee on Marking, Rendering Inert, and Licensing of Explosive Materials, National Research Council. 1998. Containing the Threat from Illegal Bombings. Washington, D.C.: National Academy Press.

2. Committee on Smokeless and Black Powder, National Research Council. 1998. Black and Smokeless Powders—Technologies for Finding Bombs and the Bomb Makers. Washington, D.C.: National Academy Press.

3. National Commission on Terrorism (established by Congress in October 1998), Ambassador L. Paul Bremer III, Chairman. 2000. Countering the Changing Threat of International Terrorism. Available on line at: http://www.terrorism.com/documents/bremercommission/index.shtml.

4. Porter, S.J. 1968. Method of Desensitizing Fertilizer Grade Ammonium Nitrate and the Product Obtained. U.S. Patent 3,366,468.

5. Fedoroff, B.T., ed. 1960-1983. Encyclopedia of Explosives and Related Items. Dover, N.J.: Picatinny Arsenal. Vols. 1-10; Urbanski, T.1964. Chemistry and Technology of Explosives. New York: Pergamon Press, Vols. 1-3; Davis, T.L. 1943. The Chemistry of Powder and Explosives. Hollywood, Calif.: Angriff Press.

CYBERTERRORISM

Computer Terrorism and
Internet Security Issues

Valery A. Vasenin and Aleksei V. Galatenko [*]
Center for Telecommunications and Internet Technologies
M. V. Lomonosov Moscow State University

INTRODUCTION

The word "terrorism" is derived from the Latin word *terror* (i.e., fear or horror). It is not a new phenomenon, but for individual countries and the world community the scale and significance of the acts now classified as terrorism have increased considerably in recent years. This fact gives special meaning to the study of the roots (causes) of this phenomenon, as well as of the technologies by which it is carried out and the methods used to do so. Also of urgent importance is the task of creating mechanisms and building tools to effectively counter this type of act.

Terrorism can be defined as the aggregate of illegal acts involving persecution, threats of violence, murder, distortion of objective information, and a number of other acts that facilitate the sowing of fear and tension in society for the purpose of gaining advantages (influence) in connection with the resolution of political, economic, or social issues.

The methodology, strategy, means of implementation, and mechanisms used by criminals to commit terrorist acts vary. Some of them are more traditional and involve the use of weapons (knives or firearms), radio, and television; others are high-tech and utilize the latest advances in science and technology. Without going into the use of various mechanisms, means, and methods—including computers—to carry out terrorist acts, let us examine those that actively affect computer systems and networks.

---

[*] Translated from the Russian by Rita Kit.

Two factors have helped to create a new communications and information environment that is potentially suitable for the commission of terrorist acts. The first is the development of computer networks (especially those using packet communications technology) and information systems, ranging from the agency and corporation level to the national and even transnational level. The second involves the processes of globalization, integration, and convergence that objectively accompanied that evolution in the late twentieth century.

What are the distinctive characteristics of this new communications and information environment? What possible areas could criminals exploit, and what are the potential damages? Let us consider some individual objectives and focuses.

1. Destruction of the infrastructure of a network at the corporate, national, or transnational level by disabling its control system or individual subsystems—if a network supports tasks of a strategic nature, the threat of such destruction could be used as blackmail, and the destruction itself could open the door to criminal acts involving information on the network (disruption of the confidentiality and noncontradictory nature of the information, not to mention its possible destruction or restriction of access to the information);

2. Unauthorized (illegal) access to network information that is protected by law and is confidential in nature or highly secret, for purposes of blackmail; and

3. Intentional distortion of information in Internet-based mass media for purposes of discrediting, inadequately reflecting reality, and so forth.

Criminals might use the following potential strategies of action to achieve the aforementioned objectives separately or in various combinations: the physical seizure of a network control center, penetration of it by accessing control systems, the traditional use of computer software inserts and viruses by malicious individuals, the usurpation of superuser rights, et cetera.

The material damages from malicious individuals' actions in each of these cases may involve the cost of restoring network control or repairing damage stemming from destructive acts during the violation, or damages involving possible losses from unauthorized use of information that is highly secret or from distortion of information. Moreover, distortion of information in one form or another is demoralizing to the owner of the network infrastructure as well as to the owner of the distorted information resources that it supports.

The Internet's present capabilities do not allow the total prevention of its use for terrorist purposes in the areas described above. The reasons are not only and not even largely technological in nature (i.e., involving the TCP/IP stack based on IP v. 4 [20-30 years have passed since its inception in 1973-1983, whereas the life span of network infrastructure is 15-20 years]), but instead are issues of a legislative and administrative nature.[1]

Given these factors, it is essential to make efforts in all areas (and at all levels) and accordingly take measures and create mechanisms that can be used to solve problems on each of the aforementioned levels.

THE INTERNET, ILLEGAL ACTS, AND TERRORISM

The development of the Internet as a transnational network infrastructure has given rise to a number of very complex problems. In the early 1970s, when the Internet's protocol base was taking shape, it was hard to imagine that eventually this "Network of Networks" would extend across more than 170 countries around the world and link approximately 100 million computers, all the while continuing to expand rapidly.[2] Many of today's needs were not envisioned in the traditional stack of Internet protocols. For these reasons today's agenda contains urgent issues relating to the exhaustion of available addresses, address mobility, and the ability of routers to prevent congestion in trunk channels and also provide the necessary speed of network packet processing. There are also problems with transmission quality for multimedia systems and with the security of information resources. The reason for these problems is that in the early 1980s, when the stack of Internet protocols became the network's technical foundation, it was hard to predict the future of the newly emerged network or envision its impact on every aspect of society. For these reasons, the implementation of mechanisms to provide information security and to protect data and network infrastructure were not that urgent. Today, concerns about information protection are not academic on the Internet, which is home to an enormous quantity of information, including information that is confidential or secret and protected by law. Access to it is a violation of the rights of an individual, organization, or agency. Nowadays we are increasingly seeing how network technologies are being used for criminal purposes, including terrorism.

Let us illustrate this point with a number of examples. Last year, a large number of computers around the world were infected by the "I Love You" virus (http://www.isec.ru.news). According to Federal Bureau of Investigation (FBI) estimates, total damages were in the range of $10 billion.

A program developer for Japan's naval headquarters turned out to be a member of the religious sect Aum Shinrikyo, which is known for acts of terrorism. The programs are now being audited. According to documents discovered during a search of the sect's headquarters, Aum Shinrikyo members could control many computers within the military establishment (www.provoslavie.ru.news/04-17/09.htm).

According to Reuters reports, in February 1999 a hacker group seized control of a British communications satellite (http://inroad.kiev.ua/prob/terror.htm).

Another group of hackers called the "Legion of the Underground" has declared cyberwar on China and Iraq (http://inroad.kievua/prob/terror.htm). Their reason is the execution of two Chinese hackers accused of financial fraud and Iraq's manufacturing of weapons of mass destruction. The group has declared that it intends to wage war until the enemy's computing resources are completely destroyed.

According to FBI reports, attempts have even been made to use computer networks to physically eliminate individuals. One criminal attempted to get rid of a witness who had consented to testify against him in court. The offender gained access to a hospital's computer network and changed the dosage of a medication to a lethal level (http://www.isec.ru.news).

Unfortunately, this list represents only a small selection from the many examples that illustrate the potential threat from illegal terrorist acts utilizing modern network technologies.

THE RUSSIAN SEGMENT OF THE INTERNET

Before we proceed to outline our views on ways of preventing or interdicting use of the Internet for terrorist purposes, let us say a few words about the current state of the Russian segment of the Internet, its place within the Internet as a whole, and potential opportunities for its use for purposes of terrorism.

According to a study on the Russian segment of the Internet conducted by the M. V. Lomonosov Moscow State University's Center for Telecommunications and Internet Technologies, the primary (integral) characteristics of its status as of mid-2001 include the following:

• The total number of hosts is approximately 400,000, of which the commercial sector accounts for 70% and scientific and educational institutions 30 percent.

• The Russian segment of the Internet is served by more than 250 Internet service providers (ISPs).

• Growth of channel capacity on the global Internet since 1996 has been exponential.

• The rates and trends of development of trunk carrying capacity in Russia are in line with those in other parts of the world.

Thus, it may be said that the Russian segment of the Internet has already completed its formative stage. The Russian Internet has all the attributes of analogous national segments abroad necessary for self-development, primary among them being a fairly large number of hosts; the existence of a national trunk infrastructure based on IP-exchanges in Moscow, St. Petersburg, and other regions that is comparable in size to average European external capacity into the global Internet; and a balance between incoming and outgoing traffic as the first sign of good information content, including content not in the Russian language.

Mechanisms of regulation (in particular self-regulation) that are common practice on the Internet worldwide have begun to be implemented within the Russian Internet, though not to a sufficient extent.

Thus, the Russian Internet has become a factor that actively affects all aspects of the country's economy, extending not only to the high-tech sectors, education and industry, but also to business, medicine, the media, leisure, and a number of other areas. This Internet's position in Russia makes it a potential arena for the commission of illegal acts, including acts of terrorism.

Potential targets of such acts with major consequences could be facilities of strategic importance in the country's defense system, as well as economic complexes at the national scale, for example, transportation systems or electric power grids. The facts indicate that the number of illegal acts directed against facilities inside Russia and from Russia against facilities outside its borders is increasing in proportion to the growth and development of the Russian segment of the Internet. An example of such an act could be actions by pro-Chechen individuals intending to distort information on the Internet regarding the antiterrorist operation in Chechnya.

GENERAL FORMULATION OF THE PROBLEM
AND POSSIBLE SOLUTIONS

Accepting the potential objectives outlined above and the methods of terrorist acts using modern network technologies, one could view the following considerations as a foundation upon which to build general approaches to formulating goals for preventing, interdicting in a timely manner, or eliminating the effects of such actions.

• Actions that pursue (i.e., are aimed at achieving) goals 1 and 2 outlined above, focusing on destruction of the network infrastructure and unauthorized access to confidential information with a high level of classification, are malicious acts that are traditionally viewed through violator models and attack models. These models are an essential prerequisite for the development of a system (program of action) for any organization, company, or corporation that is building (developing) an information security policy in networks under its control.

• Actions that pursue objective 3—"the possibility of intentional distortion of information in Internet-based mass media"—can be divided into two categories:

1. Those stemming from the unauthorized and illegal use of rights to the use of an information resource; and

2. Those resulting from the creation of an alternative information source on general-access networks.

The methodology for preventing and responding effectively to actions in the first category boils down to the traditional means of maintaining information security in networks and is supported by measures at all levels of implementation. The methodology for preventing actions that fall in the second category is less traditional and relies mainly on the legislative and administrative level of information security. However, in terms of countermeasures it also correlates with the assessment (evaluation) of the quality and functionality of resources presented on the Internet. This is a separate and complex issue for which no effective solution as yet exists anywhere in the world.

To sum up the above, one may conclude that the difference between approaches to prevention of and response to actions of a terrorist nature and other illegal and unauthorized actions on the Internet rests largely in the higher level of demands and losses from this type of malicious action.

Let us term actions intended to prevent and effectively interdict terrorist acts using network technologies "ATIS," for antiterrorist information security, in order to differentiate it from traditional IS (information security) in a network, whenever the need for such differentiation arises.

Note that here and subsequently, we are referring to problems of information security (in antiterrorist terms as well) in a narrow sense (i.e., only as it applies to network infrastructure [the network transmission medium, technologies, informational and computational resources, et cetera]). Hence the general definition of ATIS and the goal of acting to prevent and effectively respond to terrorist acts in the network environment and/or through use of information technologies may be formulated as follows: ATIS is the aggregate of mechanisms, tools, methods, measures, and activities that make it possible to prevent; detect; and, in the event of detection, effectively respond to actions intended to

- Destroy network infrastructure by disabling control systems;
- Gain unauthorized access to information protected by law and confidential or highly classified in nature; and
- Create intentional distortion of information presented in general-access networks.

The preceding definition reflects the current state of problems in the area of ATIS. It does not claim nor can it claim to be universal, all-encompassing, or complete in its description of possible objectives, areas of malicious action, et cetera. These are defined by the status of development of computer, communications, information technologies, and hosting services, which are developing very dynamically.

Note that the fundamental conceptual difference between this definition and the traditional definition of IS rests on the lack of references to reasons (premises) of nonmalicious (unintentional) actions not necessarily caused (or taken) by a human being. Those actions, including natural phenomena, should definitely be taken into account when dealing with IS issues.

This definition indicates that at its root, the stated goal of providing ATIS boils down, in methodological terms, to the similar stated goal of providing IS in the network infrastructure, in which normally the following types of threats are identified:

• A threat to confidential information (protection from unauthorized viewing);

• A threat to the integrity of information (the timeliness and non-contradictory nature of information, as well as protection against destruction and unauthorized changes); and

• A threat to information access (the ability to obtain information within an acceptable amount of time).

The main components of efforts to ensure information security are as follows:

1. Actions to eliminate opportunities to carry out an attack, and thereby prevent damage; and
2. Measures to reduce possible damage by

• Reducing the amount of information and resources accessible to a malicious individual in the event of an attack, and restoration of systems following an attack;

• Ensuring early detection of any attack on a system; and

• Implementing measures capable of detecting the perpetrator following an attack.

The order of the areas of effort listed above reflects their urgency in terms of protecting users' interests and reducing damages from perpetrators' actions.

The multifaceted nature of this goal of ensuring information security, including antiterrorist information security, defines several areas (or levels), with coordinated actions in each of them capable of supporting a comprehensive solution. These include the legislative, administrative, operational, and programming and hardware levels.[4]

LEGISLATIVE, ADMINISTRATIVE, AND OPERATIONAL LEVELS

The legislative level is fundamental to the creation of a well-designed system of measures to ensure IS at all the other levels, because it determines the following:

• Measures of direct legislative action that allow the categorization of violations and violators and also create a negative attitude in society toward IS violators; and

• Measures aimed at coordinating and facilitating better education in the field of IS, and developing and disseminating methods of ensuring IS.

With regard to Russia, among the measures taken in our country in the first category are Chapter 28, "Crimes in the Area of Computer Information," found in Section IX of the latest edition of the Russian Federation Criminal Code, as well as the law "On Information, Provision of Information Services, and Protection of Information" and a number of other laws that are currently under development ("On the Right to Information," "On Commercial Secrecy," "On Personal Data," and "On Electronic Digital Signatures").

The second group of legislative and regulatory acts includes documents that regulate licensing and certification in the realm of IS (issued by the FAPSI [Federal Government Communication and Information Agency] and the Russian Federation Presidential State Committee on Technology) and ministry and agency regulations (guidelines from the State Committee on Technology regarding protection classes for computer hardware and automated systems, regarding internetwork firewalls, et cetera).

However, it should be noted that thus far, only the initial steps have been taken toward bringing this level into compliance with the requirements of today's Internet and its role in society and the state. We have repeatedly discussed these issues at Moscow State University roundtables devoted to information security issues. One such standing roundtable discussion group was established at the initiative of M.V. Lomonosov Moscow State University with support from the Russian Security Council. It has been active for more than a year now, with participation in its sessions by scientists, technical specialists from various scientific fields, and of course representatives of the humanities.

We will not go into this in greater detail. Some issues of legislative support for information security have been discussed previously. We would simply like to focus attention once again on the importance of coordinating these measures with international practices and on the need to bring Russian standards and certification regulations into line with the international level of information technologies. The former stems from the necessity of introducing means of IS in order to interact with partners from abroad. The latter is dictated by the de facto dominance of foreign-made hardware and programs in Russian network infrastructure.

At this point in time, it must be acknowledged that not only have issues of international legal regulation not been resolved, they are not even under consideration. This is true not only in terms of preventing use of the Internet for terrorist purposes, but also with regard to broader issues of traditional illegal activities with a direct bearing on ATIS. We find that the international legal aspects of the Internet are lagging behind its infrastructure and technical capacities.

Security policy is a system of measures taken by the management of an organization or network at the administrative level. This system of measures represents the aggregate of administrative decisions aimed at protecting both information and the network infrastructure that supports it. Security policy defines an organization's strategy in this area and is based on an analysis of risks, which are systematized and acknowledged as real for the information system of the organization (or network).

Implementation of a security policy may be divided into two groups, namely, upper- and lower-level measures. The upper level includes risk management, coordination of efforts, strategic planning, and monitoring of the implementation of information security measures. The lower level is where monitoring of specific security services occurs.

The administrative level, or the level at which security policy is developed and monitored, is very important. Coordination of efforts on that level makes it possible to unify approaches and actions by specific implementers to prevent, detect, and interdict in a timely manner violations of IS in general and ATIS in particular and to reduce (minimize) damage from them. As demonstrated by the example of the Aum Shinrikyo programmer cited previously, methods of protection must be tested. There is virtually no one to "watch the watchers," and if a watcher allows terrorists into a facility, the security system is useless. A code audit and certification of the entire complex of measures at the operations level by reliable organizations proves to be very important.

Based on my own experience as a network service provider in the Russian segment of the Internet, I would like to direct your attention to a number of issues that are inherent to this level. Unfortunately, despite the existing (although overly general) standards for the purpose of developing security policy, in practice a majority of organizations that have fairly large IP networks do not adhere to those standards. Furthermore, the legislative level does not contain materials that would stimulate activity at the appropriate administrative level (by making this work mandatory). There is a lack of model standards in this area for various organizations (networks) that would take into consideration the specific nature of the goals to be achieved. For instance, in scientific and educational networks the priority is usually to ensure access to information, while ensuring its integrity and confidentiality is a goal at the second level of diagnostics. There is a different correlation of priorities regarding protection against information security threats in commercial structures' networks, and even more so in the networks of law enforcement-related government institutions.

It is essential that at least model standards be developed for the networks of such organizations.

The operational level is one of the most important in terms of implementing a general security policy in Internet networks. Operational regulators are focused primarily on people, not on technical means. They are intended to reduce damage when attacks are launched, through a timely response and high-quality system restoration. As our first example, let us examine the threat of penetration into a computer system. It would be hard to exaggerate the seriousness of this threat—examples involving attempted murder of a witness and usurpation of control over a communications satellite are sufficiently convincing (and what if the satellite had been a military one?). After acquiring superuser rights, a malicious individual can do virtually anything he likes with a system. Let us focus on the following operational measures:

- Personnel management,
- Physical control of access and minimization of privileges, and
- Maintenance of functionality and restoration of a network or network resources after failures.

However, practical implementation of these measures at the operational level in networks within the Russian segment of the Internet also creates a number of difficulties. Personnel management, for example, collides with the absence of clear-cut job descriptions and a lack of qualifications on the part of the specialists called upon to carry out such management. It is possible, out of ignorance, to make a mistake that could be fraught with serious consequences, for example, acquiring a "Trojan horse" program, disclosing a password to an unauthorized individual, and so on. One must be aware of these kinds of mistakes in order to avoid them.

The use of measures to physically control access is difficult to carry out within the limits of a large organization's network. Nevertheless, the application of such regulators to a number of key nodes is extremely desirable. This problem applies in particular to ATIS in the case of objective 1, when the cost of the issue is very high and actions taken by a malicious individual could have serious consequences. A criminal who has penetrated a system can spy on a password selected by one of the system's legitimate users and thus gain access to a confidential computer (generally speaking, one that is not externally accessible, etc.). To keep this from happening, it is essential to monitor individuals who penetrate the "security perimeter."

Each employee should have the minimum privileges necessary to perform his or her duties. In this way, even if a malicious individual penetrates an organization, that individual cannot cause real damage. Prior development of responses to violations of the network information security regime to a large extent involves backup copying and network resource restoration following failures.

Maintenance of functionality and restoration of the system following failures remains a trouble spot even for major Russian ISPs because of a lack of clarity in the way interaction with channel operators is set up, short staffing, the lack of midlevel specialists with appropriate qualifications, and a host of other problems. Response to violations of the security regime causes difficulties, usually due to a lack of any rules governing interaction not only with government ministries and agencies involved with information security (the FAPSI, the State Committee on Technology, the Internal Affairs Administration, et cetera), but even with other ISPs, which might not have people to support that kind of interaction. The current situation can be explained as the initial stage in the development of the relatively young Russian segment of the Internet. We must find approaches that will eliminate the indicated shortcomings in each of the networks that represent individual organizations.

Administrative and operational measures in support of information security, for example, depend to a considerable degree on the structure in place for organizing and specifying goals to be achieved; therefore, the development of general recommendations with regard to a solution in these areas is made much more difficult. However, efforts are being made in that direction. Moscow University's Center for Telecommunications and Internet Technologies, for example, has a working group assigned to create a methodology for protecting open scientific and educational networks. This activity addresses both administrative and operational regulators. However, the work is far from complete.

THE PROGRAMMING AND HARDWARE LEVEL

The Internet—or as it is sometimes called, the Meta-Network (a network of networks)—is the sum total of interactions between individual networks ranging from the very smallest, local networks to major networks at the corporate, national, or even transnational scale. It is precisely this task of internetwork interaction that is performed by the TCP/IP protocol stack, and that fact is the main reason for the Internet's unprecedented rapid growth and popularity. Each of these networks has (or should have) its own security policy and, based upon it, apply its own operational regulators and use the programs and hardware needed for that purpose. Of crucial importance in this hierarchy of network infrastructures are the major governmental and corporate networks. It is these that are as a rule the main target of potential attacks by terrorists.

In order to build an information security system adequate to the needs of such a network, the following protective means are necessary at the programming and hardware level:

- Internetwork firewalls (restricted access);
- Means of identification and authentication that support the concept of a single entrance into a network (the user proves his or her authenticity once upon entry and then has access to all of a network's services, subject to appropriate authorization);
- Anticopying and code audit means to provide monitoring of the network at all levels and to detect suspicious activity and implement a rapid response;
- Means of protection incorporated into applications, services and hardware or software platforms; and
- Centralized network administration tools.

The combination of these tools is intended to cover to a significant degree the protection needs of a corporate IP network at the programming and hardware level.[5] Let us briefly examine a few of these.

Firewalls. Firewalls are designed to regulate flows between the internal and external parts of a computer system. Examples of this include closing certain parts to outside access, blocking access from certain addresses, and blocking traffic containing "dangerous" commands. Thus, firewalls restrict opportunities for a malicious individual to enter a system and also make it difficult for Trojan horse programs to send information out.

Identification and Authentication. Identification allows the subject to indicate his or her name; authentication makes it possible to prove the authenticity of the identifier used. There are three main methods of authentication: based on what a person is (for example, using biometric features such as retinal scans or fingerprints), based on what a person possesses (for example, using "smart cards"), or based on what a person knows (for example, using a password). Identification and authentication prevent "strangers" from entering and also make it possible to track each action back to the subject who performed it.

Access Control. Access control tools make it possible to specify and monitor actions that subject may perform on objects. Thanks to access controls, "underprivileged" users cannot perform actions that could possibly cause significant harm. This is yet another defensive perimeter. Even if a malicious individual penetrates the lower levels, he cannot do serious damage.

Cryptography. Cryptography serves to ensure data confidentiality and integrity and is also an auxiliary service for other regulators (for example, authentication). Thanks to cryptographic methods, a malicious individual cannot view or alter critically important data.

Protocolling and Auditing. Protocolling is defined as the collection and accumulation of information about events occurring in an information system. Auditing refers to analysis of the accumulated information carried out either quickly in real or near-real time or periodically (for example, once a day). Protocolling keeps users accountable. The psychological factor is important (aware that all actions are being protocolled, some potential criminals could abandon their intentions). Analysis of the recorded logs makes it possible to detect malicious activity and take measures in time.

One of the important types of attack frequently used by hackers against Internet networks in recent years has been the denial-of-service attack. As a result of this type of attack, a system is unable to provide one or several services with the required level of quality. This is also a very serious threat and could result in the failure of large systems (transportation, power grids, et cetera).

In addition to the aforementioned methods of defense, we should also mention one common type of access management (i.e., resource quotas). Generally speaking, service failures occur due to exhaustion of some system resource. The use of quotas can limit the amount of resources available to each subject and create a reserve for the superuser, so that he or she will be able to intervene and correct the situation.

PHYSICAL EFFECTS

Physical effects can also disable a computer system. The classic examples of such effects are fires or bombs. Recently, devices have been created that are specifically designed to destroy computer systems.[6] The basic principle by which these devices operate is to cause a sharp voltage spike in power supply systems, communications, or other signals, with an amplitude, duration, and energy in the spike capable of shutting equipment down or degrading it completely. The ability to conceal this type of attack is greatly enhanced by the fact that an analysis of the damaged or destroyed equipment will not clearly identify the cause of the damage, since the cause could be either an intentional destructive power effect (an attack) or an unintentional one (for example, lightning-generated induction).

As a rule, this kind of device uses one of three methods of creating the effect:

1. Through the power grid (it is estimated that a device costing $10,000-$15,000 can disable up to 20 computers simultaneously);

2. Through wiring conduits (in this case, the devices cost only about one-tenth as much); or

3. Through the air, using short but powerful electromagnetic impulses.

Let us examine a few means of defense against this kind of destructive effect:

• The security perimeter must be wider than the space occupied by the computer so that a malicious individual cannot approach within the distance required for effective use of his weapon.

• When equipment is purchased, priority should be given to products that are more resistant to the destructive effects described above.

• Power supply panels, grounding cables, communication lines, and so forth must be closely monitored.

• A "normal" picture of the network's operations should be compiled and the network's current status compared periodically with this benchmark (similar to the use of code auditing).

• It is desirable to shield both the equipment and the rooms within which the equipment is housed.

• Fiber-optic cables should be used as communication channels whenever possible.

INTERNATIONAL INFORMATION SECURITY ISSUES

Extending as it does to all aspects of countries' affairs, the information revolution is expanding opportunities to develop international cooperation and is creating an international information space within which information is becoming a highly valuable component of national wealth and a strategic resource.

In view of this, international cooperation in the information realm is becoming timely and promising. On the one hand, this cooperation makes it possible to have access to the latest information technologies and participate in a worldwide division of labor in the fields of information services, information systems, and information-based products. On the other hand, it is becoming obvious that along with the positive aspects of this process there is also emerging a real threat that achievements in the information realm will be used for purposes not compatible with the goals of maintaining world stability and security or abiding by the principles of sovereign equality among nations, peaceful resolution of disputes and conflicts, renunciation of force, nonintervention in internal affairs, and respect for human rights and liberties. Among these threats is terrorism employing modern network technologies.

This highlights the obvious need for international legal regulation of the processes of international interaction among all subjects involved in the maintenance and development of network infrastructure and information resources. It is essential that we have an international platform on the issue of information security that will correspond to the interests of world security and take antiterrorist considerations into account.

The UN General Assembly, in its resolutions 53/70 of December 4, 1998, and 54/49 of December 1, 1999, has already addressed the need to develop international principles aimed at improving the security of global information and telecommunications systems and facilitating the fight against information terrorism and crime. Now the specific points in a program of action must be developed.

Within the framework of international (bilateral and multilateral) programs, for example, it would be possible to conduct research aimed at preventing the following threats in the realm of information security:

• Actions by international terrorists, extremists, criminal societies, organizations, groups, and individual lawbreakers that present a threat to information resources and nations' critically important structures;
• The use of information technologies and means to the detriment of human rights and liberties as exercised in the information realm; and
• Manipulation of information flows, disinformation, and concealment of information for the purpose of distorting society's psychological and spiritual environment and eroding traditional cultural, moral, ethical, and aesthetic values.

NOTES

1. Kroll, E. 1995. Vsyo ob Internet [All About the Internet] (translated from English). BNV Trade and Publishing Bureau, p. 592.

Cerf, V.G. 1991. Networks. Scientific American 265(September):72 et passim.

Kahn, R.E. 2000. Evolyutsiya seti Internet. Vsemirnyy doklad YuNESKO po kommuni-katsiyam i informatsii, 1999-2000 [Evolution of the Internet Network: UNESCO Global Report on Communications and Information, 1999-2000]. Moscow: Biznes-Press.

2. Vasenin, V.A. 1997. Rossiyskiye akademicheskiye seti i Internet (sostoyaniye, problemy, resheniya) [Russian Academic Networks and the Internet (Status, Problems and Solutions)]. V.A. Sadovnichiy, ed. Moscow: REFIA, p. 173.

3. Sadovnichiy, V.A., V.A. Vasenin, A.A. Mokrousov, A.V. Tutubalin. 1999. Rossiyskiy Internet v tsifrakh i faktakh [The Russian Internet in Figures and Facts]. Moscow: Moscow University Publishers, p. 148.

4. Galatenko, V.A. 1998. Informatsionnaya bezopasnost: prakticheskiy podkhod [Information Security: A Practical Approach]. Moscow: Nauka Publishers, p. 301.

5. Galatenko, A.V. 1999. Aktivny audit [Active auditing]. Jet Info Newsletter 8(75).

6. Barsukov, V. 2000. Zashchita kompyuternykh sistem ot silovykh destruktivnykh vozdey-stviy [Protecting computer systems from destructive power effects]. Jet Info Newsletter 2(81).

Preventing and Responding to Cybercrime and Terrorism: Some International Dimensions

Seymour E. Goodman
Georgia Institute of Technology

"Cyberspace"[1] seems well on its way to becoming a new technology-based medium for extensive human activity, joining several others that have been created and exploited over the last 100 years, including the media built up around aircraft, spaceflight, and the internal combustion engine. In little more than 30 years, cyberspace has become the locus of much of value (notably information and money), a means of passage, and an environment for extended personal and organizational presences and interactions. It has become a locus for many systems that control and manage other more traditional infrastructures, such as those for banking and finance and transportation systems.

It is also attracting a great deal of malicious activity ranging from extensive, long-range vandalism, to various types of more serious crimes, to prospective forms of terrorism and nation-versus-nation conflict. Attacks may be directed at parts of the information infrastructure itself, or through the networks against other targets with some presence in this medium. Criminals and terrorists may also value the networks as assets for themselves (e.g., for inexpensive, effective communications or as a source for intelligence gathering).[2]

The extensive internationalization of the Internet and some of the other networks is a fairly recent phenomenon. By 1984—almost half of the time since the 1969 birth of the Internet as ARPANET under the U.S. Department of Defense—the entire network consisted of only 1000 host computers located in fewer than a half-dozen North Atlantic Treaty Organization (NATO) countries. By 1989, only a few years after most of the network had migrated out of the Department of Defense and essentially become the Internet, the count had risen to fewer than 20 countries and 100,000 hosts. But the vast majority of those hosts were in the United States.

Over the last 8-10 years, international growth has been explosive. There are now about 220 countries and other semisovereign entities (e.g., Hong Kong still retains its own top-level domain name) with full TCP/IP connectivity. Worldwide growth has been 50-100 percent per year, and much higher in some years in many countries. More of the Internet is now outside the United States than inside. As of early 2001, there may have been tens of millions of host computers and 400 million users worldwide, with something like a quarter of the users located outside of the Organization for Economic Cooperation and Development (OECD) countries. Improving technology, declining cost, and the demographics of the world's under-30 population are favoring growth outside the OECD. For example, within the last four to five years, the user populations of China and India have gone from almost negligible numbers to at least 30 million and 6 million, respectively. Several countries (e.g., Turkey and Pakistan) generated a million users or more within a year or two of the start of public access. Such numbers will increase appreciably, especially if there is a massive "second wave" of people with essentially no capabilities in English.

In addition to the many positive aspects of this kind of global connectivity, it also is an extraordinary enabler of malicious people. Virtually every connected country can serve as a base for any number of such people, who have any number of motivations, and who can readily acquire technical capabilities to cause harm to others.

It is often said that cyberspace is borderless and has in some ways effectively erased borders between countries. Conversely, global connectivity has made it possible for attackers to work from almost any country against targets in almost every country, and since all of cyberspace comes to ground somewhere, it has essentially created borders between every pair of countries.

Thus, almost every country is, or potentially is, part of the problem of concern to us. Most national and local governments are incapable of dealing with, and often are largely unaware of, these problems. It is desirable to help make them part of the solution. Most will be incapable of doing this on their own. Since much of the problem of cybercrime and terrorism is intrinsically transnational, some form of international cooperation arguably should be part of the national strategies of most of the governments of the world.

The remainder of this short paper will be concerned with international cooperation to help prevent and respond to cybercrime and terrorism. We will be concerned primarily with acts against cybersystems (e.g., destroying, incapacitating, or misusing them).[3] We take the view that it is both difficult and unnecessary to precisely define "cyberterrorism." We are unlikely to get much agreement among a wide spectrum of interested parties on such a definition, given the enormous variety of malicious activity possible in this medium and the enormous range of possible motivations behind the possible attacks. It is very difficult to distinguish an early stage of an attack as either crime or terrorism. We take the approach of defining serious forms of crimes against information systems under the assumption that most forms of what would be widely considered cyberterrorism would be egregious instances of these crimes. As is the case in other contexts (e.g., safety and security in civil aviation), it is the nature of the attack itself that matters; the motivation of the attacker should not be a determining factor.

DEFENSES IN A TRANSNATIONAL ENVIRONMENT

We need to define and distinguish between two complementary forms of defense:

1. **Passive defense** is essentially target hardening. It consists largely of the internal use of various technologies and products (e.g., firewalls, intrusion detection) and procedures (e.g., governing outside dial-in or reconstitution and recovery) to protect the information technology (IT) assets owned by an individual or organization. By definition, passive defense does not impose any serious risk or penalty on the attacker. With only passive defensive measures, the attacker is free to continue assaulting the target until he either succeeds or gets bored and looks elsewhere. Given the extensive vulnerabilities of most cybersystems and the low cost of most attacks, a skilled and determined attacker may well be more likely to succeed before getting bored.

2. **Active defense** by definition imposes serious risk or penalty on the attacker. Risk and penalty may include identification of the attacker, investigation and prosecution, stopping an attack in progress, and preemptive or counterattacks of various sorts.

Note that some actions—for example, stopping an attack in progress—can be pursued using both passive and active means. Passively, one might plug a vulnerability hole in real time. Actively, one might try to get at the source of the attack.

In a transnational context, passive defense is not without problems (e.g., with regard to liability issues or information sharing). But the pursuit of active defensive measures in an international context is more difficult and will get most of the attention in this paper.[4]

At the very least, active defense involves gathering intelligence information about the attacker. It can go well beyond that to damaging the attacker's cyberassets to physically apprehending or otherwise physically incapacitating the attacker. All of cyberspace "comes to ground" somewhere (including at sea). So essentially all attackers and their assets are located within the jurisdiction of one or more nation states. For a defender to engage in unilateral active defense, in almost any transnational context, he will very likely covertly reach into computers and other places located outside his legal jurisdiction.

Since much of the information infrastructure is owned, operated, and used by the private sectors around the world, they and their assets are, and will continue to be, primary targets. Many private entities are technically capable of trying to engage in active defense. But they do not have much legal basis for doing so in an international context, and the state of technology is such that there is considerable likelihood that they may incorrectly identify their attackers, cause undesirable collateral damage, or result in some other kind of messy mistake. In so doing, they may become greater and more readily identifiable offenders than their attackers and may be subject to considerable liability, publicity, and criminal penalties. Furthermore, few governments anywhere officially condone any form of vigilantism.

Thus, the pursuit of active defense would necessarily fall to governments. Governments are not subject to the liability risks of private entities. A good case can be made to the effect that national governments would be justified in engaging in active defense under the international legal principles of proportionality and response-in-kind. But few if any nations would welcome another government's intrusions into information systems located within their sovereignty, and the intruding government would largely have to do so covertly. Under these circumstances, particularly if the volume of serious cyber-attacks is high, sooner or later this will result in messy and visible misidentifications and collateral damage and would likely generate international friction between governments. The government engaging in active defense would also be at a serious disadvantage with regard to apprehending or otherwise physically dealing with the attackers. Furthermore, it would seem unwise for any country to establish precedents for aggressive international behavior in this arena.[6]

The U.S. government, in particular, should have reservations in this regard. Because of presumed technical prowess and other reasons, it will be held to higher standards of accountability and suspicion than other governments when it intrudes. It will suffer serious blame in public opinion and elsewhere when its intrusions inevitably result in undesirable collateral or other damages. The United States is home to far more information systems and hosts much more of the Internet than any other country. It is physically home to a larger number of attackers and is a third-party transit country for more network traffic than any other country. As such, it is likely to be a target of a great many active defensive measures by other countries, and we might expect some large fraction of these to be carried out relatively incompetently. We can be sure that the U.S. government, not to mention the private-sector owners and operators and users of these information systems, will very much resent such intrusions by other governments.

FINDING A SUITABLE FRAMEWORK FOR INTERNATIONAL COOPERATION

These arguments and constraints lead us to conclude that the ideal international arrangement would have to look something like the following. First, each of the governments of the world would have considerable competence to deal with the problem. This includes capabilities and policies in passive defense to provide substantial security for those portions of cyberspace within its purview. Second, all of the connected countries would share a common baseline perception of what constitutes serious (felony) criminal behavior in this new medium. One of the manifestations of this shared perception would be in the form of a similar set of laws defining such behavior in each country. Third, each country would have some substantial capability in active defense and a competent national authority for engaging in active defense. Finally, international responses to transnational attacks would be covered under a near-universal umbrella convention that would permit timely action, among any combination of countries, under established procedures.

Under these ideal circumstances, we might expect the following standard scenario if a serious cyber attack is launched from country X against targets in country A. The victims in A immediately seek help from government A. Government A determines that there is reason to suspect that the attack originates from, or at least passes through, X. Under the umbrella international convention, it immediately contacts the competent authority in X, where the attack is equally viewed as a crime. Government A can count on government X being willing and able to investigate the extent to which the attack is taking place from X. The competent authority in X will act in a timely manner to help stop the attack and proceed with other forms of defense in essentially the same way that government A would if it had the jurisdictional authority to do so itself.

Because of all the ideal commonalities under the near-universal arrangement just described, this procedural scenario scales. So, for example, it extends in a straightforward manner if the attack is simultaneously launched from countries X, Y, and Z against targets in countries A and B, and the attack is routed through M, N, P, and Q.

As far as we can determine, this is the only unambiguously legal way to handle active defense on the global scale of the Internet and other large transnational networks. It is also the only way we can conceive of avoiding what is potentially an enormous amount of essentially covert actions on the parts of governments against systems and citizens in other countries. It would tend to minimize the errors, collateral damage, and other forms of friction that might arise between nations as a result of all that covert activity.

The present reality is very far from this ideal situation. Perhaps most importantly, the great majority of the governments of the roughly 220 countries or other semisovereign entities with Internet connectivity have very little awareness, and far less capability, in this area.

So how may we try to proceed from the current reality to something closer to the ideal international situation? We would argue that we should start to think about the desired structure and content of such an international convention. The time scale associated with conducting and dealing with malicious cyber-activities varies from months (e.g., the time for new tactical attack modes to emerge) to the comparatively glacial time scales for building extensive and effective international agreements. So it is necessary to start thinking about the long and iterative process of the latter, even though it is too early to expect solutions to some specific problems and questions. We might look to a framework that builds in an expectation and means for dealing with the detailed problems of changing technology, et cetera, over an essentially unbounded time into the future, as well as one intended to help build the capabilities of weaker nations.

So what might be included as necessary top-level features in such an international convention? We would suggest the following:[7]

• The focus should be on **serious crimes against computer networks**. The primary concern is protecting the infrastructure, both the IT-based infrastructure itself and the other infrastructures that may be accessed and damaged or manipulated through IT-based control structures. This is not the place to address content crimes (e.g., pornography or intellectual property rights).

• There should be a **harmonization of laws**. Each State Party to the convention must adopt a complete set of national laws defining and punishing serious crimes against computer networks. Although the wording of this set does not have to be identical for each country, each must establish all of the collectively defined malicious behavior specified in the agreement as felonies within the country. Having such a set of laws on the books would be considered a necessary condition for admission to the convention. We believe that this would be sufficient for most extradition purposes. What is necessary is to get near congruence of national laws widely accepted and to make the subject a legitimate concern on a broad international level.

• There should be a **near-universal set of States Parties**. The problem is intrinsically global, and at least some element of a partial solution has to be global. Near-universal participation makes the problem legitimate globally, and tries to eliminate safe havens. Each country connected to the Internet is part of the threat problem, and an effort must be made to try to make each a part of the solution, which is decidedly not the case now.

• A major goal should be to **build international capabilities** to deal with the problem. To this end we would propose a working organization, somewhat similar to the International Civil Aviation Organization for that transportation infrastructure, to help develop standards, determine best practices, provide training, and so forth, on a global scale, especially for the large number of countries that have little or no capacity to do anything for themselves in the cyberdomain at this time. This applies to both passive and active means of defense. We tentatively call this organization the Agency for Information Infrastructure Protection (AIIP).[8]

• **Avoid building too much technical and procedural detail into the basic agreement**. At this time, nobody understands the technological and procedural means and costs well enough to appreciate what it would take to require them on a large scale. It will take some time for thoughts and technology to mature to the point where such might be recommended or required. We recommend setting up a forum and means (e.g., through the AIIP) for the necessary discussions and work to take place. As is the case in other international domains, industry participation in these efforts would be highly desirable.

• The prospective convention is **not meant to apply to the actions of states**. We suspect that there are dozens of governments investigating the possibilities of so-called information warfare. Few of those would presumably be interested in constraining themselves at this early stage. This is not meant to be an arms control convention, just as the various widely accepted agreements on safety and security in civil aviation are not meant to ground the air forces of the countries of the world.

• States Parties would **not violate the civil or human rights** of their citizens. No State Party would be expected to compromise its own laws in this regard. So, for example, assume that both the United States and Iran are signatories. Say that an American citizen is suspected of attacking an Iranian system in a manner that is against the laws both countries have agreed upon in signing the convention. If the United States suspects that this person's human rights would be at risk if he were to be extradited to Iran, then the United States is obligated to try the person for that crime in the United States or to extradite him for trial to a third country that has a claim to jurisdiction but observes civil or human rights laws similar to those in the United States.

We briefly note that our views on all of these points differ to a greater or lesser extent from those expressed or omitted in the draft agreement being developed under the purview of the Council of Europe (CoE).[9] We feel that the CoE draft is focused too much on matters of content violation and prosecution. We believe a broader spectrum of needs should be addressed to protect infrastructure and build defensive capabilities.

We also briefly note that reasonably effective agreements exist in other domains along the lines enumerated in the above list. Perhaps the closest analogy is with civil aviation, which itself also happens to be extensively and increasingly dependent on cybersystems.[10] There are others covering intrinsically transnational domains such as maritime transportation, health, and pollution.

We are a long way from having such an agreement, and there will be considerable difficulties along any path to an effective approximation. We touch on a few of the difficulties below.

• As with many international agreements, questions arise as to forms of enforcement and sanctions against signatories who are not living up to the conditions or who are in conscious violation.

• Work needs to be done on estimating the costs of such a convention. Just two examples of such costs include an estimate of the volume of requests and investigations (and their growth rates) that would have to be handled, and the cost of standing up and running an organization such as the AIIP. In terms of savings, we note that many major cyber-attacks (e.g., via virus or denial of service) have been estimated to cost hundreds of millions of dollars. So, as in the case of averted airline disasters, every prevented major incident represents a huge "savings."

• How do we effectively scale up to a near-universal sign-up? In addition to the obvious approach of simply starting with a small number of countries, possibilities include the use of more limited agreements as "building blocks" to acquire subsets of partners and experience in "what works." These more limited agreements might be done bilaterally, or multilaterally based on sector (e.g., for the cyberdimensions of civil aviation) or regional (e.g., for Europe) distinctions.[11]

• A related question is what to require of a State Party as a condition for admission? Two possibilities are a set of harmonized domestic laws and the existence of a competent national authority. Another issue is what to do with nonsignatories? For example, should (could?) an effort be made to create a form of quarantine?

We believe that some kind of extensive international convention is inevitable. Given the time scales involved and how long it takes to work out effective agreements, we also believe it is prudent to pursue serious deliberations on the matter, with the intent of developing an initial "greatest common denominator" that has a strong likelihood of finding broad acceptance among a large and diverse set of countries. The realistic issue is not whether we can achieve an ideal agreement, but rather how to get something that is far better than what exists now and that can be updated and improved over time. Can anything be proposed that is significantly different from and better than what has been outlined here and in the Stanford Draft? In this regard, it may be appropriate to recall and adapt to the current context Churchill's classic statement that "democracy is the worst form of government except all those others that have been tried from time to time."[12]

NOTES

1. We simply define "cyberspace" to include the Internet and all other extensive wide-area networks with similar architectures and protocols. Many of the latter are sector specific (e.g., the global money transfer systems used by the international banking and finance industries).

2. Soo Hoo, K., S. Goodman, L. Greenberg. 1997. Information technology and the terrorist threat. Survival 39(3):135-155.

3. These are defined in Articles 3 and 4 in Sofaer, A.A., S.E. Goodman, et al. 2000. A Proposal for an International Convention on Cyber Crime and Terrorism. Stanford: Center for International Security and Cooperation, Stanford University. Article 1, Paragraph 2, which unnecessarily attempts

to define "cyberterrorism," should be considered deleted. Hereafter this is referred to as the Stanford Draft.

4. Grove, G.D., S.E. Goodman, S.J. Lukasik. 2000. Cyber-attacks and international law. Survival 42(3):89-103.

5. Goldsmith, J. 1999. Paper presented at the Conference on International Cooperation to Combat Cyber Crime and Terrorism, Stanford University, December 6–7, 1999.

6. Such issues are already becoming problematic. See, for example, Brunker, M. Cyberspace evidence seizure upheld. FBI downloaded data from suspects' computers in Russia. MSNBC, May 30, 2001.

7. Sofaer et al., op. cit., discussed throughout the text.

8. Lukasik, S.J. 2000. What Does an "AIIP" Do? Presentation notes, Georgia Institute of Technology, Atlanta, May 27.

9. European Committee on Crime Problems, Committee of Experts on Crime in Cyber-Space, Council of Europe. 2000. Draft Convention on Cyber-Crime, Draft No. 25, Rev. 5. Strasbourg, December 22, 2000.

10. See Goodman, S., M. Cuellar, H. Whiteman. 2001. In The Transnational Dimensions of Cyber Crime and Terrorism, A.D. Sofaer and S. E. Goodman, eds. Stanford: Hoover Institution Press, pp. 69-124.

11. Whiteman, H. 2001. International Institutions and Agreements to Combat Serious Cyber-Crime. Presentation at the Georgia Tech-Stanford Workshop on Protecting Cyberspace: The International Dimension, Washington, May 1, 2001.

We might also note that a set of bilateral agreements will be unworkable as a long-term solution. Global connectivity enables too many countries. For N countries, a perfect set of bilateral agreements that would allow any two to work together would number $N(N - 1)/2$. In our case, $N = 220$, necessitating 24,090 bilateral agreements. If one recognizes that attacks could involve three or more countries, the number of multilateral agreements short of a universal agreement becomes exponential.

12. Ibid. Whiteman is Assistant Deputy Minister, Security, and Emergency Preparedness, Transport Canada.

AGRICULTURAL TERRORISM

Problems of Biological Security in Agriculture

Georgy A. Safonov and Vladimir A. Gavrilov[*]
Pokrov Biological Preparations Plant

First of all, we would like to say a few words about the Pokrov Biological Preparations Plant. The plant was built in 1978 for two main purposes: (1) producing diagnostic and prophylactic preparations used against especially dangerous diseases, including exotic varieties (all types of foot-and-mouth disease, cattle plague [rinderpest], classical swine fever, Newcastle disease, avian influenza, and others); and (2) stockpiling necessary reserves of biological preparations for use in emergency measures to combat disease. The plant was part of the special system of the USSR Ministry of Agriculture intended for organizing and carrying out efforts to respond to emergency situations arising in the agricultural sphere during outbreaks of especially dangerous diseases. Leading specialists at the plant include scientists working on matters related to eliminating the consequences of unforeseen situations, including biological terrorism.

Over the past decade, the world has seen the exacerbation of the situation between individual countries and groups divided by their various political, territorial, and religious views regarding coexistence: Israel-Palestine, Yugoslavia, Chechnya in Russia. Existing contradictions grew into military confrontations with unpredictable consequences with regard to the methods and means of action used. In fact, we have already seen a case in which the religious sect Aum Shinrikyo carried out a terrorist act using chemical weapons and attempted to initiate production of biological weapons.

In many countries, the public has been concerned about the possible consequences of terrorist acts in our high-tech society, and attempts are being made to develop effective methods of combating these phenomena. A number of sources

---

[*] Translated from the Russian by Kelly Robbins.

in the literature provide rather complete coverage of various aspects of the use of pathogens to cause economic, moral, and physical harm to a healthy population.[1]

It is generally known that for the majority of countries, agriculture serves as the main source of foodstuffs and raw materials. A sharp reduction in food resources is always accompanied by demoralization and the worsening of demographic indicators regarding the health of the population.

The economic costs involved in fighting epizootic diseases are practically always enormous, not to mention the costs of protecting health and preventing financial damages associated with quarantine measures and reduced labor productivity. One must also consider the additional costs of maintaining personnel to monitor the appearance of infection foci, diagnose animal diseases, quarantine infected individuals, restrict the transport of animals, test the quality of meat and milk, and certify these and other livestock-related products as unfit for sale if necessary. This is a far from complete list of the economic costs borne by the state and counted on by the terrorists. It does not take into account the psychological trauma suffered by farmers and the population as a whole.

Broad-scale movements of people and migrations of animals could serve as the basis for widespread contacts with contaminated food, feed, and water. The population is becoming increasingly mobile (due to tourism and searches for work and new places of residence), while international shipments of animals and livestock-related products are also on the rise. Often, the appropriate safety measures are not taken. Refugees, victims of natural disasters, participants in massive pilgrimages and other religious observances, and individuals temporarily living in crowded conditions represent a favorable target for acts of bioterrorism, especially those involving animal-borne pathogens. In such situations, control and monitoring of animals is usually weakened or completely lacking; therefore, animals in such circumstances can represent a likely source for the transmission of zoonoses.

The destruction of food supplies could be the consequence not only of climatic anomalies, but also of the inadvertent or intentional spread of diseases among animals or plants. For example, practically all the cattle in the Philippines died as a result of a foot-and-mouth disease outbreak in 1917-1927. Outbreaks of foot-and-mouth disease in England (2001) and classical swine fever in Denmark and Holland (1998-1999) not only caused enormous economic losses of more than 3 billion U.S. dollars, but also completely paralyzed economic life in these countries. An outbreak of African swine fever in Cuba (1976) was no less grievous. Another example is the epidemic of Rift Valley fever in Egypt (1977), in which by the most conservative estimates more than 500 people died and another 18,000 became ill in just one year, not to mention the cases suffered by animals.[2]

The spatial (territorial) or varietal rotation of pathogens always inflicts the heaviest consequences. This can occur not only by means of evolution, but also as a result of the accidental or intentional spread of an active agent.

In recent years, the world community has become increasingly concerned over the possible use of biological agents in the commission of terrorist acts. History provides no small number of examples in which human corpses, animal carcasses, or infected clothing were used to create micro-outbreaks with the aim of producing major foci of infections. Today, the overwhelming majority of states and their leaders actively oppose the use of pathogens as a means for the mass destruction of people, plants, and animals.

Thanks to the activism of many politicians advocating controls over work with especially dangerous pathogens, you will not hear any strategists of warfare or terrorist acts saying that biological weapons are not only the most economically accessible, but also the most humane of weapons from the standpoint of preserving material valuables or the environment.

The world is still divided into hostile opposing groups based on religious, racial, political, economic, or merely moral-ethical views on coexistence.

It should always be kept in mind that the use of biological agents such as foot-and-mouth disease, cattle plague, African or classical swine fever, avian influenza, or anthrax could initially go unnoticed—and furthermore unprovable—or be explained away as a result of spontaneous external transmission, as has happened on more than one occasion. For example, explanations for the foot-and-mouth disease outbreak in England postulate that it occurred because a restaurant was supplied with infected pork.

But how can one differentiate between happenstance and intention—a terrorist act? This is practically impossible to do. The very fact of an unprovable accusation being made would be an intentional insult to individuals and even states.

The concept of terrorism relative to agriculture seems at first glance to have little applicability, because it is aimed not directly at the physical destruction of people, but only at human food sources. At the same time, we are well aware of the fact that a country left without agricultural resources finds itself in extreme conditions that could lead not only to the removal of a government or change of political course, but also to mass deaths of people due to starvation.

The Chechen conflict has already led to a clearly expressed terrorist action, namely, the bombing of apartment buildings used by the civilian population and subsequent heavy human casualties. The world would not be surprised if tomorrow it heard the news that pathogens had been used in one of the above-mentioned states to destroy not only people, but also animals and crops. However, in this case we would be dealing with an organized action affecting primarily the psyches of the population and government with the aim of changing opinions on a specific issue—territory or independence, for example. In such a case we are fully justified in calling such an action terroristic.

The situation that arose in England with regard to the foot-and-mouth disease outbreak is another matter. At first glance, we see no connection with terrorism. On the other hand, England and surrounding countries have long been free of foot-and-mouth disease. The question is, How and from where did the foot-and-mouth disease agent arrive in England? It is supposed to have arrived in infected meat, but how did infected meat reach the market? Why was it not discovered by veterinary services in the country of export? And how did it end up in England?

The effectiveness of the international system for monitoring especially dangerous infections largely depends on the responsible attitudes of national veterinary services and governments of UN member countries.

The system for providing notifications of cases of zoonotic disease and quarantine infections is presented in some detail in the reports of an FAO-WHO (Food and Agriculture Organization-World Health Organization) joint expert committee on veterinary sanitation.[3] However, in certain cases this system is ignored for reasons of economic constraints, which usually follow after the issuance of official FAO notifications on the presence of quarantine infections in a country. This creates a precedent for the wide-scale spread of especially dangerous infections. We propose viewing such situations of concealment of quarantine disease as a latent form of terrorist action on the part of a state.

A state that has not instituted the appropriate quarantine (intentionally or not, which is another question), not notified other countries in a timely manner, and not taken active measures to recall infected products for heat treatment or other decontamination processing should bear the corresponding responsibility for any consequences.

Bioterrorism can be painstakingly planned and carried out by individuals aware of the consequences of their actions with regard to the chosen target.

In a number of cases, where states in which quarantine infections are present take a passive attitude with regard to preventing the spread of the infectious agent beyond their borders, this should also be viewed as a special form of terrorism that can be termed "latent." Like intentional terrorism, it can lead to the deaths of people and losses of crops and animals on a massive scale. In this case, such a state—we shall call it a "passive terrorist"—is guilty of spreading pathogens to other territories and is obligated to bear the economic and moral responsibility for the damage caused to the other country, for example, England. In cases of aggressive terrorism, the question must be viewed as a criminal matter in accordance with the existing laws of the country affected.

If in the course of analyzing the causes of an infectious outbreak it can be established and proven that an individual or group is to blame for spreading the pathogen by means of infected food or feed products to another country or to a firm located on the territory of another country, then charges of latent terrorism should be addressed in an international court of law. As for punishment, a decision could be rendered to include not only payment of damages, but also a temporary economic embargo (full or partial) with regard to the guilty country.

The proposed approach and measures for punishment of those to blame for spreading pathogens should reduce the potential threat that such situations will arise.

In addressing possible situations involving the spread of pathogens, we first of all wish to attract attention to the discussion of bioterrorism-related questions by the maximum possible number of scientists and specialists working in the legal field so that in the end, there will be a clear-cut definition of various situations associated with the spread of pathogens.

At a minimum, the following four aspects of the biological threat should be kept in mind:

1. The spread of an agent beyond the borders of states where a particular disease or pathogen is present;

2. The unintentional release of a pathogen from scientific-research or production facilities;

3. The spread of infection by products from infected livestock; and

4. The intentional spread of infection aimed at causing economic pressure or changing the political course of a country.

We have seen dozens of examples in which agents from so-called natural foci infections appeared far beyond the borders of the areas in which they are traditionally found: African swine fever, Venezuelan equine encephalitis, Rift Valley fever, and others.

The territorial rotation of pathogens always causes significant difficulties in the areas where the pathogens have newly arrived. The unexpected appearance of African swine fever in Portugal (1957) and Spain (1957) caused well-founded alarm in many European states. To this day, Portugal and Spain have been unable to rid themselves completely of this uninvited guest.

There are a number of examples of the release of pathogens from institutions or enterprises working with them. For example, during testing of a new foot-and-mouth disease vaccine in 1965, the foot-and-mouth disease virus escaped from the Kursk Biological Plant, causing one of the most severe epizootic outbreaks in the European part of the USSR. It took years to eliminate this outbreak, and the country's economy suffered significant damage.

We are well aware of the fact that industrial or research work with pathogens also requires special safety equipment and technical conditions, depending on their individual properties.[4]

Today in Russia, not only technologies, but also pathogen strains used in production are being sold off. In a number of instances, industrial strains of pathogens differ little from field strains. For example, the majority of technologies for the production of killed vaccines are generally based on field strains of pathogens (foot-and-mouth disease, avian influenza, rabbit hemorrhagic disease, etc.). Furthermore, it seems to us that this technology in no way differs from that used in the production of raw materials for biological weapons. We are certain that one might find no small number of businessmen who, for a relatively small payment, would sell active raw material without even thinking of the possible consequences of such a deal.

It is commonly known that within Russia, not only are individual people being killed, but entire apartment buildings full of completely innocent people are also being blown up. The Chechnya crisis has not yet passed, and no one can predict the future turn it will take or when it will end.

Furthermore, the entire agricultural sector (including the raising of both livestock and crops) is practically unprotected from terrorism. Foot-and-mouth disease, African and classical swine fever, avian influenza, and anthrax are obviously the most likely and most accessible biological agents for local application against animals.

Highly infectious material can be produced in quantities sufficient for the commission of terrorist acts even in the most primitive conditions—barns, caves, or even animal pens. Doing this would require just 1-2 ml of a pathogen and a susceptible animal. The sick animal could be introduced unnoticed into a large herd, or one might wait for the infected animal to die and then extract highly concentrated material from it (spleen, liver, lungs, etc.), which could then be used to infect feed, pastures, or water supplies or else be sold to the population.

On the territory of the Russian Federation, there are more than 10,000 sites where anthrax spores lie buried. The detonation of any one of these could become a nightmare for the population within a radius of 5-10 km or more.

We would not like to go into detail regarding all possible ways of using biological agents as terrorist weapons, so that this work does not become a textbook for people who have lost their minds for whatever reason.

We have already mentioned the transmission of foot-and-mouth disease from the territory of a biological plant in 1965. Even today, a repeat of such a situation cannot be ruled out, particularly in view of the fact that institutes working with especially dangerous infections are engaged in the production and sale of biological preparations. Furthermore, production discipline has deteriorated significantly during the recent years of economic restructuring. The stream of visitors has grown immeasurably, and protective alarm systems have aged or broken down entirely.

At the same time, many countries are taking a responsible approach to the question of bioterrorism. For example, an international seminar on increasing the level of security for work with dangerous pathogens and other materials was held in October 2000 in the city of Albuquerque, New Mexico. Participants in the seminar included scientists and specialists from the United States, Great Britain, Canada, Sweden, Russia, Ukraine, Kazakhstan, Uzbekistan, and Georgia. The seminar featured discussions of new approaches to the physical protection of institutions working with potentially dangerous materials. Questions regarding the storage, accountability, control, and transport of biologically hazardous materials represented a significant focus of discussion. Personnel-related work was addressed in detail, including the hiring of personnel for responsible positions, reliability, professional skill, and readiness to work in emergency situations. Several potential situations that might arise at facilities were reviewed:

- The theft of biomaterials for the purpose of committing acts of terrorism or blackmail;
- Terrorist acts aimed at disrupting the functions of production facilities or premises housing security personnel; and
- Incursion onto the territory of a facility in the aim of committing illegal acts and other situations.

Illegal actions could be committed not only by terrorists or criminals, but also by disgruntled or bribed employees or even representatives of animal rights groups. In this regard, any system for protecting dangerous facilities must feature multiple levels of security: a reinforced concrete wall with two alarmed perimeters and video surveillance. Each critical building, floor, material storage room, and container of biomaterials must be equipped with an alarm system.

In conclusion, we feel it is necessary to discuss the most important problem from our point of view, that of the bioprotection of agriculture. First, legislative limits must be placed on the number of scientific institutes and biological enterprises that are authorized to work with especially dangerous pathogens and with infectious materials in general. The international community must develop methods for monitoring the safe operation of biological enterprises regardless of their ownership. State agencies must bear responsibility for ensuring compliance with international safety standards for the operation of biological enterprises. They bear this responsibility not only to their own countries, but to the world community in general.

Of course, the most complex aspect of this problem involves the effectiveness of control, especially internationally or bilaterally. In this regard, concrete steps are already being taken in Geneva to create an agreement on a mechanism for such control. We believe that resolving the question of effective control over biosecurity will be possible only after normal partner relations are established between countries, peoples, and first of all, state structures.

The difficulties of biocontrol can be overcome only as a result of procedurally unrestricted exchange visits and contacts between scientists and production personnel and their colleagues abroad. One should not follow the thesis that private firms cannot be controlled by international agencies. In visiting other countries, we have always been surprised by such a convenient method of limiting access to this or that firm. Our colleagues also probably find it hard to understand when they are restricted from visiting facilities. How can we speak of any sort of trust here? Fear over so-called industrial secrets cannot be the reason for refusing access. Citizens of any country must be subject to the laws of their own country, as well as to international laws. If not, neither mutual trust nor appropriately effective control will ever exist. Disagreements over issues concerning exchanges of visits could become a basis not only for mistrust, but also for political blackmail.

It is also essential to strengthen the 1972 convention on the prohibition of biological weapons, first of all by creating an atmosphere of international trust.

From the first years of its production activity, the Pokrov Biological Preparations Plant of the USSR Ministry of Agriculture operated on a self-financing basis, requiring no budget support from the government. This was made possible not only by the plant's large-scale production of vaccines against practically all viral infections existent in the Soviet Union, but also by centralized state orders for the production and stockpiling of reserves of vaccines for foot-and-mouth disease, cattle plague, classical swine fever, Newcastle disease, sheep pox, and avian pox.

The plant is a potentially dangerous enterprise with regard to the livestock industry. The range of viral infectious agents with which the Pokrov Biological Preparations Plant worked, as well as the location of the plant in a region with many livestock farms and enterprises, determined the need for a special closed operating regime. Admission to the plant required showing a badge or pass, visits were restricted, and a security system was in place around the perimeter of the plant. Indeed, the size of the area occupied by the plant and the special construction characteristics of several earthquake-resistant buildings on the site attract heightened interest regarding the nature of work being carried out there.

The plant produced more than 40 biological preparations, the lion's share of which were unique, patented products. This made it possible for the plant to produce biological preparations worth 50 million dollars or more each year. The collapse of the Russian economy in the transitional period led to a significant reduction in livestock numbers and a sharp drop in demand for biological preparations. Today the output volume at the plant totals 10 percent of capacity. The high energy demands of the production process have become a sort of Achilles' heel with regard to the profitability of products manufactured in small volumes. In connection with this problem, the plant is experiencing a critical period. A significant portion of the employees have moved on to other jobs in private firms. The plant currently employs more than 700 people, 150 of whom are scientists or specialists with a higher education.

In the aim of increasing the profitability of production and improving its financial position, the plant plans to carry out a substantial modernization and reconstruction project. This will involve reducing energy costs in the production shops by dismantling the centralized refrigeration and compressed air systems and replacing them with small localized units in each individual shop. More than 20 fermenters will be dismantled in order to retool the shops to manufacture pharmaceutical products. In the space freed up after removal of the fermenters, plans call for installing production lines for liniments, medicine tablets, and intravenous solutions.

The production of veterinary probiotics and immunomodulators is also to be established in the buildings to be freed up after the renovations. Equipment for feed production and quality control will be installed in the decrepit older buildings, along with a storage facility for animal embryos. With financial support from partners, plans will be carried out to establish a poultry farm processing and storage facility with a capacity of 2 million eggs per year.

A number of research and implementation projects have recently been developed in cooperation with the International Science and Technology Center (ISTC) and the Defense Threat Reduction Agency. Implementation of these projects will facilitate the reconstruction of the plant's production capacities and the reduction of tensions regarding issues of mutual trust and site visits.

Completion of the entire range of planned reconstruction projects at the plant will make it possible to convince the public of the peaceful nature of our production facility. The planned long-term strategic cooperation with a number of U.S. organizations will also promote an improved political atmosphere between our countries. Moreover, the plant hopes to make a concrete contribution to the prevention of especially dangerous infections not only within Russia, but also in other countries. We are convinced that international cooperation on the issue of biological security will promote collaboration among scientists of various countries in preventing other types of terrorism.

In accordance with the Initiatives for Proliferation Prevention (IPP) Program, the plant will be able to cooperate with the United States Industry Coalition (USIC) and the European Union programs INTAS, Tacis, and others. The financial support provided by ISTC in the form of grants makes it possible to host foreign colleagues at the plant and openly show our production capabilities, which will reduce concerns with regard to hidden or closed facilities.

We have always taken a serious approach to critical comments from the international commission that visited the plant in 1993 regarding its concerns about the plant's technical capabilities. We believe that international cooperation will enable us to remove these worries on the part of the public.

Even today, a potential danger exists regarding the appearance and spread of panzootic outbreaks of such infections as monkeypox, Marburg disease, Ebola, prion encephalopathies, foot-and-mouth disease, African and classical swine fever, and others. These infections have really appeared on the horizon of the twenty-first century in connection with the growth of international trade, tourism, ethnic conflicts, natural and technological catastrophes, and an ever-increasing number of militarized conflicts.

Given the real threat of biocatastrophes, efforts must be stepped up to create international institutions that will focus their activities on rendering practical assistance to states in eliminating even small foci of especially dangerous exotic diseases. First of all, the WHO and FAO must resolve the problem of creating emergency stockpiles of preventive and curative medicines for dealing with wide-scale infectious outbreaks. Consideration must also be given to questions of strategy and tactics in combating such outbreaks, including universal slaughter, the destruction of infected animal carcasses, and comprehensive vaccination campaigns in the event that a localized outbreak becomes epizootic.

Let us wish for all of us a strong sense of responsibility not only for the fate of our own peoples, but also for that of our beautiful planet Earth. Let us not forget the opinions of our cosmonauts—that Earth as a cosmic body is but an infinitely small speck of dust in the limitless ocean of the universe. The natural harmony of living nature on Earth has continued for many millions of years, but today life on Earth depends on the reason and will of mankind, including all of us here.

NOTES

1. Rozbern, T., E. Kabat. 1955. Bacteriological War. Moscow: Voenizdat.

Rotshild, D. 1966. Tomorrow's Weapons. Moscow: Voenizdat.

Sokolov, G.A. 1968. Thermonuclear, chemical, and biological weapons: means of mass destruction. Mendeleev Chemistry Journal.

Timakov, V., F. Koroshkov. 1969. Protecting people from the threat of chemical and bacteriological war. Medical Newspaper.

Thant, U. 1970. Chemical and Bacteriological (Biological) Weapons and the Consequences of Their Use. Report of the UN Secretary General at the 25th Session of the UN General Assembly.

Baroyan, O.V. 1971. The Fate of Conventional Diseases. Moscow: Meditsina.

Georgievsky, A.S., O.K. Gavrilov. 1975. Social Hygiene Problems and Consequences of War. Moscow: Meditsina.

FAO-WHO. 1975. The Veterinary Contribution to Public Health Practice. Technical Report Series No. 573. Geneva.

2. FAO-WHO. 1982. Bacterial and Viral Zoonoses. Technical Report Series No. 682. Geneva.

3. FAO-WHO. 1982. Bacterial and Viral Zoonoses. Technical Report Series No. 682. Geneva; WHO. 1985. *Laboratory Biosafety Manual.* Geneva.

4. WHO. 1985. *Laboratory Biosafety Manual.* Geneva; Drozdov, S.G., N.S. Garin, L.S. Dzhindonyan, V.M. Tarasenko. 1987. Fundamentals of Safety Equipment in Microbiological and Virological Laboratories. Moscow: Meditsina.

Agricultural Bioterrorism

Martin E. Hugh-Jones
Louisiana State University School of Veterinary Medicine

BIOLOGICAL ATTACKS

Any biological attack on agriculture will differ significantly from one that primarily targets human beings, since any human deaths will at worst be coincidental, even when zoonoses are concerned. Any agricultural impact may be delayed significantly and only become obvious after weeks or even months; and the major losses follow from the disease and are not those directly from the disease itself, which in comparison may be relatively trivial.

An effective "attack" does not necessitate massive death and destruction; quite the reverse. **It is the necessary responses to agricultural disease—to contain and clean up, to prevent further spread, and then to reclaim the previous level of disease control or freedom, lost exports, and international recognition—that eat up effort and funding.** There is a very different time scale and series of available tools than those involving public health and human biological attacks. The desired results from an agricultural biological attack are much more complicated than the simple widespread terror induced in a human target population.

A biological attack is the deliberate use of microorganisms or toxins derived from living organisms to induce death or disease in humans, animals, or plants. Biological attacks can include biological warfare, bioterrorism, and what we might call "biocrimes." The main differences in these three are in breadth, motivation, target, route, transport and logistics, and potential countermeasures.

Biological warfare (BW) is defined in the North Atlantic Treaty Organization (NATO) *Handbook on the Medical Aspects of Nuclear, Biological, and Chemical (NBC) Defensive Operations* as the "employment of biological agents to produce casualties in man or animals or damage to plants." Biological warfare is, therefore, a specialized type of warfare conducted by a government against a target.

Terrorism has been defined as "the unlawful use of force or violence committed by an individual or group of individuals against persons or property to intimidate or coerce a government, the civilian population, or any segment thereof, in furtherance of political or social objectives." By extension, then, bioterrorism is a terrorist activity that employs a biological agent as the means of force.

Biocrimes are illegal activities in which the perpetrators used biological agents as weapons, but in which no political or social objectives were involved. Unlike the bioterrorist, the biocriminal's motivation is usually murder, extortion, sabotage (usually for economic reasons), or revenge.

The potential terrorist or criminal has many more agents available that could produce visible results against a relatively small target than the military bioweaponeer has that could produce large-scale results on a battlefield.

The targets for any of these attacks could be humans, livestock, or crops. Many people think that it would be too difficult for a terrorist to produce and disperse enough agent to do any significant harm. Although that might be true to some extent for most terrorists with human targets, an attack that causes even *one* casualty will be counted a success if it becomes known. And an attack on agriculture could potentially affect the lives of everyone in the affected nation.

WHY ATTACK THE AGRICULTURE INDUSTRY?

Why would anyone want to use biological agents against animals or plants? We can think of several instances in which attacks against the agriculture industry would be particularly effective.

If a key agricultural industry were undermined sufficiently, particularly in a nation highly dependent upon one main crop such as rice, food shortages could arise. This could escalate into widespread unemployment, starvation, civil unrest, and destabilization of the government. This is more likely to affect developing nations with limited food resources than industrialized nations that have more options.

Causing an export ban (as in the recent outbreaks of foot-and-mouth disease in the United Kingdom) is certainly an effective means of damaging a government without directly causing physical injury to any of its citizens.

One would expect attacks such as these to be carried out mainly by enemy nations (or by terrorists backed by such states), and the possibilities are numerous. According to the Chemical and Biological Arms Control Institute Web site:[1]

• The United States, during the days of its offensive biological warfare program (1943-1969), investigated agents of anthrax, brucellosis, Eastern and

Western equine encephalitis, foot-and-mouth disease, fowl plague, glanders, late blight of potato, Newcastle disease, psittacosis, rice blast, rice brown spot disease, rinderpest, Venezuelan equine encephalitis, wheat blast fungus, and wheat stem rust as potential biological weapons.

• The Soviet Union/Russia (1935-1992) worked with African swine fever, anthrax, avian influenza, brown grass mosaic, brucellosis, contagious bovine pleuropneumonia, contagious ecthyma, foot-and-mouth disease, glanders, maize rust, Newcastle disease, potato virus, psittacosis, rice blast, rinderpest, rye blast, tobacco mosaic, Venezuelan equine encephalitis, vesicular stomatitis, wheat and barley mosaic streak, and wheat stem rust. They also experimented with parasitic insects and insect attractants.

• Germany's biological weapons program (1915-1917, 1942-1945) worked with anthrax, foot-and-mouth disease, glanders, potato beetle, and wheat fungus. During World War II they also experimented with turnip weevils, antler moths, potato stalk rot, potato tuber decay, and miscellaneous anti-crop weeds.

• France (1939-1972) investigated potato beetle and rinderpest.

• Japan (1937-1945) worked with anthrax and glanders. During World War II they experimented with miscellaneous anti-crop fungi, bacteria, and nematodes.

• Iraq (1980s to probably present) investigated weaponizing aflatoxin, anthrax, camelpox (which may have been investigated as a surrogate for smallpox), foot-and-mouth disease, and wheat stem rust.

While all these countries are supposed to have ceased production of biological weapons with the signing of the Biological Weapons Convention in the mid-1970s, the possibility of some "nations of concern" still maintaining offensive BW programs remains. For instance, the Iraqis are believed to retain elements of their program despite UN disarmament efforts.

Other goals are also possible. In the United States, for example, the government has a responsibility to provide safe and wholesome food. A terrorist or criminal might seek to undermine the public's confidence in the government to provide a safe food supply. This could affect the outcomes of elections and lead to changes in laws and policies.

A criminal, or a criminal organization, might wish to cause losses in a particular crop to manipulate commodities futures and affect stock market prices.

The first two goals are long-standing national and international implications of biological attacks on food, with economic and political implications. The latter two are more recent goals adopted by activist groups seeking to manipulate public behavior.

Yet there is yet another kind of possible "bio-user"—one who can bring about unintended consequences by using biological agents as a form of pest control: deer or rabbits eating the garden, feral pigs tearing up the ranch, and so forth. This person does not see himself as a criminal but rather as someone who had to take action because the authorities would not. Depending on the agent used, this individual's act might trigger rampant disease outbreaks in this country's livestock industry or even cause disease in humans.

For a variety of reasons, agricultural bioterrorism is easier and safer to do, and, in the view of many, is much more likely than attacks against humans.

So why would people think of agricultural bioterrorism? Well, first of all, it's **low tech**. It is much easier to develop capability without a lot of extensive sophisticated infrastructure. There is a **lower profile for detection** because of the kind of agents you would be working with. **Personal safety**. You know there's something to be said for working with something that will kill animals or plants, and not people. If you have a little accident in your laboratory, you're probably not going to kill yourself. **Easier delivery**. In places like Colorado and Kansas and the great agricultural areas of our country, it will be significantly easier to distribute biological agents with virtually no chance of detection. **Lower retaliatory risk**. I believe that if someone decided to take a shot at Uncle Sam, they could decide to wipe out our pork or beef, or wheat industry. The retaliatory decisions we would have to make would certainly be more difficult in the event of a proven agricultural attack. It is difficult to envision a lethal-type retaliation in response to an agricultural attack. I don't think world or public opinion would tolerate it. So, for a rogue state, this would be a much more acceptable way to fight that asymmetric battle. **Plausible deniability**. This is one of the hallmark reasons that bio is such a tough nut to crack. You can say we've had a serious outbreak, but where did it come from? Was it naturally occurring? Virtually all of these agents are naturally occurring some place. You nearly always would have that kernel of doubt as to whether it was intentional or naturally occurring. And, of course, once again in the retaliatory phase, that would be a very significant aspect. I believe that there is a **reduced moral and ethical burden** associated with perpetrating an agricultural attack. There are many people who would accept the idea of killing all our hogs, wiping out our wheat crop, or wiping out a rice crop. However, those very same people might never accept the thought of killing innocent people, but might consider ways to damage our economic infrastructure for political or other reasons.[2]

OUR VULNERABILITIES TO AGROTERRORISM

In the United States, agriculture is no longer spread more or less evenly throughout the country. Today's highly concentrated agricultural systems, coupled with the decreasing genetic diversity of livestock and crop plants, heighten the vulnerability of our agricultural economy to terrorist acts.

In 1970 there were about 500,000 dairy farms in the United States; by 1988 this had decreased to 160,000. Beef production has followed the same trend, with 120,000 feedlots in 1970 and only 43,000 in 1988. Today's processing plants operate at extremely high volume: a plant that produces ground beef may produce 4 to 12 tons per hour and operate on a 20-hour day. A single line can

---

BOX 1   Our Vulnerabilities to Agroterrorism

- Few states raise more than 30% of what their residents eat.
- Most cities have only a five-day food supply or less.
- On average, a person's food travels 1,300 miles from field to table.
- Current agricultural and food production trends make agroterrorism easier.
  - Concentration
  - Decreasing genetic diversity
  - Consolidation of support industries
  - Urbanization
  - Internationalization

---

turn out 20 million ground beef patties per day, and a single hamburger patty can contain meat from a minimum of 51 to a maximum of 1,400 different cattle that originated in many different states and/or countries.

In such high-speed, high-volume operations the potential for accidental contamination of meat with rumen or intestinal contents is enormous; if contamination were to be intentionally introduced, the results could affect an untold number of consumers.

Strangely, as the world has grown richer, farming more intensive and agricultural research more sophisticated, we have concentrated food production on just a few varieties. Ninety-five percent of the world's calories now come from only 30 crops, and fifty percent from just four: rice, maize (corn), wheat, and potato.

—Editorial, *New Scientist*, September 2, 2000

BOX 2   Who Is at Risk?

At risk are states that
- Practice high-density, large area agriculture
- Have heavy reliance on monoculture and restricted range of genotypes
- Are free of serious plant and animal pathogens or pests
- Are major agricultural exporters
- Are suffering domestic unrest or have unfriendly neighbor nations with BW programs
- Have weak plant and animal epidemiological infrastructure

SOURCE: Adapted from Wheelis, Mark. Agricultural biowarfare and bioterrorism. Federation of American Scientists Chemical and Biological Arms Control Program Web site, http://www.fas.org/bwc/agr/main.htm.

Box 3   Consequences

- Direct losses affecting relatively few farms
- Costs of containment efforts (national in scope)
- Restrictions on international trade (international in scope)
- Indirect effects
  - Shareholder losses
  - Revenue losses to processors and shippers
  - Market destabilization
  - Feed and forage producers

According to Mark Wheelis,[3] the potential consequences of an attack on the agricultural sector are many:

Direct losses due to disease. Direct financial loss due to mortality or morbidity of domestic animals or crop plants can vary from insignificant to catastrophic. In many cases the direct losses would be modest and would fall on a small number of farms. One of the major determinants of the magnitude of the direct losses will be the rapidity with which the disease is noticed and diagnosed. In developed countries, most of the foreign diseases of greatest concern would likely be identified fairly early, allowing the direct disease losses to be kept modest.

Losses due to efforts to contain outbreaks. An outbreak of an imported, highly contagious animal or plant disease is routinely controlled by the destruction of all potentially exposed healthy host organisms. With animal diseases, this normally means the slaughter of all host animals in the immediate vicinity. With plants, thousands of acres of crop plants may have to be destroyed to contain an outbreak. Thus, the losses attendant on outbreak control can exceed, often by several orders of magnitude, the direct losses due to the disease itself.

Destruction of exposed hosts is often the only option when the agent is bacterial or viral. However, for fungal agents, destruction of exposed crops may be reduced by the use of fungicides. However, this is an expensive process itself, so it adds significantly to the cost of the outbreak, and it may cause environmental damage.

A number of important threats to crop plants are from insect pests, rather than microbial pathogens. These outbreaks are usually controlled by the use of pesticides rather than the destruction of exposed plants, which, as with control of fungal disease, can cost large amounts.

Widespread broadcast of insecticide may cause environmental or human health damage as well. The Biological and Toxin Weapons Convention (BTWC) certainly could cover pests as well as pathogens, since Article I refers to "microbial or other biological agents" and the consultative process of the BTWC has been used to address concerns about a pest infestation in Cuba. However, this coverage has never been made explicit, and it would be useful to do so since there are so many insect pests of great potential for agricultural biowarfare or bioterrorism.

Losses due to sanitary or phytosanitary restrictions on international trade. Under the World Trade Organization (WTO), member states are allowed to impose import restrictions on agricultural products to prevent the importation of pests or disease agents. Thus, importing countries free of a particular disease are usually quick to block imports from countries in which that disease breaks out. This happens frequently, because these diseases periodically resurface in areas from which they have been absent; trade restrictions typically last a month or two when control of the outbreak is rapid, or they may endure much longer if disease control is slow and difficult (e.g., the European Union restriction on the import of beef from the United Kingdom due to the bovine spongiform encephalopathy [BSE] outbreak).

Thus, major agricultural exporters are particularly vulnerable. For instance, the Taiwan foot-and-mouth disease (FMD) outbreak in swine in 1997 probably only cost tens of thousands of U.S. dollars in direct losses, but it cost $4 billion in eradication and disinfection costs, and a cumulative $15 billion in lost export revenues. An FMD outbreak in Italy in 1993 again had trivial direct costs, but nearly $12 million in eradication and disinfection costs and $120 million in lost trade revenues.

Alternatively, the introduction of a disease into a country previously free of it would undermine the legitimacy of that country's import restrictions under the WTO, forcing the lifting of the restrictions and opening up the market. This could bring significant additional losses to domestic producers.

Losses due to indirect effects (market destabilization, etc.). The substantial market effects of a widespread outbreak, or one that has major impacts on international trade, could have secondary effects, such as shareholder losses, revenue losses to processors and shippers, and so forth. In the extreme, if losses are very large and if future losses appear likely, significant levels of investor panic could lead to market destabilization.

ANTI-ANIMAL AND ANTI-PLANT AGENTS

An effective agent to be used against animals will be highly contagious, virulent, able to survive well in the environment, and will result in economic hardship and an import ban by other countries. What types of agents might fulfill some, if not most, of the above criteria? Foot-and-Mouth Disease, Hog Cholera, Velogenic Newcastle Disease, African Swine Fever, Highly Pathogenic Avian Influenza, and Rinderpest. It is estimated that if FMD became established within the U.S. that it would cost our nation over $27 billion in trade losses alone each year. Add to this the costs of depopulating infected herds, disinfecting premises, quarantines, surveillance, higher prices of meat—it all adds up to a heavy price.

—from Biological Warfare and Terrorism Web site,
  http://www.vetmed.iastate.edu/Faculty&Staff/RDavi current_interests.htm

Biological weapons may be used not only against humans, but to attack plants or animals to harm the nation's economy. Some diseases are so feared, and so closely guarded against international transmission, that the appearance of even one infected animal in this country could cause serious economic repercussions if other countries banned the importation of U.S. meat products. Any potentially exposed animals would have to be slaughtered immediately. As mentioned in the previous section, our intensified livestock production system makes us particularly vulnerable. More and more animals are kept in fewer and fewer places, so the potential for a great number of animals becoming infected with a disease is high. One such feared disease is the so-called Mad Cow Disease (BSE). We will discuss two others in this section.

Likewise, certain plant diseases could result in the forced destruction of entire crops, even if only a few plants are infected, and many countries might ban the import of U.S. wheat, rice, or soybeans. In addition, some plants, when infected by certain organisms, produce toxins that can cause illness in humans or animals consuming them. Any contamination of this sort could lead to loss of confidence in the safety of our food supply, which would harm farmers, consumers, and business. And a hoax could be as effective here as an actual attack.

Newcastle Disease

Newcastle disease is a viral infection that causes a respiratory or nervous disorder in several species of fowl including chickens and turkeys. Different types or strains, varying in their ability to cause nervous disorders, internal lesions and death, have been recognized. The most severe is velogenic viscerotropic Newcastle disease (VVND) (also called "exotic Newcastle disease"), which until the1970s had not been seen in the United States.

The U.S. Animal Health Association's Web site gives the following account of the first U.S. outbreak:

> Around Thanksgiving of 1971, an outbreak of VVND began in southern California from the importation of infected exotic birds (parrots and mynah birds). The disease spread to a nearby poultry ranch via escaped infected exotic birds or by cats taking infected dead birds that were improperly disposed of back to the poultry ranch. The disease then spread throughout eight counties in Southern California via importation of infected exotic birds, movement of live commercial chickens, and movement of people from infected ranches. Within two months, the disease spread to 34 flocks. The spread was then explosive,

with 75 more flocks becoming infected within one month. A total of 45,000 square miles was subsequently quarantined. From March 14, 1972, to November 1, 1972, a total of 101,909 flocks (exotic birds and poultry) [comprising] 406,078,000 birds were inspected. Two hundred seventy-nine flocks comprised of about 7,856,860 birds were found to be infected, and 369 flocks and 306,155 birds were found to be exposed. All infected and exposed birds were destroyed and indemnified at a cost of more than $15.5 million.

In addition to the indemnification cost of this outbreak, there was a severe financial and economic burden on many poultry producers. The quarantine blocked movement of any poultry product out of the quarantine area, resulting in millions of dollars in losses. Many producers were forced out of business because they no longer had a market for their product even if their birds were not infected nor exposed. The quarantine area was reduced from 45,000 square miles to about 2,300 square miles on October 27, 1972 — almost 1 year after the outbreak started. It is estimated that the total expense to eradicate this VVND outbreak was $52 million.

> —Report of the United States Animal Health Association
> Committee on Foreign Animal Diseases, 1998 committee reports.
> *http://www.usaha.org/reports98/r98fredi.html#vvnd*

Highly Pathogenic Avian Influenza

Avian influenza affects a wide variety of farmed and wild birds—predominantly of chickens and turkeys, but also game birds such as pheasants, partridge, and quail; ratites (ostrich and emu); psittacines (parrots); and passerines (songbirds and perching birds).

With virulent strains, losses can be up to 100 percent. The virus is so tiny and so virulent that one gram of fecal material, just enough to cover a dime, contains up to 10 million particles, which is enough virus to infect all of the chickens in the world.

Lethal strains of the virus can strike quickly, particularly in young chickens. There may be no signs other than sudden death. In cases of highly virulent virus, clinical signs may simply be seen as sudden high mortality rate (exceeding 90 percent), possibly preceded by severe depression or fever in the flock. Affected birds may show conjunctivitis, runny eyes, sinusitis, and swollen dark blue heads. Milder forms may be associated with nonspecific respiratory signs, depression, loss of appetite, blue combs and wattles, diarrhea, or blood-tinged discharge from the nostrils. There may be a severe and sudden drop in egg production in breeder birds with an increase in soft-shelled or shell-less eggs. Treatment is usually ineffective and inappropriate because birds that have been affected tend to be weak and in poor condition. Virulent disease is controlled by immediately stamping out and disposing of infected and in-contact birds to remove the major source of the virus. Even though recovered flocks shed less virus than clinically ill flocks, recovered flocks will intermittently shed and should be considered infected for life.

The potential economic impact of this disease is huge: Pennsylvania had an outbreak in 1883-1884 and it cost more than $50 million to control the disease. Adjusted for inflation, losses to producers and increased costs to consumers resulting from the 1883-1884 outbreak would today equal approximately $85 million and $490 million, respectively. A coordinated attack using H5 AIv simultaneously against poultry farms in the five major areas—Georgia, Alabama, Mississippi, California, and the DelMarVa peninsula—could halt all poultry consumption (thanks to a "panic" factor), with follow-on effects of extensive layoffs in the slaughter and processing plants; grossly affect feed grain production and the farming community; and stop exports. If an attack were against only one region, there would still be significant price disturbances and an increase in consumer costs.

In May 1997, Hong Kong officials reported the death of a three-year-old boy from respiratory failure due to influenza. In August, authorities identified the strain of influenza virus isolated from the boy as H5N1. H5N1 previously had been known to exist in shorebirds and occasionally to infect chickens, but this was the first time a person had been found to be infected with this particular influenza strain. The virus had jumped directly from a bird to a human, an unprecedented event. Public health officials worldwide continue to monitor the situation closely, still not certain whether human-to-human transmission can occur, which would increase the likelihood of epidemic spread. Laboratory researchers are pursuing studies to determine the source of the virus and the properties that allowed it to infect humans. Since that initial case was identified, seven additional cases (total of eight) of influenza A (H5N1) have been recognized in humans in Hong Kong. Two of the seven have died.

Foot-and-Mouth Disease

Foot-and-mouth disease is an extremely contagious virus that affects all cloven-hoofed animals. (Although rare, humans can become infected; human FMD is not a serious disease.) Numerous different strains exist, some of which are more virulent for some animals than for others. The disease is endemic to much of Africa, Asia, and South America, as well as parts of Europe. The United States has not had an outbreak of FMD since 1929, but one has only to look at the outbreaks in the United Kingdom that appeared in February 2001 to imagine the devastating economic effects such an event would cause.

After an incubation period of one to ten days, FMD produces lesions in the mouth and on the feet of infected animals, among other symptoms. Although the disease is infrequently fatal, it can result in enormous losses in productivity. This accounts for the considerable efforts undertaken by FMD-free countries to remain that way.

FMD is resistant to common disinfectants and can persist for more than a year in infected premises and up to 12 weeks on clothing or in feed. The virus can also be carried in uncooked meat and in dairy products from infected animals; virus-laden exhalations from infected swine herds can be carried on the wind for distances of 100 km or further.

Fungal agents are the most likely group of agents to be used against plants. Many fungal agents are able to be easily disseminated over large areas, reduce yields, and disseminate widely each repeating cycle. They can be produced in large quantities, many in simple nutrient culture. Most are obligate parasites on plants in the field. They are relatively inexpensive to procure and propagate and can easily be stored for long periods in plant tissue or under refrigeration.

Rice Blast

Rice blast is one of the most important diseases affecting rice worldwide. It is caused by a fungus that can attack the rice plant at any stage of growth. It is characterized by the appearance of lesions on the leaves, nodes, and flowers. On the leaves, lesions are typically spindle shaped—wide in the center and pointed toward either end. Large lesions usually develop a grayish center, with a brown margin on older lesions. When a node is infected, all parts above the infected node may die. When this occurs, yield losses may be large because few seeds (the part we know as rice) will develop. Yield loss estimates from various parts of the world have ranged from 1 to 50 percent. Aside from rice, this fungus can also attack more than 50 other species of grasses and sedges. Many developing nations whose populations are heavily dependent upon rice as a source of food would be extremely vulnerable to a disease that seriously threatened their rice harvests.[4]

Stem Rust

Rusts are among the most damaging diseases of wheat and other small grain crops. In the Great Plains of the United States, stem rust and leaf rust epidemics often have caused yield losses in wheat far exceeding 20 million bushels. As recently as 1993, leaf rust destroyed more than 40 million bushels of wheat in Kansas and Nebraska. In 1985, Texas and Oklahoma lost 95 million bushels of wheat to leaf rust. The country can ill afford such losses, especially for wheat, a major export commodity.

Wheat stem rust occurs worldwide wherever wheat is grown. It is most important where temperatures are warm, 18-30°C (64-86°F), and dews are frequent during and after the heads of wheat form. Losses are often severe (50 to 70 percent) over a large area, and individual fields can be totally destroyed. Damage is greatest when the disease becomes severe before the grain is completely formed. In areas favorable for disease development, susceptible cultivars cannot be grown. Grain is shriveled due to the damage to the conducting tissue, resulting in less nutrient being transported to the grain. Severe disease can cause straw breakage, resulting in a loss of spikes with combine harvesting.[5]

CHARACTERISTICS OF AN AGRICULTURAL BIO-ATTACK

Any or all of the following may characterize a biological attack on agriculture:

Unusual time and/or place (i.e., at extremes of normal distribution). Based on informed epidemiological experience, literature, and databases, 99 out of 100 suspicious outbreaks will be normal events and fully explicable from existing knowledge. Events at the extremes of normal probabilities are by their nature infrequent but not ipso facto abnormal. An event having a low probability will acquire persuasion only when matched or unmatched with other events. "Experience" may indicate that certain infrequent events are commonly associated with a specific set of circumstances, and these may be missing in a contrived and not-normal outbreak. Therefore, the events leading up to the "incident" must be carefully analyzed by experienced investigators.

Unexpected strain of agent, or multiple strains. Isolates from the initial outbreaks should be compared rapidly with known isolates in the pathogen archives. Does the agent exactly match a known strain with a documented origin? Are there genomic markers that are associated with a specific ecology and/or host species, further defining its natural origin? If multiple strains are identified, are they logical? Do they have any other characteristics, such as resistance to a number of antibiotics, a documented collective availability to one institute, or an unusual common ability (e.g., to successfully withstand freeze-drying while others do not)? Are any possible "attacker(s)" or their contractees capable technically and scientifically of mounting such an offense?

Marked reversal of an otherwise steady progress in disease control or freedom. One should carefully and objectively investigate the situation and the existing control program's surveillance system. The setback is probably 100 percent predictable in hindsight, especially if the outbreak has revealed embedded defects in program design, implementation, reporting cycle and response time, funding, training, or tactical control. Many national disease control programs work well until they are challenged by a real epidemic. However, a new case in an area well cleared of disease for a number of years—and with farmers experienced and knowledgeable of the costs to be incurred if the condition were to be reintroduced—must get one's attention. One should also never lose sight of the possibility of unintended outbreaks following illegal importation of fruit and livestock, which by definition lack the appropriate certificates and health guarantees. What characterizes these events is that there are no external beneficiaries other than those individuals directly involved in the illegal activities.

Epidemiologically "weird" event. An epidemiologically weird event is one that in no way matches normal experience or knowledge and goes far beyond expectations, such as Venezuelan equine encephalitis in Switzerland, vector-borne diseases in areas without appropriate vectors, normally feed-borne diseases in stock not receiving feed, et cetera. Other things to consider include evaluation of the outbreak to see if it was independent of normal commercial or industrial activities, marketing, weather, and/or livestock and crop densities. For example, if an infection is normally windborne (e.g., certain FMD virus strains), was the initial spread downwind or across the prevailing wind direction? If it is density dependent, as with bovine brucellosis, was it first noted in one or more small herds with less than 10 cows? Was the outbreak in the dry season while the local vectors are all wet-season breeders?

Forced diagnosis. How did we hear of this case? Was this a normal outbreak discovered in a normal manner, or were there circumstances that ensured diagnosis? Following from this, were there any circumstances relating to the announcement or news releases that indicated an unusual amount or kind of publicity? Most agricultural costs from outbreaks are self-inflicted by the host country in responding to the outbreak and the need for rapid resolution. This is usually out of proportion to the number of index or primary cases. The initial hit can be singular or numerically trivial, and in these cases the attacker must aid the diagnostic process to make sure the event is (1) recognized and (2) reported. Therefore, what were the circumstances that led to the initial recognition of the event and its subsequent diagnosis and laboratory confirmation?

RECOGNIZING A BIOLOGICAL ATTACK

One must always be aware that biological events will be rare, and therefore any suspicious incident is most likely to have a normal if not prosaic explanation whatever the initial impression or belief. Similarly, the implications of a proven attack are so far reaching that any investigation resulting in such a conclusion must be so thorough as to survive the most rigorous of examinations.

Therefore, unless the circumstances are blatantly those of an obvious biological event—the biological equivalent of the Oklahoma City bombing, such as 10 widely separated cases of rinderpest across the United States within one week[6]—the primary investigative position is that the situation was normal and, if unexpected, merely unusual. Thus, Rule One: "Rule out normality." And Rule Two: "Try harder to rule out normality." Only if that fails does Rule Three apply: "Round up the usual suspects."

THE 1973 NEWCASTLE DISEASE OUTBREAK IN NORTHERN IRELAND: A CASE STUDY

The event itself was certainly unexpected, since Northern Ireland did not and does not import animal proteins or by-products, such as bone meals or poultry offal meals. In retrospect, this outbreak probably is traceable to contamination of European feed grains by the then-pandemic Newcastle disease virus strain in Western Europe. Although there were 15 feed-compounder mills involved, importation was via only two known agents. All of the initial isolates were identical except for the "known" overvaccination-related outbreak.

The outbreak directly resulted in an economic cost of £668,994 (or £4.7 million to £5.1 million in 1997 terms), but the benefits were diffuse because the province returned to full production quickly. Most countries in Europe had Newcastle disease problems at that time, which would have limited their trading capacity. The demand for table eggs was declining rapidly in the United Kingdom. In reality, there was slight benefit to anyone outside Northern Ireland in this outbreak. There were no obvious social or political impacts inside the country. In fact, the outbreak brought all those involved closer together.

There are no additional aspects of this case, which is indicative of a non-BW, but natural, source. (Of course, if viewed from the opposite direction, varied Newcastle disease virus strains would be characteristic of an aggressive group with tight security and three separate teams, each with their own infected eggs to be placed broken in the targeted flocks so that they would be eaten by the chickens; or however else delivery was to be achieved—a Roswell interpretation, in the opinion of the writer.)

NOTES

1. Ban, J. 2000. Agricultural biological warfare: an overview. Chemical and Biological Arms Control Institute website, http://www.cbaci.org.

2. Jaax, J. 2000. Non-lethal technology in a comprehensive homeland defense program. Presented at Non-Lethal Technology and Academic Research (NTAR) Symposium II, November 14-17, 2000, Portsmouth, http://www.unh.edu/ntar/Transcripts/EDjaax.htm.

3. Wheelis, M. Agricultural biowarfare and bioterrorism. Federation of American Scientists Chemical and Biological Arms Control Program Web site, http://www.fas.org/bwc/agr/main.htm.

4. Rice BlastDB, A database for the rice blast fungus, *Magnaporthe grisea*, http://ascus.cit.cornell.edu/blastdb/index.html.

5. U.S. Department of Agriculture, Agricultural Research Service Cereal Disease Laboratory, http://www.crl.umn.edu/index.htm.

6. Even this might be explainable if it were found to be related to a recent importation of wildebeest from Africa that somehow were cleared from quarantine early and shipped to widely dispersed "wildlife parks" with resident beef cattle or nearby dairy farms. Then the incident is downgraded from an intentional attack to an egregious example of negligence or stupidity (never an inconsequential consideration).

FUTURE TRENDS AND INTERNATIONAL COOPERATION

Terrorism in a High-Tech Society: Legal Aspects and Contemporary Methods of Preventing and Countering Terrorist Activity

Aleksandr V. Zmeevsky [*]
Ministry of Foreign Affairs of the Russian Federation

Humanity's entrance into the twenty-first century is significantly clouded by the growth of terrorist danger. Each year, hundreds of people fall victim to terrorist acts. The methods used by terrorists are becoming ever more diversified and refined. As the number of terrorist and extremist groups rises, these groups are also becoming better equipped technically. The threat of "terrorism of mass destruction" is becoming ever more realistic. The danger of terrorists penetrating computer networks is increasing many times over. On the whole, the "information boom" has become a sort of springboard in the development of terrorism. The interweaving of terrorism, narcobusiness, and other manifestations of organized crime causes deep concern. The financial base of contemporary terrorism is widening. The border between terrorist acts committed in peacetime and those carried out in the context of armed conflicts is being erased. On the whole, international crises and conflicts are providing favorable grounds for terrorism. Terrorists are easily able to use interethnic conflicts and interreligious contradictions to achieve their goals. They are able to unite. The reality of our day is that the terrorist international is creating a threat not only to the security of individual states, but also to international stability on the whole. It is possible to fight this common enemy only by working together.

In the general effort to counter the terrorist danger, it is difficult to overestimate the role of international law. It is on the basis of international law that the international community has succeeded in rising above political-ideological, national-ethnic, religious, and other contradictions and prejudices and forming a system of global countermeasures against various terrorist challenges. This sys-

---

[*] Translated from the Russian by Rita S. Guenther.

tem currently includes 12 active, universal, antiterrorist treaties on combating various manifestations of terrorism on land, at sea, and in the air.

The contemporary system of multilateral cooperation in the fight against terrorism took shape primarily in the last four decades. On the global level, it functions under the aegis of the United Nations and its special institutions, first and foremost the Institute for International Relations, the International Civil Aviation Organization, and the International Atomic Energy Agency.

Antiterrorist conventions contain provisions defining the general legal framework necessary for the organization of an effective international rebuff to terrorism. These provisions include obligations to suppress terrorist acts, including to disarm and detain persons suspected or found guilty of perpetrating such acts, to exchange appropriate information, and to provide the maximum degree of mutual legal assistance. Undoubtedly, there is great significance in the convention provisions calling on signatories to ensure inevitable punishment for criminals by affirming so-called universal criminal jurisdiction based on the principle of *aut dedere aut judicare*. This requires the state in which a criminal is found either to subject him to criminal prosecution or to extradite him to another state for this purpose.

Terrorism is an extremely multifaceted phenomenon: there are political, legal, psychological, philosophical, historical, technical, and other aspects involved. It is no coincidence that the international community has not managed to develop a universally accepted legal definition of terrorism, although the essential nature of this phenomenon is understood by all. These characteristic features include illegal violence (using weapons, as a rule), a desire to intimidate broad segments of the population, and innocent victims. There is also an international element, when the matter concerns terrorist acts that cross state borders.

It is within the framework of this global system for antiterrorist cooperation that the underlying principles of international collaboration in the battle against this phenomenon were formed and are developing. The first such principle is that generally recognized principles and norms of international law are to be followed steadfastly in the struggle against terrorism. Another very important principle is that there should be universal condemnation and acknowledgment of the illegality of terrorism in all of its manifestations, wherever and by whomever terrorist acts may be committed. Another key point is the principle of international cooperation in the struggle against terrorism. This includes active cooperation to eliminate the root causes lying at the foundation of this phenomenon, cooperation within the framework of international treaties, development of new agreements, the taking of practical measures to prevent attempted acts of terrorism (by exchanging information and coordinating necessary measures), and the rendering of mutual criminal procedural assistance. The effectiveness of antiterrorist cooperation is directly connected with the principle of ensuring that those persons who have committed crimes are inevitably held to criminal responsibility.

The United Nations has made historical contributions to the formation of the basic parameters for global antiterrorist cooperation and has become the center of global opposition to terrorism. Various aspects of cooperation among states in the fight against terrorism are regularly discussed at the UN General Assembly and its subunits, UN special institutions, the UN Commission on Human Rights, and UN congresses on crime prevention and the treatment of offenders.

Countering terrorism is not among the key areas of activity of the UN Security Council. The focus of its attention, according to the UN Charter, lies primarily in questions of maintaining international peace and security. At the same time, as terrorism has gone beyond the limits of national boundaries and individual regions, it has gradually become a real global challenge. The Security Council is therefore devoting more attention to searching for responses to the growing terrorist threat, especially where it impacts questions of peace and security. Until recently, the Security Council dealt with antiterrorist problems for the most part in the context of specific situations related to the scope of its primary interests.

One of the first attempts in the Security Council at considering specific situations where the terrorist threat had consequences for peace and security was the July 1976 operation by Israeli commandos to free hostages being held at Entebbe. Due to the divergent positions of its members, the Security Council could not produce a clear-cut position regarding this action.

UN Security Council Resolutions 1269 (1999) and 1333 (2000) may be considered the clearest examples of the imposition of sanctions according to Chapter VII of the UN Charter in reaction to the threat of international terrorism in connection to a specific situation. They are aimed at the Taliban movement, which refuses to comply with the demands of the Security Council regarding the termination of support for terrorism on the territory it controls in Afghanistan. Among other points, the sanction limitations call on the Taliban to stop granting asylum to international terrorists and their organizations, to hand over Osama bin Laden, and to close all terrorist training camps.

The most severe measure established by Resolution 1333 (2000) is the unilateral embargo on the shipment of weapons to the Taliban. That step completes a wide range of sanctions, including a ban on flights by Taliban aircraft, the freezing of Taliban financial accounts, limits on embassy and consular staffs, the closure of Taliban offices abroad, et cetera.

As stipulated in Resolution 1333 (2000), the mechanism of international monitoring of compliance (particularly with those sections concerning observance of the embargo on arms shipments and the closing of terrorist training camps) is intended to be an effective means of putting the sanction decisions into practice.

In addition, paragraph 18 of Resolution 1333 contains an appeal to states to institute criminal proceedings against persons or entities within their jurisdiction that violate the measures of the given resolution, with appropriate measures of punishment to be applied.

In 1999, on the initiative of Russia, the Security Council for the first time began a comprehensive examination of the topic of terrorism unrelated to any specific situation, which would create a threat to peace and security. The council was spurred to take this action by the global scale of the terrorist danger, including its capability to create a threat to the peace and security of all states.

Adopted at the conclusion of this session, Resolution 1269 (1999) contains an unconditional condemnation of all acts, methods, and practices of terrorism as criminal and unjustifiable, regardless of motives, in all forms and manifestations, wherever and by whomever they are committed. This especially pertains to those who could threaten international peace and security. The Security Council calls upon all states to carry out international antiterrorist conventions in full and to join forces with other states that are cosignatories to these agreements. It also proposes that as-yet-unratified conventions be adopted as soon as possible. The council pays special attention to the vitally important role of the United Nations in strengthening international cooperation in the fight against terrorism. It contains urgent strategic and practical measures that should be undertaken by states in the area of antiterrorist cooperation. These include the following: strengthening the legal bases for international cooperation in the struggle against terrorism by fully implementing existing antiterrorist conventions and ratifying new agreements; improving coordination among governments and international and regional organizations; facilitating coordinated activities to protect citizens from attempted terrorist acts; preventing and suppressing acts of terrorism; ensuring the inevitability of punishment for terrorists; and preventing the granting of asylum to them.

The preamble of the resolution touches on the topic of state-supported terrorism. Specifically, it points out that suppressing acts of international terrorism in which states are involved "is an essential contribution to the maintenance of international peace and security."

In the development of this resolution, the Security Council ratified a statement from its chairman regarding the struggle against terrorism. Adopted at a meeting on December 6, 2000, which was convened on the initiative of Russia, the statement expresses deep concern over the increasing frequency of terrorist acts in many regions of the world. The Security Council condemns all such acts regardless of where or by whom they are committed. The council once again confirmed its readiness to take appropriate measures in accord with its obligations under the UN Charter to counter threats to international peace and security resulting from terrorism. In the aim of strengthening international antiterrorist cooperation, the Security Council called on all states that have not already done so to immediately examine the question of adhering to existing antiterrorist conventions. The council has resolved to continue to study this question.

Under the aegis of the United Nations, states have succeeded on the whole in defining the general political-legal framework for joint opposition to terrorism. Under the influence of this framework, various configurations of influential antiterrorist coalitions have formed. However, it would be premature to speak of the formation of a universal antiterrorist front of states.

Unregulated conflicts are exerting serious negative influence on the effectiveness of cooperation in this sphere, first and foremost under the aegis of the United Nations. Appeals continue to be made to the effect that the struggle of national liberation movements should not be equated with terrorism, although it is clear that the entire question is that this struggle should not be conducted with terrorist methods. That is to say, one must not hijack civilian airplanes, shoot at buses full of tourists, or conduct similar activities. Appeals are being made just as insistently to equate terrorism with those activities of states that are contradictory to international law, although it is obvious that aggression, occupation, or violation of the Geneva Convention is very bad, but not terrorism. Time passes, political regimes fade into the past, and new leaders appear, but the fuse of confrontation still remains.

The task now is to move international cooperation in the battle against terrorism once and for all under the aegis of the United Nations, as well as to move other forums from the plane of political-ideological opposition to the sphere of practical action. The legacy of confrontation can be surmounted through concrete work.

A new, extremely important, and hopeful moment in the fight against terrorism has been the development of parameters for specific joint actions in the given sphere by the Group of Eight (G-8) countries. Naturally, these states by virtue of their political, economic, and other influence possess considerable capabilities for eradicating the terrorist threat on our planet.

We highly value the 25 practical recommendations worked out in 1996 by the Paris Conference of G-8 Ministers of Foreign Affairs and Security, which addressed not only these countries, but also the entire world community. In final documents of subsequent G-8 summits, a program of further actions was formulated in the sphere of combating terrorism, including a number of new elements. Specifically with regard to the possible use of computer systems by terrorists to accomplish their goals, these elements include the prevention of terrorist acts aimed at the electronic and computer infrastructure.

In recent times, it seems that fresh impulses to breathe new life into global cooperation in fighting terrorism have come primarily from efforts being undertaken on the regional level.

Impressive political-legal potential has accumulated on the European continent. The 1977 European Convention on the Suppression of Terrorism operates under the aegis of the Council of Europe. Russia recently became a participant. A mechanism also exists for joint antiterrorist actions by the countries of the European Union (specifically, within the framework of the so-called Trevi Group). Problems of antiterrorist cooperation are regulated by the corresponding provisions of final documents from the Helsinki, Madrid, Vienna, and Istanbul conferences of the Organization for Security and Cooperation in Europe.

Cooperation in the battle against terrorism was also strengthened within the framework of conventions of the South Asian Association for Regional Cooperation (SAARC), the Organization of American States (OAS), and the Organization of the Islamic Conference (OIC).

The realities being confronted by Russia and the other states of the former Soviet Union demand that they too take immediate joint measures to create an effective legal mechanism for antiterrorist cooperation.

Within the Commonwealth of Independent States (CIS), a system of multilateral security mechanisms has taken shape, and this system is already being used or could be used to repel terrorist threats.

A Treaty on Cooperation in the Fight against Terrorism is in effect. The June 2000 CIS summit saw the ratification of an intergovernmental Program of Cooperation on Combating Terrorism and Other Manifestations of Extremism for the period through 2003. The CIS Antiterrorist Center has begun its operations. Plans also call for the possibility of opening branches of the center in various regions of the CIS if necessary.

An important result of the process of consolidating efforts within the CIS framework and developing cooperation with the world community was the conference "International Terrorism: Sources and Prevention," which was held by the CIS Interparliamentary Assembly on April 17-19, 2001, in St. Petersburg.

Conference participants included parliamentary delegations from CIS Interparliamentary Assembly member states; leaders and staff of law enforcement, military, and security agencies of CIS members; representatives of international organizations; and prominent scholars.

The results of the conference demonstrate that today, within the framework of the CIS, a defined system of norms and rules has been created to regulate cooperation among the law enforcement agencies of CIS member states in combating international terrorism and other manifestations of extremism. At the same time, the extent of development of a unified legal space to support such efforts still does not fully correspond to the extent of the terrorist threat within CIS territory. Emphasis was placed on the need for legislative bodies of CIS states to focus their efforts on forming a unified and well-ordered legal base as a foundation for effective cooperation among the law enforcement agencies of CIS countries.

In particular, the conference definitively condemned the practice of terrorism as criminal and without justification, regardless of its motives. It called on all parliaments of the Interparliamentary Assembly member states to ratify and carry out other procedures within their own countries to ensure the implementation of documents on combating international terrorism ratified at the highest CIS levels. The provisions of international antiterrorist conventions must also be fully implemented. The conference also recommended that the Interparliamentary Assembly Council define a principle of standardizing and harmonizing to the maximum extent the national legislation of Assembly member states in the fight against this evil. It appealed to all conference participants to step up efforts to prevent the planning and financing of any acts of terrorism on the territory of their states and to facilitate international cooperation in this sphere.

The 1999 Collective Security Treaty is a tried and tested instrument in countering international terrorism, having proven its effectiveness during the events in southern Kyrgyzstan. The steps taken by its participants to adapt the treaty to current geopolitical realities are substantially reinforcing its antiterrorist components. For instance, the Committee of Secretaries of the CIS Security Council has been created. Among its tasks is coordination of cooperation among CIS member states in the fight against terrorism and extremism.

The Shanghai Forum is becoming an increasingly weighty component of interstate cooperation in the interests of security, stability, and development in the region. At the Dushanbe meeting of the heads of state of the five member countries in June 2000, the parties confirmed their determination to fight jointly against international terrorism, religious extremism, and national separatism, which represent "the main threat to regional security, stability, and development," as emphasized in the meeting's final declaration. They committed themselves to develop an appropriate cooperative program and to conclude the necessary multilateral treaties and agreements that will create an organizational-legal basis for cooperation in this sphere. The parties agreed to organize multilateral antiterrorism training exercises, taking into account the development of the situation, and they supported the initiative of Kyrgyzstan on creating a regional antiterrorist unit to be headquartered in Bishkek.

Naturally, cooperation in fighting terrorism is also developing on a bilateral level. It is a very important element of global efforts of states in this sphere. In such cases, where the level of trust between partners is highest, the practical return from their cooperation increases accordingly.

One clear example of such cooperation is the activity of the Russian-American and Russian-Indian working groups on countering the terrorist threat emanating from Afghanistan, which were created as a result of decisions by high-ranking officials. These groups are studying the challenges to regional and international stability arising as a result of Taliban support for terrorism and developing concrete measures aimed at countering this threat. Thus, in the course of the third meeting of the Russian-American group, which was held in Washington in May 2000, Russia and the United States agreed to continue both on a bilateral basis and in international forums their consideration of specific measures to counter the threats of terrorism and narcotics coming from Afghanistan. They will also continue joint work in support of further efforts aimed at developing an effective monitoring mechanism with regard to sanctions imposed by the Security Council with the goal of spurring the Taliban to stop supporting terrorism and to close terrorist training camps in Afghanistan.

Current international cooperation in the fight against terrorism is developing in a relatively dynamic fashion. However, its potential is by no means exhausted. We believe that the fundamental areas for increasing the effectiveness of antiterrorist cooperation are as follows.

First of all, the question must focus on strengthening the legal foundation for such cooperation. In the aim of making cooperation truly universal, it is important that every effort be made to expand the circle of participants in existing global antiterrorist treaties, which serve as a kind of common denominator of the joint opposition of states to the threat of terrorism. Russia actively supports the annual appeals of the UN General Assembly aimed at achieving this goal. We also participate in collective G-8 demarches addressed to countries that have not yet adhered to such treaties.

Also important is the quickest possible implementation of the acts recently ratified under the auspices of treaties in this sphere, including the international conventions on the suppression of terrorist bombings and the financing of terrorism.

An adequate response to terrorism presupposes the development of a basis in law and in treaties for cooperation among states in the fight against this challenge. It is important that the United Nations complete work as soon as possible on the draft of the international convention on combating acts of nuclear terrorism, which was submitted by Russia. The United Nations must also continue the process of reaching agreement on a comprehensive draft convention submitted by India on the struggle against international terrorism.

The process of filling in the international-legal gaps regarding antiterrorist cooperation must also be encouraged on the regional and bilateral levels.

The Achilles' heel of terrorism lies in the financial sources from which it feeds. Reliably blocking these sources means inflicting a destructive blow on terrorism. It is essential that the mechanism adopted by the United Nations in the 1999 International Convention on Suppression of the Financing of Terrorism be implemented as soon as possible. This treaty must become a truly universal instrument of effective antiterrorist cooperation. It is important to support efforts at the regional and other levels to carry out the provisions of the convention, without waiting for it to formally go into effect.

Exchanges of information aimed at preventing terrorist acts and reducing the degree of terrorist danger must become an integral component of antiterrorist cooperation. Taking into account the specifics of the battle against terrorism, requirements of confidentiality and mutuality must be applied to all forms of such exchanges and all categories of transmitted information.

A high level of trust is one distinguishing characteristic of effective interaction in this sphere. This is also completely applicable with regard to cooperation of states in rendering mutual legal assistance, including extradition. It is important not to permit the development of negative tendencies toward concealing from justice persons suspected of committing or being involved in terrorist acts because they are of a certain ethnicity or hold particular religious or other convictions. Otherwise, the very foundations of antiterrorist cooperation will be placed in doubt—its effectiveness, the inevitability of responsibility for illegal actions, and ultimately the confidence of states in one another. To prevent this from occurring, every effort must be made to cultivate predictability with regard to partners, for example, by clearly outlining in national legislation procedures for the implementation of general international norms and standards for rendering legal assistance and extraditing suspected criminals.

It would be deeply incorrect to reduce problems of international cooperation in this sphere to the mere development of its legal framework. It is necessary to develop a general philosophy for combating terrorism as a criminal act, placing at its foundation the need to unite the efforts of the international community in opposing this phenomenon. This philosophy must also stipulate the ultimately uncompromising nature of this struggle, the inevitability of responsibility for the crime of terrorism, the rendering of aid to its victims, and finally the formation and maintenance of a worldwide atmosphere that actively rejects terrorism.

It is important to make people realize that any terrorist act, regardless of its motives, brings with it evil and constitutes a crime, for which legal punishment will inevitably follow. It is necessary to deprive terrorists of the halo of fighters for faith and justice and against any form of oppression and discrimination.

The United Nations, its specialized institutions, and well-known state and public figures could make their own contributions to these efforts. It would be useful if a brochure could be published with information on the threat of terrorism and its negative consequences for international security, for the normal development of relations between states, and for the fulfillment of basic human rights and freedom. Such a brochure could also reveal the contribution of the United Nations and its institutions to countering this dangerous phenomenon.

Representatives of science are called upon to make a notable contribution to these efforts. It is from this standpoint that the significance of this seminar should be evaluated. Such experience is useful and should be developed.

The theme of including the media in mobilizing international public opinion in the struggle against terrorism and possibly even in developing appropriate international recommendations obviously merits a separate study.

However, the social delirium of terrorism cannot be eliminated through propaganda efforts alone. It requires daily efforts on the part of the state to show concern for the population and for each person, primarily with regard to defending his or her socioeconomic rights, freedoms, and dignity and ensuring each individual's physical protection from the threats of terrorists. That is the prime duty and obligation of the state.

Neglect and disregard of human interests create the grounds for destabilizing tendencies and lead to the appearance of separatist and other disintegrating processes linked with the criminal world. These factors also promote the consolidation of extremist forces that rely on outside support, as has happened in Chechnya and is happening in Central Asia and other regions that have become hotbeds of increased terrorist activity.

A serious danger is presented by acts of so-called technological terrorism— that is, those involving the use of the latest scientific-technological developments. Issues of countering terrorism in the realm of computer space have recently moved to the forefront. We intend to continue supporting efforts, including within the G-8 framework, aimed at finding an effective antidote to this refined variety of terrorism, which unfortunately has not bypassed Russia.

Our country initiated efforts at the United Nations to develop an international convention on the suppression of acts of nuclear terrorism, the adoption of which would markedly enhance the international-legal potential to fend off the threat of "terrorism of mass destruction." We also intend to continue actively encouraging international, regional, and bilateral efforts to counter terrorism involving the use of chemical and bacteriological substances.

Having raised the bar of international cooperation, Russia is simultaneously making stricter demands of itself. The Federal Law "On Combating Terrorism" was adopted in our country on June 25, 1998. It creates a firm normative-legal foundation for the enhancement of activities by Russian law enforcement agencies in fighting terrorism both within the country and at the international level. The fundamental goals of the law include protecting the individual, society, and the state from terrorism; preventing, discovering, suppressing, and minimizing the consequences of terrorist activity; and uncovering the causes and conditions that promote terrorist acts. The law outlines jurisdictions and assigns general parameters for coordinating the efforts of law enforcement agencies and intelligence services of the Russian Federation in combating terrorism, along with general methods and means of conducting counterterrorist operations. The law regulates questions of compensation for damages resulting from terrorist acts and deals with the social rehabilitation of victims of acts of terrorism.

With the passage of this law, Russian legislation for the first time has defined the procedure for classifying an organization as terrorist and has determined measures of criminal responsibility for such organizations.

I am sure that this seminar will contribute to the development of specific recommendations for increasing the effectiveness of international cooperation in combating terrorism and strengthening the role of Russia and the United States in that process. It will also serve as a stimulus for the appearance of new scientific and engineering developments oriented toward the achievement of real results in opposition to terrorism.

Cooperation Among Ministries of Internal Affairs of CIS Member States in the Fight Against Terrorism and Other Manifestations of Extremism

Igor L. Dimitrov *
Main Administration for Legal Work and External Affairs,
Russian Ministry of Internal Affairs

Having directly encountered the problems caused by the process of the breakup of the USSR, field personnel from internal affairs agencies and other law enforcement structures were the first to conclude that joint efforts and coordinated actions are required in the fight against crime, which recognizes no boundaries. Therefore, measures to create an organizational-legal basis for cooperation with colleagues from neighboring states were undertaken right at the interagency level.

As early as the first meeting of internal affairs ministers of the Commonwealth of Independent States (CIS) member countries, which took place in Almaty in April 1992, participants signed an Agreement on Cooperation among the internal affairs ministries of the various independent states in the fight against crime. This treaty outlined the commitments of the parties first to work jointly to combat gangsterism, terrorism, and international crime and second to create a coordinating body, the Conference of Internal Affairs Ministers (SMVD).

At the same time, because the conference could not function on a continual basis, the Office for the Coordination of the Fight Against Organized Crime and Other Dangerous Types of Crime on the Territory of CIS Participant-States (BK-BOP) was created on September 24, 1993. This action was taken on the initiative of the conference and on the basis of a resolution of the Council of CIS Heads of Government. This structure essentially became the working arm of the SMVD and began regularly coordinating all areas of the fight against crime, including crime of a terrorist nature. Thus, the organizational-legal foundations for interagency cooperation in this field were successfully created at that time.

---

* Translated from the Russian by Kelly Robbins.

The question of the need to intensify cooperation in the fight against terrorism given the situations developing in the Caucasus and Central Asia was first raised separately at the April 1996 regular meeting of the Council of Ministers of Internal Affairs of CIS Member States in Dushanbe. As a result of discussion of these problems, participants in the meeting adopted a resolution consisting of practically 30 points, which specifically stipulated the following:

• Identifying within each ministry an agency responsible for coordinating antiterrorist activities within the framework of the ministries of internal affairs, with the BKBOP to be informed of this selection as soon as possible;
• Ensuring the systematic exchange of operational and other information about uncovered or developing terrorist organizations and individuals inclined to commit terrorist acts or involved in the manufacture of explosive devices;
• Carrying out coordinated activities to work out plans of actions to be taken to prevent and suppress terrorist acts;
• Instituting measures to discover and suppress the channels by which illegal armed formations, organized crime societies, and individuals obtain money and other assistance used in the commission of terrorist acts;
• Carrying out in 1996-1997 a comprehensive inventory of rifles in the possession of enterprises, organizations, institutions, and citizens as well as a listing of locations where explosive materials are stored, with operational coverage to be ensured regarding these locations; and
• Developing a standard checklist for urgent actions to be taken by duty officers of internal affairs agencies when reacting to cases of terrorism.

It should be noted that a substantial amount of joint work was done in implementing the stipulations of this document, and the results of this work were summarized at the June 1998 meeting of the council in Tashkent.

The next notable step in the strengthening of cooperation in this sphere was the resolution "On Cooperation in the Struggle Against Crimes of an Extremist Nature Committed on Religious Grounds," which was adopted during the next regular SMVD meeting in Moscow in December 1998. This resolution calls for carrying out a whole series of specific joint activities in this regard.

The Kiev meeting of the council on October 1, 1999, saw the passage of the resolution "On Combating Terrorism on the Territory of CIS Member States" and the Appeal to Heads of State and Heads of Government of CIS Countries. The first document stipulated the establishment of a Provisional Anti-terrorist Center under the auspices of BKBOP, with the new center to be given the functions of coordinating the activities of internal affairs agencies in combating terrorism and other manifestations of extremism. This unit was soon in fact created. The second document specifically called for the Council of CIS Heads of State to take a top-priority look at the problems of combating international terrorism.

In Moscow on January 25, 2000, the leaders of the CIS countries reviewed these questions and adopted a resolution that later served as the basis for the passage of the Program of CIS Member States to Combat International Terrorism and Other Manifestations of Extremism through 2003. The resolution also created the CIS Antiterrorist Center (a representative of SMVD was appointed first deputy director of the center). It should be emphasized that the same day saw the adoption of the Intergovernmental Program of Joint Measures to Fight Crime for 2000 through 2003, which was developed with our active participation. Among other elements, the program calls for carrying out targeted interagency operational-preventive activities and special operations to suppress acts of terrorism and other manifestations of extremism.

The Council of Ministers of Internal Affairs met for the next time in Moscow on March 10, 2000, with the meeting being devoted entirely to issues regarding the strengthening of cooperation in the antiterrorist sphere. At the meeting, participants passed the appropriate resolutions, in particular calling for the following:

• Preparation of a multilateral interagency agreement on fighting terrorism and other manifestations of extremism;
• The regular holding of coordinated operational search and prevention exercises, especially the special operations entitled "Border-Barrier";
• The holding of joint training exercises for special militia (police) units and internal affairs troops to work out coordinated actions in the struggle against acts of terrorism;
• The facilitation of close interaction in the development and contracted provision of special means, technology, and equipment for carrying out antiterrorist activity; and
• The exchange on the basis of mutual agreement of specialists to render consultative and other assistance in the fight against terrorism.

The next meeting of SMVD, which was held in Cholpon-Ata in September 2000, saw the signing of the Agreement on Cooperation Among Internal Affairs Ministers in the Fight Against Terrorism. Participants also adopted corresponding resolutions aimed primarily at the full and absolute implementation of the above-mentioned intergovernmental programs. A council plan for carrying out these programs was later prepared and approved, and implementation of the plan has already been discussed at the regular SMVD meeting held in Yerevan in June 2001 (the appropriate joint resolutions were also passed as a result of consideration of this question).

In noting the basic stages in the development of cooperation on the given issue among the internal affairs agencies of the CIS countries within the framework of such multilateral bodies as the SMVD and BKBOP, one should also mention the very important work being done by other organizations. These include the "Borzhomi Four" (the Conference of Internal Affairs Ministers of Azerbaijan, Armenia, Georgia, and Russia), the "Bishkek Group" (the Conference of Leaders of Law Enforcement Agencies and Intelligence Services from the "Shanghai Five" Countries), and the Conference of Internal Affairs Ministers of the Black Sea Economic Cooperation Organization member states, as well as activities being conducted through the International Criminal Police Organization (Interpol). The notable role played by bilateral coordinating institutes—for example joint boards—should also be mentioned.

At present, such Russian Internal Affairs Ministry boards have been created with the internal affairs ministries of Armenia, Belarus, Georgia, and Tajikistan. For instance, within the framework of the Russian-Belarusan Joint Board, a Program of Joint Measures to Combat Terrorism and Other Manifestations of Extremism for 2000-2001 has been approved and is being carried out successfully. The Russian-Armenian Board has a Plan for Joint Actions on Combating Terrorism and the Illegal Trade in Weapons, Ammunition, Explosive Substances, and Explosive Devices for 2000-2001.

In addition, another sort of coordinating institution, the conference of heads of internal affairs agencies of border districts, has recently been developed. In the fall of 2000, such conferences, including the participation of the relevant internal affairs ministers, were held for Russian and Ukrainian officials (in Donetsk) and Russian and Kazakhstani officials (in Novosibirsk). During the meetings, these conferences were given permanent operating status.

Therefore, a very solid organizational basis for cooperation has been created along with the necessary treaties and legal arrangements. At present, a significant number of multilateral and bilateral agreements are in effect in the anticrime sphere at the interstate, intergovernmental, and interagency levels, and this process is continuing.

The internal affairs agencies of the CIS countries are working actively on the investigation of criminal cases; on questions of extradition and the protection of social order; on the development of information systems and special means, technology, and equipment; and on the training and continuing education of personnel. A system has been put in place for the exchange of operational information. Comprehensive investigations are being conducted regarding organizations and individuals suspected of involvement in the activities of terrorist or other extremist formations and criminal groups and societies.

In cooperation with other military structures, prevention and search operations are regularly conducted, along with special operations to prevent, uncover, suppress, and reveal crimes. There are a multitude of examples, including most importantly such activities as "Border," "Border-Barrier," "Channel," "Transit," "Passenger," and "Foreigner."

Despite the fact that the development of interagency cooperation within the CIS framework regarding the struggle against terrorism and other manifestations of extremism is going well on the whole, work on the further intensification of joint efforts in this regard is actively continuing. This is connected primarily with the fact that these extraterritorial phenomena, which do not recognize the boundaries of state or political systems, today represent an enormous problem and a real force capable of opposing state institutions and threatening national security. This has been shown by events occurring in the Caucasus and Central Asia.

Therefore, it is difficult to overestimate the role and significance of close international cooperation in this sphere on the whole, including within the framework of the Commonwealth of Independent States. On this basis, we must continue to move forward on the road to a new millennium free from the threat of international terrorism and other manifestations of extremism.

International Centers as a Basis for Controlling Infectious Disease and Countering Bioterrorism

Lev S. Sandakhchiev, * *Sergey V. Netesov, Raisa A. Martynyuk*
Vector State Research Center for Virology and Biotechnology
Russian Federation Ministry of Health

The task of our panel is to examine the role of international collaboration in countering terrorism. In my presentation, I would like to address the need for international cooperation in combating bioterrorism.

During the past decade, policy makers and military and civilian experts have shown more and more interest in the bioterrorism issue. Much discussion and analysis has centered on possible biological agents of viral or bacterial etiology, scenarios of how to prevent and respond to the use of these agents, and epidemic response capabilities in terms of the availability of competent personnel and diagnostic and therapeutic products.

As a rule, the scenarios of bioterrorism incidents are far from optimistic in terms of both human casualties and costs associated with containing the direct consequences of such actions, not to mention the resulting economic breakdown in the region affected and the lasting psychological effect on the population.[1]

Terrorism is now a growth industry, and the possibility of a chemical or bioterrorist attack is increasingly defined as "not if, but when." However, even the United States, which has longstanding experience in infectious disease control worldwide, developed its response plan, *Biological and Chemical Terrorism: Strategic Plan for Preparedness and Response*, only in the year 2000.[2] This plan, which involves coordinated response to and elimination of such events by more than 10 agencies, is focused on five major areas:

- Preparedness and prevention,
- Detection and surveillance,

---

* Presenting author. Any comments should be sent to lev@Vector.nsc.ru.

- Diagnosis and characterization of biological and chemical agents,
- Response, and
- Communication.

Included in all of these areas are proposals for personnel training as well as investigation of and total preparedness for detection and elimination of consequences of possible attacks using chemical or biological agents in all states and cities. The key point is to design a multilevel laboratory network to efficiently warn public health authorities at the community, state, district, and city levels if biological and chemical agents are detected. This plan is aimed at significantly reengineering the existing infrastructure for infectious disease response and control.

I would like to especially emphasize certain features that differentiate bioterrorism from other kinds of terrorism.[3] Explosive substances are fairly widespread and not very diverse. Chemical agents that could be used for terrorist purposes are well studied as potential chemical weapons, and detection procedures have been developed for many of them, along with measures for the treatment and decontamination of those affected. In case of biological agents, however, it is an absolutely different situation. In nature, there are a great variety of viruses, bacteria, and fungi that cause diseases in humans, animals, or plants. Experts estimate that currently we are aware of far less than one percent of existing viruses and several percent of microbes. Nature is continuously creating new pathogens, the so-called emerging infections, and this potential is simply inexhaustible. During the last 20 years alone, scientists have discovered more than 30 new infectious agents (e.g., HIV, Marburg, and Ebola viruses) against which neither cures nor preventive drugs are yet available.

As a result of their ability to change, known diseases such as influenza, tuberculosis, malaria, and some others can relatively easily overcome conventional immunization and drug-based approaches to prevention and therapy.

Humankind has been fighting a biological war against microbes since its emergence, and even now infectious diseases account for almost 30 percent of worldwide mortality. Although experts on biological weapons and bioterrorism often operate with a limited list of several dozen infectious agents, we should not underestimate the possible terrorist use of any of the diverse pathogens existing in nature.

Thus, the task of establishing a global system of surveillance for possible natural or artificial outbreaks is far more difficult than for chemical agents or explosives.

It is important to realize that biological agents act over time and have a latent period during which the carrier of infection may find herself or himself in another city or even another country, where the outbreak of disease may be actually identified. It may take much time to prove the bioterrorist use of microorganisms since it will require a comprehensive epidemiological analysis (e.g., investigation of all stages involved in the manufacture and distribution of foodstuffs, in the case of food poisoning). The well-known case of the terrorist use of *Salmonella* in a salad bar in Oregon in 1984 resulted in sickening more than 700 individuals. However, it was initially regarded as a natural outbreak, and only one year later it was proven that *Salmonella* had been used by religious cult extremists to prevent voting in Oregon. By the way, the U.S. public learned about that case many years after it occurred.

Therefore, it is medical personnel that are the first to have to deal with biological incidents, and it is public health capabilities that determine the preparedness of a country, region, or city for timely detection and elimination of consequences of the use of biological agents. For this reason, financial and organizational efforts should be focused on civilian rather than military agencies.

The nation must be prepared to deal with the detection and elimination of consequences of outbreaks caused by any biological agent, including both conventional and exotic species of microorganisms. The existing systems for nationwide epidemiological surveillance and control of infectious diseases should be capable of identifying, containing, and eliminating an infectious disease outbreak regardless of whether it is the result of the natural manifestation of a pathogen or its deliberate use.

All these features require that international collaboration be established in order to set up a system of efficient alert and response. This issue was specifically addressed at the May 2001 54th World Health Assembly in the report by the Secretariat entitled "Global Health Security—Epidemic Alert and Response." It was noted that in 1995 the World Health Assembly adopted resolutions WHA48.13 on new, emerging, and reemerging infectious diseases and WHA48.7 on the revision and updating of the International Health Regulations. The World Health Organization (WHO) totally realized the need for enhancing epidemiological and laboratory surveillance at the national level as "the main defense against the international spread of communicable diseases."

Increased population movements (through tourism or migration or as a result of natural or technologic disasters or conflicts), growth in international trade in food and biological products, social and environmental changes associated with urbanization, and changes in food processing technologies, food distribution networks, and consumer habits determine the likelihood that an infectious disease will emerge in a given country and so create a real threat to the remaining countries worldwide.

The Secretariat pointed out the increased possibility of the intentional use of infectious disease agents and emphasized that natural epidemics and those due to the deliberate use of biological agents may manifest themselves in the same manner. The Secretariat also noted that the need for international cooperation on this issue appears far more important now than when this idea was discussed at the first International Sanitary Conference in 1851. Such cooperation has been maintained by WHO since its establishment in 1948.

In 1997, WHO established a special system to seek, collect, and verify information on reported outbreaks. Based on the close cooperation of WHO Collaborating Centers with governmental and nongovernmental agencies, the system provides information on confirmed disease outbreaks on the WHO web site (www.who.int/disease-outbreak-news) and in the WHO *Weekly Epidemiological Record* (www.who.int/wer). At global level, laboratory networking takes place (www.who.int/emc), focusing on such infections as hemorrhagic fevers (including Ebola virus) and poliovirus. Efforts are also devoted to preparation of databases such as the WHO antimicrobial resistance data bank (ARInfoBank) (www.who.int/emc/amr.html), influenza FluNet (http://oms2.b3e.jussieu.fr/flunet/), rabies RabNet (www.who.int/emc/diseases/zoo/rabies.html), and others. WHO has called on its member states to establish partnerships to involve both civilian public health and military medical capabilities.

WHO continuously draws the attention of its member states to the ultimate role of national potential in ensuring the epidemiological welfare of other countries, so it plans to expand national training programs in intervention epidemiology worldwide as well as the Training in Epidemiology and Public Health Interventions Network (TEPHINET). Major conclusions based on discussions of the Secretariat report were reflected in Resolution WHA54.14 entitled "Global Health Security: Epidemic Alert and Response" (http://www.who.int/wha-1998/EB_WHA/PDF/WHA54/ea54r14.pdf). A good example that deserves serious attention and similar action is the establishment of the WHO Bureau in Lyon (France) as a model for using national potential to contribute to the training of personnel for countries at high epidemic risk (www.who.int/emc/lyon).

At the global level, huge resources are already available to combat infectious diseases. Certainly, these will also be used to counter bioterrorism incidents.[4] They include hundreds of WHO Collaborating Centers worldwide specializing in certain infections; a Pan-American Health Organization (PAHO) laboratory network; the International Clinical Epidemiology Network (INCLEN); the Pasteur Institutes network; an international research centers network of the National Institutes of Health (NIH) that involves many universities across the United States; and the Centers for Disease Control and Prevention (CDC) offices in numerous countries, many of which conduct epidemiological surveillance and provide field epidemiology training for different regions. The U.S. Army and Navy have also established a specialized network of research centers in several countries. It should be noted that this particular resource is very much focused on specific tasks and, except for the Epidemiologic Intelligence Service (EIS) centers, is not oriented toward detection and identification of the entire pathogen range.

As a matter of fact, to localize and contain unusual outbreaks posing a threat to global public health, WHO has set up task forces to be deployed during such outbreaks. A number of epidemics have been eliminated in this way in recent years, although this has required tremendous efforts in terms of coordination, material supply, transportation, communication activities, and so forth.

Another approach was proposed by the outstanding epidemiologist Dr. D. A. Henderson,[5] who, based on many years of experience as a leader and actual participant in the global smallpox eradication program, arrived at the conclusion that fixed-site international centers should be established in 15 regions of the world. These should include the following:

- Inpatient and outpatient capabilities to deal with infectious diseases;
- Research and diagnostic laboratories;
- Epidemiological teams to function like the EIS to cover regions with populations of 2 million to 5 million; and
- Education and training capabilities to provide training to national and international personnel.

Systematic studies of a specific region make it possible to obtain invaluable databases, investigate different factors that can influence the epidemiological situation, and identify unusual cases requiring careful examination.

According to Henderson, this network of regional centers should involve collaboration with such organizations as CDC, the National Institute of Allergy and Infectious Diseases (NIAID), and academic research centers. To provide stability and a legal framework, they should work closely with WHO and government authorities in the countries where they would operate.

The leader of the U.S. Emergency Interagency Working Group, Jewellyn J. Legster, evaluates Dr. Henderson's proposal very highly, though the former believes that prior to realizing this idea it is necessary to work to analyze existing regional capabilities and choose geographic regions at high epidemic risk. Such regional centers should also have research programs in epidemiology and the region's key problems in terms of infectious diseases, diagnostic, and therapeutic means, as well as personnel training.[5]

As a follow-up to the U.S. Institute of Medicine recommendations, the WHO Department of Communicable Disease Surveillance and Response together with the International Center of Genetic Engineering and Biotechnology (ICGEB) and several nongovernmental organizations (Program for Appropriate Technology in Health [PATH], INCLEN, and TEPHINET, the so-called Alliance against Infectious Diseases) prepared a program proposal in 2000 entitled "Global Monitoring, Research and Training to Control Infectious Diseases."

In the initial stage of the program, 10-12 laboratories or institutes would be identified in strategically important regions at high epidemic risk and with insufficient surveillance capabilities. Those laboratories should have laboratory and clinical study capabilities and a potential for conducting epidemiology work, access to air and ground transport, possibility of telecommunications installation, and prospects for future expansion.

Centers thus identified would have status as WHO Collaborating Centers and preferred access to WHO programs and those of Health Ministries in WHO member states. They would be coordinated by the WHO Office of the Strategic Alliance.

Each center would in turn be established by taking into account the region's specific needs and, in the initial stage, would be provided with the necessary resources to create the most advanced potential for diagnostic, clinical, and epidemiological activities. It also would be provided with telecommunications equipment to be able to communicate with the other centers, as well as with regional, federal, and international agencies involved in infectious disease surveillance and response.

Each center would establish regional networks to include clinics, institutes, education establishments, and others, and it would participate intensively in the region's infectious disease programs. The regional network would involve enterprises manufacturing specialized pharmaceutical products that, through technology transfer, would be given an opportunity to meet the region's needs for standard diagnostic tests and therapeutic products.

The regional network should also involve research laboratories that develop diagnostic and therapeutic products and vaccines, as well as biosafety research laboratories studying the safety of biological substances and microorganisms to humans and the environment.

The program envisages that within 8-10 years, a worldwide network of regional centers would be up and running, and thus a long-term sustainable regional potential for communicable disease control would be created. It is proposed that some of these centers would become centers of excellence like CDC, NIAID, and ICGEB.

The authors note that the proposed approach would represent the most reliable way of preventing and dealing with possible future pandemics (for more information, send a message to WHO at allaid@who.int).

In the above WHO Secretariat report, it was noted that possible mechanisms to support the initiatives to enhance epidemiological surveillance may be based on Article X of the 1972 Biological and Toxin Weapons (BTW) Convention. This article seeks to enhance international cooperation on the peaceful use of biological material, equipment, and technologies. Within the measures envisaged, state parties would receive assistance in strengthening their potential in infectious disease surveillance and response, including research and development activities.

Therefore, it is crucial that the above-mentioned international institutions not only provide the region's epidemiological protection in case of natural or terrorist events using microorganisms, but also contribute to efforts in the extremely difficult political task of confidence building, which is an important factor in enhancing the 1972 BTW Convention.

For many years, our institute—Vector State Research Center for Virology and Biotechnology of the Russian Federation Ministry of Health—has been involved in combating viral infectious diseases. In recent years we have been discussing the prospects for reorganizing the institute into a regional center similar to those described above.

The institute was established in 1974 with the task of conducting basic and applied research on extremely pathogenic viral agents such as the less-studied Marburg, Ebola, Lassa, and other viruses related to potential biological weapons (BW) agents. The research was aimed at assessing the potential threat posed by these agents and developing means for their diagnostics, prevention, and therapy. Maximum biological containment laboratory facilities and clinical and epidemiological capabilities were built, in addition to the standard engineering infrastructure and a set of scientific and supporting facilities, including a laboratory animal breeding and holding facility. The total area of existing buildings and facilities amounts to 250,000 square meters.

Before 1992, Vector received all of its funding from the federal budget and was just beginning to establish manufacturing activities. Access to workplaces by and communication with foreign scientists were limited. The same limitations applied to the participation of Vector scientists in international conferences and the publication of scientific papers.

In 1989, it became obvious that Vector should be restructured[6] to adapt to changing economic conditions that ultimately resulted in a significant cutback of federal budget funding. A program was prepared for Vector's long-range development, with the focus on conducting much more public health and veterinary medical research on infectious diseases such as HIV/AIDS, tick-borne encephalitis, viral hepatitis A and B, measles, and others. This would include development of diagnostic tests, vaccines, and antivirals as well as establishment of manufacturing facilities for diagnostic, therapeutic, and prophylactic products.

In 1993, Vector became a State Research Center and started to receive federal budget funding to support its R&D activities through government civilian programs. The development of pharmaceutical manufacturing activities was supported by government investments and credits, which allowed us to renovate and upgrade several facilities and purchase necessary equipment.

Currently Vector is a scientific center consisting of six scientific research institutes and three daughter companies manufacturing a broad range of products. We have managed to retain most of our key scientific personnel and establish sustainable manufacturing activities. During recent years, Vector's income pattern has changed dramatically. While in 1990 78 percent of funds came from the federal budget, in 2000, 77 percent of total income came from product sales.

I would like to say a few words about the role of international foundations and organizations in Vector's reorientation toward public health and agriculture-oriented programs.

In 1992, the International Science and Technology Center (ISTC) was established as a nonproliferation-targeted program for the Newly Independent States (NIS). The same goal was set for the U.S. Civilian Research and Development Foundation (CRDF), which was established by the National Science Foundation in 1995, and for the Newly Independent States Industrial Partnering Program (IPP, currently known as Initiatives for Proliferation Prevention), which is operated through the U.S. Department of Energy with the involvement of the United States Industry Coalition (USIC). Collaboration with the European Union programs INTAS, Tacis, and others is opening up big opportunities.

During 1995-2000, we completed 29 projects with these organizations. Today, we have 26 active projects, including 23 ISTC-funded projects. In 1998, these projects began to play a significant role in Vector's budget, whereas the contribution they made amounted to 30 percent of funds provided from the Russian federal budget. In 2000, the funding under these programs had grown to almost twice as much as the funding provided from the Russian federal budget, and this year the amount of funding under project agreements that have been concluded is approximately $10 million.

Grant funding and a transparent character of work allow us to receive our foreign colleagues and, in turn, travel ourselves to get acquainted with foreign laboratories. Vector employees have attended dozens of international conferences and workshops. Hundreds of our scientists have visited their foreign counterparts on-site. This has made it possible to create an atmosphere of openness and transparency at Vector, which is critical to science and scientists. Thanks to support provided for our scientific staff, we have been able to maintain our relationships with NIS scientists and scientists from other regions in Russia.

Our employees attend international refresher courses, including English language training, patent and R&D commercialization classes, and training programs in good laboratory, manufacturing, and clinical practices. These activities helped us realize that without implementing international quality standards in science and production, we could hardly hope that our R&D products would be competitive on the world market.

Thanks to grant funding, our scientists are able to conduct research using up-to-date equipment and supplies as well as the latest techniques to gain world class results. I would especially like to mention the Biotechnology Engagement Program (BTEP) of the U.S. Department of Health and Human Services (DHHS). BTEP involves the study of infections such as HIV/AIDS that represent serious public health problems, field epidemiology of hemorrhagic fevers, (multi-) drug-resistant forms of tuberculosis, and research on hepatitis, measles, and variola viruses under an international program under the aegis of WHO. At Vector, we have one of the two WHO Collaborating Centers on smallpox (the other is at CDC, Atlanta), and we collaborate with WHO and our U.S. colleagues on a regular basis on this important program. The study of this infection is of special importance to current efforts to counter the bioterrorism threat.

Very focused efforts are also being planned and implemented under the Defense Threat Reduction Agency (DTRA) Cooperative Threat Reduction (CTR) program with regard to bringing physical security and biological safety systems at the maximum biocontainment facilities at Vector up to the highest modern standards. Serious efforts are being undertaken to bring laboratory work with research animals and pharmaceutical manufacture at Vector's daughter enterprises up to GLP and GMP standards, respectively.

We take very seriously the criticisms concerning the alleged use of U.S. government funds by Russian institutes for whatever prohibited purposes. These concerns have been voiced in the recent study prepared by the U.S. General Accounting Office and a study conducted by the Henry L. Stimson Center, and others.[7]

Despite the lack of evidentiary support for these statements, we should admit that it could change the situation in principle if the recipient institution were operating on an international regimen ensuring confidence and transparency. For several years, we have been discussing this problem with representatives of the U.S. State Department, DTRA, DHHS, and Russian authorities, as well as with the scientific community at several international conferences.[8] We are now in the process of discussing with DHHS experts a BTEP-ISTC project entitled "Development of Concept of an International Center for the Study of Emerging and Re-emerging Infectious Diseases." This project proposes to define in greater detail the ways in which the above-mentioned approaches could be implemented.

By an "International Center," we mean an international organization established by an intergovernmental agreement, similar to those of ISTC or the Joint Institute for Nuclear Research in Dubna, the European Organization for Nuclear Research (CERN) in Switzerland, or the International Center for Genetic Engineering and Biotechnology in Trieste (Italy). Nonproliferation and threat reduction goals can be achieved only through transparency and confidence building when the International Center is established and operated with free access to the program and results obtained, and with free access to financial information and to all facilities and all staff of the center. Continuous involvement of foreign scientists in work at this center would be a powerful instrument of confidence building.

Although the process of establishing the International Center is complex and may take several years to complete, the proposed arrangement would provide for a long-term strategic collaboration, which is far less subject to political or economic fluctuations in member states. International partnership would accelerate the study of dangerous pathogens and the development of state-of-the-art public health products for diagnosis, prophylaxis, and therapy, as well as integration of our institution into the WHO international infectious disease control network proposed by the Strategic Alliance Initiative.

The establishment of the proposed International Center would allow us to join our efforts to counter bioterrorism. It is, however, important to establish an appropriate regimen for the use of infectious agents and scientific results obtained to avoid their possible misuse for illicit purposes.

I take this opportunity to emphasize the key role played by the staff of the Russian Federation Ministry of Industry, Science, and Technologies; the Russian

Federation Ministry of Health; RAO BIOPREPARAT; the Russian Academy of Sciences; the Russian Academy of Medical Sciences; the Institute of International-al Security of the Russian Academy of Sciences; the U.S. Department of State; ISTC; DTRA-CTR; the U.S. Department of Energy; DHHS; CDC; NIH; the U.S. National Academy of Sciences; USDA; and CRDF in the development of international collaborations at Vector.

ACKNOWLEDGMENTS

I wish to thank Mr. V.V. Ryabenko and Mr. A.V. Mironov for their help in editing this presentation.

NOTES

1. Preston, R. 1998. The bioweaponeers. The New Yorker (March 9): 52-65.
Preston, R. 1998. Bio-warfare: fiction and reality. Genetic Engineering News (March 1): 6-39.

2. Biological and Chemical Terrorism: Strategic Plan for Preparedness and Response Recom-mendations of the CDC Strategic Planning Workgroup. April 21, 2000 / 49(RR04); 1-14.

3. Committee on R&D Needs for Improving Civilian Medical Response to Chemical and Bio-logical Terrorism Incidents. Health Science Policy Program. Institute of Medicine and Board on Environmental Studies and Toxicology. Commission on Life Sciences. National Research Council. 1999. Chemical and Biological Terrorism. Research and Development to Improve Civilian Medical Response. Washington, D.C.: National Academy Press.

Proceedings of the Eleventh Amaldi Conference on Problems of Global Security. 1999. (Moscow, November 18-20, 1998). Moscow: Nauka.

4. Lederberg, J., R.E. Shope, S.C. Daks, Jr., eds. 1992. Emerging Infections: Microbiological Threats to Health in the United States. Washington, D.C.: National Academy Press.

5. Morse, S.S., ed. 1993. Emerging Viruses. New York: Oxford University Press.

6. General Accounting Office. 2000. Biological Weapons: Effort to Reduce Former Soviet Threat Offers Benefits, Poses New Risks. Report [NSIAD-00-138].

7. General Accounting Office. 2000. Biological Weapons: Effort to Reduce Former Soviet Threat Offers Benefits, Poses New Risks. Report [NSIAD-00-138].

Chemical and Biological Weapons Nonproliferation Project. 1999. Stimson Center Report No. 32. Toxic Archipelago. Preventing Proliferation from the Former Soviet Chemical and Biologi-cal Weapons Complexes. Available on-line at http://www.stimson.org.

8. Sandakhchiev, L.S., S.V. Netesov. 2001. Strengthening the BTWC through R&D restructur-ing: the case of the State Research Center of Virology and Biotechnology "Vector." The Role of Biotechnology in Countering BTW Agents. Amsterdam: Kluwer Academic Publishers; Netesov, S.V., L.S. Sandakhchiev. 1999. The development of a network of international centers to combat infectious diseases and bioterrorism threats. ASA Newsletter 70 (February 19): 2-6; Sandakhchiev, L.S. 1998. The need for international cooperation to provide transparency and to strengthen the BTWC. In Conversion of Former BTW Facilities. E. Geissler et al., eds. Amsterdam: Kluwer Academic Publishers, pp. 149-156.

Terrorism Future:
Tactics, Strategy, and Stealth

Peter S. Probst
Institute for the Study of Terrorism and Political Violence

It is a pleasure to be here in Moscow and to have an opportunity to share my thoughts with such a distinguished group of experts. I want to focus my remarks on future trends, because the better we anticipate future challenges the more effectively we can marshal and allocate our resources. The world as we know it is in a state of flux and transition and, therefore, it should come as no surprise that terrorism, too, is undergoing fundamental change. Terrorism has become the tactic of choice for extremist groups and rogue states. This is because it is effective and cheap, and sponsorship can often be disguised or denied.

STATE-SUPPORTED OR STATE-SPONSORED TERRORISM

In recent years, state-sponsored terrorist attacks against U.S. interests have significantly declined—a trend I attribute to our improved methods of detection, our demonstrated capability to fix responsibility, and most importantly, our tenacity and commitment to hunt down the perpetrators and bring them to justice.

We tracked, captured, tried, and convicted Ramzi Yousef, the architect of the 1993 World Trade Center bombing. We tracked, captured, tried, and convicted Mir Amal Kanzi, the assassin of two Central Intelligence Agency employees murdered as they sat trapped in their cars waiting to enter the Agency compound. We tracked, captured, tried, and just a week ago convicted four Bin Laden operatives, three of whom directly participated in the bombings of our embassies in East Africa. And we tracked and captured six others involved in the plot, who currently are awaiting trial.

Because we have demonstrated our ability to determine and fix responsibility for such acts, I believe states will be much more selective in their use of terrorism against American personnel and installations, reserving the terrorist card for times when they believe their vital core interests are threatened—or for times they believe a terrorist act can significantly advance their strategic agenda and, therefore, is worth the risk. And there is risk. States have territory, vital infrastructure, and economic interests—all of which are vulnerable to retaliatory measures that run the gamut from disruption to destruction.

Because state-sponsored terrorism will be an increasingly high-stakes game, such state-sponsored attacks, although fewer, will likely be massive in order to rivet attention and exert maximum leverage. And because, if caught, the price to pay would be so high, such attacks will likely exhibit increased sophistication and more professional tradecraft to maximize deniability and deflect responsibility. In fact, we may not even be able to assign blame or determine that the catastrophe that occurred was, indeed, the result of a terrorist operation. Disguising a terrorist operation as an act of God or an unfortunate accident may well become the terrorist's preferred method of operation because it maximizes plausible denial and the work of the security services if they are even brought into investigate the incident.

The only area in which I see state-sponsored terrorism increasing is operations directed against dissidents and regime critics living abroad. This is because, to date, no world power has taken serious, sustained action to penalize state perpetrators.

MOTIVATION

In general, we see religiously motivated terrorism as increasingly ascendant, and politically motivated terrorism in decline. Religious zealots whether members of a group or cult are generally less constrained than are their politically motivated counterparts and, therefore, are more likely to engage in operations that cause mass casualties. The religious extremist answers to a constituency of one—his guru or his god.

Political terrorists, in contrast, answer to multiple constituencies. Most politically motivated terrorists have made the operational calculus that the murder of hundreds of innocents would only alienate the less violence-prone members of their group, supporters on the periphery, potential recruits, and other constituencies in a position to advance their political agenda and with whom they could make common cause.

WEAPONS OF MASS DESTRUCTION

We are currently facing an unprecedented challenge. Religious zealots (i.e., terrorists with the "will" to carry out mass casualty operations) are now in a position to build or buy improvised weapons of mass destruction. Zealotry provides the "will" to inflict horrendous carnage; proliferation provides the "means." This nexus of will and means has forever changed the face of terrorism and the nature of the threat that confronts us all.

DEVOLUTION OF POWER AND WEAPONS
OF MASS DESTRUCTION

An emerging and significant threat is represented by improvised biological, chemical, and radiological devices that exploit technologies that once were the sole preserve of world and regional powers. The ability to decimate large population centers and wreak havoc on an unprecedented scale has devolved from nation-states to groups and now even to the individual.

The possibility of an individual's acting alone and employing such a device is an emerging reality and as close as tomorrow's headlines. Whether they be nations or lone individuals, proliferation enables those traditionally at the margins to play a major role on the world stage. Improvised weapons of mass destruction will be the great equalizers of tomorrow, providing the means for the disaffected and deranged to directly impact the core interests of world powers. Proliferation has changed the nature of terrorism and elevated it to a strategic threat. Cults and single-issue groups that respond to a religious imperative (such as violence-prone antiabortion groups) will likely be drawn to such operations and use them to extort concessions and significant political advantage from governments and other target groups.

ETHNICITY AS A MOTIVATOR

Just as religiously motivated terrorism is increasingly ascendant, I believe ethnically driven terrorism may soon represent a challenge of near-similar magnitude, particularly if it has a religious or mystic overlay and is grounded in real or perceived historic oppression and injustice. For decades, when immigrants settled in a new country, they tried and were often able to integrate themselves into the society of their adopted land.

More recently, a new trend has emerged wherein immigrant populations, even when encouraged to meld with the society of their new country, opt to segregate themselves from the mainstream and to retain and reinforce their ethnic identity. They view their new home as a temporary "home of convenience" adopted for economic or other advantage—their emotional, political, and cultural loyalties belonging to their country of origin.

The prime reason for this attitudinal change, I believe, can be traced directly to the technological advances of the twentieth century. Rapid, relatively inexpensive air travel makes visits to the homeland and the family left behind almost routine. Also contributing to the maintenance and strengthening of such ties is the continuing drop in the cost of international phone calls. To regularly hear the voice of one's mother or sister recount their very personal heartaches and those of the homeland immeasurably strengthens the emigrant's emotional bond to his country of origin and to the family members left behind.

Yet perhaps the most important technological advance has been the development of the Internet, which permits inexpensive, real-time communication via e-mail, on even a daily basis. Internet-based telephone transmissions will soon cost little more than a local telephone call and be ubiquitous.

Emotional ties to the homeland are also reinforced by satellite television, which keeps the emigrant informed of homeland developments often via vivid and lurid video clips and incendiary commentary, as well as through more benign cultural programming that features traditional music and drama of the emigrant group in its native language.

Throughout the Western world, enclaves are developing that to varying degrees are ethnic and political outposts of the home country or region and mirror the attitudes and anger that spur the home-grown conflicts. Even as a child growing up in New York City, I saw my home town not so much as coherent entity but as a series of contiguous ethnic enclaves divided by language and culture where, most often, the issues of the enclave were the issues of the homeland.

Many ethnically based terrorist groups draw their financial and political strength from communities of the diaspora and often a continuing stream of recruits as well. Militants from the home country often are on a continuing circuit. They visit and speak at a variety of meetings where they solicit donations, mobilize political support, and recruit the most promising. In my own country, a whole range of terrorist groups draw from their respective expatriate communities.

Traditional ethnic rivalries and hatreds no longer stop at national borders, but are played out in the streets and media of countries far removed from the site of conflict. Few major ethnic conflicts remain local. Most have become increasingly transnational—a trend that I believe will increase. The once vaunted homogeneity of European countries such as Germany and France has long been a thing of the past. Instead, large immigrant populations that to varying degrees have been excluded from the political process will, I believe, successfully challenge traditional elites and the political power brokers. A Europe without borders is increasingly a reality, but I believe it will evolve into a panorama of city-states that most closely will resemble an ethnic patchwork quilt. As a consequence, ethnic rivalries, tensions, and hatreds, many of Middle Eastern, North African, and Balkan origin, will be played out with increasing ferocity on the European landscape.

NEW ARENAS OF CONFLICT

Cyberspace is one of the most challenging new arenas of conflict not only for nations but for terrorists as well. We already have caught a glimpse of the future in the recent "Hacker War" between the Palestinians and Israelis. The success of some of these operations went beyond defacing home pages, but included some fairly sophisticated denial-of-service attacks. Nations as well as terrorist groups, I am sure, closely monitored these developments to identify "lessons learned" and determine how best these could be applied to refine their respective cyberwar capabilities.

As countries modernize, they become increasingly dependent on sophisticated technologies, with computers both running and linking vital, once disparate systems into a national infrastructure. Technological advances, although increasing efficiency and dictated by economy, may have the unintended consequence of increasing system vulnerability through the elimination of redundancy and accelerating centralization. (Having all our eggs in one basket may make economic sense but creates unnecessarily lucrative targets for our terrorist adversaries.)

Because of its complexity and interdependence, critical infrastructure presents unique targeting opportunities to a technically sophisticated adversary. Complex national infrastructures are vulnerable in that they all have critical nodes or choke points that, if properly attacked, will result in significant disruption or destruction. Such an attack may be computer generated. For the technically challenged, more conventional assaults employing truck bombs, dynamite, or cable cutting may be used to unleash a chain of events whereby a service grid, pipeline, or air traffic control system collapses in a cascading effect.

Major power failures that black out large parts of a country, systemic problems with the air traffic control systems, and breaks in highly vulnerable gas and oil pipeline systems are covered in exquisite detail by the press and industry publications and are dissected and analyzed on the Internet. Terrorists, as part of the attentive public, are increasingly aware that national infrastructure represents a lucrative and vulnerable target.

Most significant terrorist groups and movements have home pages on the Internet and use the Internet to propagandize, fund-raise, and recruit. Some use the net for near real-time operational communication. They may employ encryption and steganography—routing their messages through a series of anonymous remailers and multiple service providers as a strategy to enhance their security. Increasingly such organizations view the Internet as an offensive weapon—what might be called a "weapon of mass disruption." Cadres are being trained in the exploitation of viruses, worms, Trojan horses, and sniffers—all of which can serve as significant force multipliers.

There well may come a day when some terrorist groups will exist only in cyber-space, never meeting face to face, each member insulated from the other and communicating only through the Internet to carry out denial-of-service attacks and other offensive operations against net-dependent countries and target groups. Assassination by computer is only a keyboard away.

PRIVATIZATION OF TERRORISM

Another emerging phenomenon is the privatization of terrorism as personified by Osama bin Laden. Individual players such as bin Laden increasingly operate as virtual state sponsors. They provide significant financial, logistical, and operational support that traditionally were the province of a rogue state's security apparatus. Figures such as bin Laden, however, have an advantage over traditional state supporters of terrorism in that they have few equities or offer few levers that we can manipulate to exert pressure. Not being a state, they have no territory we can bomb or vital infrastructure that we can hold hostage, disrupt, or destroy.

NEW ORGANIZATIONAL MODELS

To avoid capture, terrorists, I believe, will increasingly adopt new organizational models and move toward a form of organization called "leaderless resistance." The premise is that if there are no chain-of-command and no communications between headquarters and operatives in the field, the risk of penetration and discovery is minimized—assuming basic principals of tradecraft are practiced. The idea is that small, totally independent cells of individuals will strike when they find a lucrative target and believe the moment propitious.

The lone-actor model—the singleton—is the most difficult adversary to identify and apprehend. Until recently such an operator was more of a nuisance than anything else, but with the proliferation of knowledge concerning improvised weapons of mass destruction such an individual may, on occasion, represent a strategic threat. We cannot arrest him because we do not know who he is or, in truth, if he even exists. Since we cannot go to him, we will have to induce him to come to us and self-identify. This is a difficult but not an impossible task. Some thoughts on how this might be accomplished can be explored during the discussion period.

I think we have to keep in mind that foremost terrorism is a tactic and form of psychological warfare. It usually is part of a broader ideological campaign. If we are to improve our counterterrorism capabilities, we not only have to apprehend the bombers and assassins but more importantly deal to effectively with the ideological motivations and psychological needs that draw new recruits and inspire them to die for a cause. To effectively combat terrorism, I believe we must embrace the stiletto over the broadsword. This means increased reliance on covert action with heavy emphasis on deception, black operations, gray and black propaganda, in-depth psychological and motivational studies of key personnel, and a thorough understanding of the rational and nonrational factors that influence the decision making calculus of the terrorist leadership and the motivational commitment of the rank-and-file. Too often, we are handicapped by our professional mindset.

A primary objective is to create an operational tool kit of interrelated, complementary capabilities and programs that are woven into an operational tapestry as part of an overarching campaign. One task is to identify, exacerbate, and ultimately manipulate to our advantage the paranoia, schisms, and rivalries that are rife within any terrorist group. Our objective is to cause the group to turn on itself and, ultimately, self-destruct in a paroxysm of paranoia. Such tactics work, unlike brute military power, which history has shown to be counterproductive particularly when used alone in ethnic or religious conflicts. Such a one-dimensional approach sows the seeds of future conflict, perpetuates the cycle of violence, and ultimately plays into the hands of our adversaries.

To be successful, we must think imaginatively—what Americans call "thinking outside the box." To be successful, we must understand what motivates key members of the terrorist groups we are targeting. We must learn what they value, what they fear, and how they weigh operational decisions, and we must study their operational predilections. We must also learn to see ourselves through the eyes of our terrorist adversaries.

The world as we know it is forever changed. Our strategies, tactics, and capabilities need to reflect these new realities if we are to successfully navigate the treacherous waters of this "brave new world." How well we succeed will ultimately determine the winners, the losers, and the price paid by each.

New Opportunities for Bilateral Cooperation

Glenn E. Schweitzer
National Research Council

During the workshop, we considered many suggestions for future cooperation—between governments, between academies, and between individual specialists. I will highlight a few of the suggestions that seem to offer particularly
promising themes for such cooperation. Of course, successful cooperation will
depend on the level of enthusiasm of our specialists and the interest of sponsors.
But there is no doubt that we have addressed some of the most important issues
that will confront our two countries, and indeed the world, during the next decade and longer.

First, in accordance with the suggestion of Academician Velikhov, we have
provided a number of publications about high-impact terrorism to the Institute of
Nuclear Safety, which in cooperation with other institutes will take the first steps
in providing an information center for future interacademy activities in this field.
We will try to obtain additional copies of these documents for other interested
organizations, and we look forward to receiving similar documents concerning
related developments in Russia. Of course we should try to modernize this information exchange quickly—from exchanges of hard copies of documents to exchanges of electronic databases. We hope to be able to report progress in this
area in the near future.

Also of special interest is the recommendation of Academician Velikhov to
establish a standing interacademy committee that can serve as an umbrella for
discussions among American and Russian specialists on many of the topics that
have been considered. He undoubtedly will expand on this proposal in the discussion period.

Turning to the specific themes of the workshop, there clearly is a considerable difference in American and Russian understanding of the term "terrorism."

We do not want to engage in an endless debate over definition. Yet further discussion of the types of activities that are considered by specialists in the two countries as terrorism will undoubtedly be helpful in avoiding misunderstandings. Of special interest is the intersection of terrorism and organized crime. This is not simply a question of definition, but it is especially important to improve understanding of how terrorists and criminal organizations fit together and how they operate in separate domains.

Although much of our focus has been on the technical aspects of terrorism, we must give continuing attention to the legal dimensions of efforts to thwart terrorism—international legal regimes and also national legislative and regulatory frameworks. While our academies are not the best organizations to analyze all aspects of the legal underpinnings of counterterrorism efforts, surely as we address specific forms of terrorism the legal frameworks should be carefully considered along with the many technical, economic, social, and political dimensions.

A number of participants underscored the importance of discussions of the policy issues as well as sorting out technical aspects of the threats, detection of the threats, and appropriate responses. Such discussions that bring together science and policy would seem to be a particularly appropriate role for our academies.

Our Russian colleagues have made several detailed suggestions for major cooperative initiatives:

- A working group of American and Russian specialists to address a range of currently neglected issues affecting the likelihood of radiological terrorism, with the purpose of such deliberations being to stimulate actions by the Russian and U.S. governments and by the International Atomic Energy Agency to strengthen international capabilities to combat this threat;
- A joint experiment to test the vulnerability of electrical and electronic connections to electromagnetic pulsed power attacks; and
- Development of scientific guidance for the establishment of an international center at Vector near Novosibirsk to investigate the epidemiological, diagnostic, and treatment aspects of outbreaks of infectious diseases.

Other suggestions of themes for joint efforts that were set forth by American and Russian specialists and that are based on preliminary analyses by the specialists include the following:

- Studies of the many dimensions of information security, including the clarification of the importance and scope of national strategies to improve protection of critical networks and the identification of areas where international cooperation should be strengthened;
- Assessments of the types of potential terrorist threats directed at facilities that produce or store dangerous industrial chemicals;

- Development of methodologies for evaluating engineering and other security enhancements that will reduce the vulnerability of a broad range of industrial facilities (e.g., nuclear power plants, gas pipelines, airports, metallurgical plants);
- Consultations of experts on the technical aspects of both marking and tagging of explosives, including record-keeping requirements for taggants and the associated costs;
- Development of new concepts for more cost-effective destruction of poorly secured chemical weapons stockpiles in Russia;
- Investigations of the feasibility of terrorist groups' assembling radiological weapons and methods for preventing and detecting such activities;
- Consideration of the technical details of discriminating between natural outbreaks of diseases and the acts of bioterrorists as well as consideration of the preparations for dealing with the consequences of a bioterrorism attack;
- Studies of methods for prevention and early detection of animal diseases and for determining the cause of disease outbreaks;
- Studies of the role of the mass media in terrorism situations and in shaping public attitudes toward terrorism; and
- Joint activities aimed at adapting to the Russian environment the American experience in training specialists to deal with terrorism, in developing organizational mechanisms for coordinating activities of many organizations in preventing and responding to terrorist attacks, and in using forensic techniques to assist in the search for the instigators of terrorist acts.

The foregoing themes are just the beginning of a long list of topics that are clearly of interest to our academies, and the list will undoubtedly grow and be continuously refined. There are of course more ambitious schemes that should be considered by our governments, such as proposals for joint investigations of incidents and joint training exercises. But my comments have been limited largely to interacademy cooperation. Of course, the academies must narrow the list and select several areas where they can indeed have an important impact on international security.

In conclusion, I would like to underscore two important points that have been raised by participants. First, any work undertaken in this field must avoid giving terrorists important technical information that could facilitate their efforts to turn hostile intentions into destructive actions. Second, our academies have strong capabilities to provide conceptual approaches and sound methodologies for addressing terrorism concerns; and they can make recommendations to governments. However, it is the government ministries and departments, and not the academies, that must translate general approaches to counterterrorism into actions at specific facilities, at our borders, and indeed throughout our societies.

Concluding Statement

Yevgeny P. Velikhov
Kurchatov State Research Center of Atomic Energy

This workshop has been very useful. It has been said that terrorism is determining the face of the twenty-first century, and this workshop indicates that this is indeed a reality. Terrorism is a global issue and should be targeted by all available methods, not only by force. I am glad to see that on the Russian side of the workshop, representatives from all involved agencies have been in attendance.

As a next step for this workshop, we must seek additional funding for future workshops, possibly as often as twice a year. We will also need to develop a mutual agreement in order to formalize this activity as an interacademy effort.

I have spoken to other academicians, and we believe it would be useful to form a committee similar to the Committee on International Security and Arms Control and possibly to sign a joint agreement. I feel that for subsequent activity on this project, it is also important to develop centers both here and in the United States that allow for the exchange of information though joint databases and other means.

Once again I would like to offer my thanks to all participants and to the Carnegie Corporation for its support. We have agreed on the production of a final report in both Russian and English, and we will exchange these reports once they have been completed.

APPENDIXES

APPENDIX
A

Goals of Russian Federal Program on Problems of Natural and Technological Security

Konstantin V. Frolov *
Russian Academy of Sciences

1. Creating and developing a Unified State System for Combating Technological Terrorism.

2. Developing legislative and normative-legal foundations for ensuring the comprehensive security of individuals, society, and the state in the struggle against technological terrorism and protection of the population, facilities, and territories from technologically based accidents, catastrophes, and natural disasters.

3. Developing a conceptual and terminological framework for the problem of ensuring the comprehensive security of individuals, society, and the state in the struggle against terrorism (including technological terrorism) and protection of the population, facilities, and territories from technologically based accidents, catastrophes, and natural disasters.

4. Creating a set of special technical and programmatic means for ensuring the comprehensive security of individuals, society, and the state in the struggle against technological terrorism and protection of the population, facilities, and territories from technologically based accidents, catastrophes, and natural disasters.

5. Developing a social-psychological support system for the population and those involved in the struggle against technological terrorism.

6. Developing a methodology and mechanisms for the interaction of state administrative agencies with all participants in the struggle against technological terrorism and for protection of the population, facilities, and territories against technologically based accidents, catastrophes, and natural disasters.

7. Ensuring the ecological security of Russia in the struggle against techno-

---

* Translated from the Russian by Kelly Robbins.

logical terrorism and for protection of the population, facilities, and territories against technologically based accidents, catastrophes, and natural disasters.

8. Promoting international cooperation with the Russian Federation in the struggle against technological terrorism and for protection of the population, facilities, and territories against technologically based accidents, catastrophes, and natural disasters.

9. Developing robots and technical diagnostic means to provide warnings of accidents and disasters.

APPENDIX
B

Terrorism in a High-Tech Society and Modern Methods for Prevention and Response

June 4-8, 2001
Moscow, Russia

Monday, June 4

Opening of the Seminar
Nikolay P. Laverov, Vice President of Russian Academy of Sciences
Siegfried S. Hecker, Los Alamos National Laboratory
Yevgeny P. Velikhov, Kurchatov State Research Center of Atomic Energy

Session 1: Terrorism and the Law

The Legal Basis for Counterterrorism Activities in the United States
Raphael F. Perl, Congressional Research Service

Russian Legislation and the Struggle Against Terrorism
Mikhail P. Kireev, Academy of the Ministry of Internal Affairs (MVD)

Russian Legislation and the Fight Against Terrorism
Viktor E. Petrishchev, Security Committee of the Russian State Duma

Organized Crime and Terrorism
Viktor Luneev, Russian Academy of Sciences Institute of State and Law

International and Domestic Terrorism
L. Paul Bremer III, MMC Enterprise Risk

The Role of Internal Affairs Agencies in Efforts to Fight Terrorism Under High-Technology Conditions
Oleg A. Stepanov, Academy of Administration, Russian Ministry of Internal Affairs

From the Experience of the Intelligence Services of the Russian Empire in Combating Terrorists
Dmitry M. Aleksenko, Commonwealth of Independent States Antiterrorist Center

The Chechen Crisis: A New Phase of the Response to Terrorism
Valery Tishkov, Institute of Ethnology and Anthropology

On Historical Experience in Combating Terrorism
Oleg M. Khlobustov, Regional Society Strategic Security Assistance Fund

Electromagnetic Terrorism
Yury V. Parfyonov, Russian Academy of Sciences Institute of High Energy Densities and Institute for High Temperatures

Tuesday, June 5

Session 2: The Types of High-Impact Terrorism

Biological Terrorism

Molecular Epidemiology as a New Approach to Detecting the Terrorist Use of Infectious Agents
Sergey V. Netesov, Vector State Research Center for Virology and Biotechnology

Bioterrorism: Threat and Response
Michael L. Moodie, Chemical and Biological Arms Control Institute

Bio-terrorism: A View from the Side
Oleg S. Morenkov, Russian Academy of Sciences Institute of Cell Biophysics

Chemical Terrorism

Chemical Terrorism
Anatoly Kuntsevich, Center of Ecotoxic Monitoring, Institute of Chemical Physics
Chemical Terrorism: Assessing Threats and Responses
Jonathan B. Tucker, Monterey Institute of International Studies

Nuclear Terrorism

Radiological Terrorism
Leonid Bolshov, Russian Academy of Sciences Nuclear Safety Institute

Nuclear Terrorism
Siegfried S. Hecker, Los Alamos National Laboratory

Could Terrorists Produce Low-Yield Nuclear Weapons?
Stanislav Rodionov, Russian Academy of Sciences Space Research
Institute

Problems of Preventing Acts of Nuclear and Radiological Terrorism
Vladimir M. Kutsenko, Russian Ministry of Atomic Energy

Terrorism Utilizing Explosives with Particularly Destructive Force

Selected Technologies and Procedures Intended to Restrict Unauthorized
Access to Explosives
Bronislav V. Matseevich, Federal State-Owned Unitary Enterprise
Krasnoarmeisk Scientific Research Institute of Mechanization

Terrorism: Explosives Threat
Ronald L. Simmons, Naval Surface Warfare Center

Cyberterrorism

Computer Terrorism and Internet Security Issues
Valery A. Vasenin, M.V. Lomonosov Moscow State University

Preventing and Responding to Cybercrime and Terrorism: Some
International Dimensions
Seymour E. Goodman, Georgia Institute of Technology

State Policy to Respond to Cyberterrorism
G. Ivashchenko, Russian National Security Council

Wednesday, June 6

Technological Terrorism

Technological Terrorism
Konstantin V. Frolov, Russian Academy of Sciences

Agricultural Terrorism

Problems of Biological Security in Agriculture
Georgy A. Safonov, Pokrov Biological Preparations Plant

Agricultural Bioterrorism
Martin E. Hugh-Jones, Louisiana State University School of Veterinary
Medicine

**Session 3: Future Trends and International Cooperation in the Struggle
against Modern Terrorism**

Terrorism in a High-Tech Society: Legal Aspects and Contemporary
Methods of Preventing and Countering Terrorist Activity
Aleksandr V. Zmeevsky, Ministry of Foreign Affairs of the Russian
Federation

Cooperation Among Ministries of Internal Affairs of CIS Member States
in the Fight Against Terrorism and Other Manifestations of Extremism
Igor L. Dimitrov, Russian Ministry of Internal Affairs

International Centers as a Basis for Controlling Infectious Disease and
Countering Bioterrorism
Lev S. Sandakhchiev, Vector State Research Center for Virology and
Biotechnology

Terrorism Future: Tactics, Strategy, and Stealth
Peter S. Probst, Institute for the Study of Terrorism and Political Violence

New Opportunities for Bilateral Cooperation
Glenn E. Schweitzer, National Research Council

Conclusion of the Seminar

Siegfried S. Hecker, Los Alamos National Laboratory
Yevgeny P. Velikhov, Kurchatov State Research Center of Atomic Energy

June 7, 2001

Site Visits

Ministry of Foreign Affairs

Vyachaslav Ivanov Trubnikov, Deputy Minister of Foreign Affairs
Ambassador A.V. Zmeevsky, International Agreements

Ministry of Atomic Energy

Lev Dmitrovich Ryabev, First Deputy Minister
Vladimir Ivanovich Limonaev, Head of the Department of Information Security, Nuclear Materials and Objects
Vladimir Maksimovich Kutsenko, Deputy Head of the Department of Information Security, Nuclear Materials and Objects
Vladimir Vladislavovich Shidlovsky, Head of the Department of Nuclear Fuel Cycles
Igor Yevgenevich Zababakhin, Deputy Head of the Department of Projection and Testing of Nuclear Arms
Aleksandr Vladimirovich Kashirsky, Deputy head of the Department of International and Foreign Economic Collaboration
Svetlana Aleksandrovna Timoshina, Chief Specialist of the Department of International and Foreign Economic Collaboration

June 8, 2001

Ministry of Internal Affairs, All Russian Scientific Research Institute

Vladimir Yakovlevich Kikot, Head of the MVD Scientific Institute of Research
Vladimir Yurevich Golubovsky, First Deputy Director, MVD Scientific Institute of Research
Igor Dimitrov, CIS Cooperation
Vyachaslav Knyazev, Foreign Relations Department